Praise for Sanity Savers

The very presence of a book like Sanity Savers tells n
that we working women are not alone in our efforts t
"have it all." When the going gets tough ... the tough
get tips from Ann Douglas!

Ann Rohm
Host, Breakfast Televisi

Ann Douglas' guide to survival in the working-mom
trenches is for every woman who has served her child-
ren reheated pad thai for breakfast, used red Crayola
Scentsation marker in place of lipstick, or seriously
contemplated cashing in her RRSPs and splitting for
Corfu with her son's soccer coach. In other words,
for (almost) every one of us.

Kathy Ullyott,
Modern Woman

Useful advice and information delivered in a fun,
reassuring and practical way.

Laura Bickle,
Senior Editor, Canadian Living

An excellent resource for women who are desperate to
restore some sanity to their too-busy lives.

Cheryl Embrett,
Senior Editor, Homemaker's

Sanity Savers not only helps mothers keep all those
balls in the air, but it helps us relax when one
inevitably drops.

Louise Brown,
Parenting Columnist,
Toronto Star, Life Section

Woman's Work

Mom and Dad were watching TV when Mom said, "I'm tired, and it's getting late. I think I'll go to bed."

She went to the kitchen to make sandwiches for the next day's lunches, rinsed out the popcorn bowls, took meat out of the freezer for supper the following evening, checked the cereal box levels, filled the sugar container, put spoons and bowls on the table and started the coffee pot for brewing the next morning. She then put some wet clothes into the dryer, put a load of clothes in into the wash, ironed a shirt and secured a loose button. She picked up the newspapers strewn on the floor, picked up the game pieces left on the table and put the telephone book back into the drawer. She watered the plants, emptied a wastebasket and hung up a towel to dry. She yawned and stretched and headed for the bedroom. She stopped by the desk and wrote a note to the teacher, counted out some cash for the field trip, and pulled a textbook out from hiding under the chair. She signed a birthday card for a friend, addressed and stamped the envelope and wrote a quick note for the grocery store. She put both near her purse. Mom then creamed her face, put on moisturizer, brushed and flossed her teeth and trimmed her nails. Hubby called, "I thought you were going to bed." "I'm on my way," she said. She put some water into the dog's dish and put the cat outside, then made sure the doors were locked. She looked in on each of the kids and turned out a bedside lamp, hung up a shirt, threw some dirty socks in the hamper, and had a brief conversation with the one up still doing homework. In her own room, she set the alarm, laid out clothing for the next day, straightened up the shoe rack. She added three things to her list of things to do for tomorrow.

About that time, the hubby turned off the TV and announced to no one in particular "I'm going to bed," and he did.

— as circulated recently on email

SANITY SAVERS

The Canadian
Working Woman's Guide
to Having it ALL
almost

Ann Douglas

 McGraw-Hill
Ryerson

Toronto Montréal New York Burr Ridge Bangkok Bogotá Caracas
Lisbon London Madrid Mexico City Milan New Delhi Seoul
Singapore Sydney Taipei

McGraw-Hill
Ryerson Limited

A Subsidiary of The McGraw·Hill Companies

ISBN: 0-07-560539-2

1234567890   W   99
Printed and bound in Canada.

Canadian Cataloguing in Publication Data

Douglas, Ann, 1963 –
        Sanity Savers: the Canadian working woman's guide to almost having it all

Includes bibliographical references and index.
ISBN 0-07-560539-2

1. Working mothers – Canada.   2. Married women – Employment – Canada.
3. Work and family – Canada. I. Title.

HQ759.48.D68   1999   640'. 852   C99-931878-0

Publisher: Joan Homewood
Editorial Co-ordinator: Catherine Leek
Production Co-ordinator: Susanne Penny
Editor: Tita Zierer
Interior Design and Electronic Page Composition: FiWired.Com
Cover Design: Sharon Matthews

To my friends:

For saving my sanity on more occasions than I'd care to admit and for not laughing too hard when I told you I was writing this book.

Table of Contents

Introduction: Operation Overload —
Why a Woman's Work is Never Done
Life in the Fast Lane 2
Working Woman's SOS .4
What You Won't Find in this Book 5
So What Makes Me So Perfect? 6
Survey Says … 8
Genuine One-of-a-Kind .8

Chapter 1: Post-it Notes from the Edge
Earning Less, Doing More 9
Is Your Job Making You Sick? 13
Lifestyle 101 14
One More Thing 25

Chapter 2: Juggling on the Job
Allow Yourself to Drop Some Balls 27
Take a Good, Hard Look at Your Priorities 28
Tame Your To Do List .29
Declutter Your Desk 33
Avoid Meetings like the Plague 35
Watch Out for Other Time Wasters 36

Chapter 3: Winning at Office Politics
Tales from the Trenches 39
How to Win at Office Politics 45

Chapter 4: When Worlds Collide – Easing the Friction
               between Your Personal and Working Life
The Work-Family Crunch 54
Get a Life 55
Job Sharing 56
Flextime 58
The Compressed Work Week 60
Tele-working 61

Child Care-related Benefits 64
Other Family-friendly Benefits 69
What Work-life Programs Have to Offer 71
How to Approach Your Employer 72

Chapter 5: Flying Solo: Is Self-employment the Answer?

Do You Have What it Takes to Run Your Own Business? 76
The Nine Biggest Myths about Self-employment 83
The Most Common Mistakes Small Business Owners Make
   — and How to Avoid Them 87
The Top Five Home Office Motivation Zappers —
   and How to Avoid Them 90

Chapter 6: Mom's the Word

The Mommy Track: How Having Children can Affect Your
   Career 96
Strategies for Dealing with Your Co-Workers 105
Reality Check: How You May Feel about Being a
   Working Mother 105
The Truth about Express-line Parenting 110
Solutions Unlimited 112

Chapter 7: Mary Poppins, Where are You? Finding The
        Right Child Care

Your Search for Child Care 123
Easing Your Child into a New Child Care Arrangement 126
What to do When Your Child is Sick 128
Dealing With Other Child Care Problems 129

Chapter 8: The Parental Ties That Bind

Be Prepared 139
Getting the Support You Need at Work 142
It Takes an Entire Village 144

Chapter 9: For Better and For Worse: Inside the Modern
        Marriage

Time Out! 148
The Stranger in Your Bed 150
Career Tug-of-War 155

Chapter 10: Making Room for Family, Friends and Community
The Theory of Relativity 159
Girlfriend Power 162
Projects and Causes 164

Chapter 11: The Martha Stewart Syndrome: Who Says it's a Good Thing?
The New Domesticity: Why You Can't Stencil Your
    Way to Happiness 171
Learning to Love the Dust Bunnies 174
Conquering Clutter 175
Cleaning 101 180
Taming the Laundry Monster 184
Dine and Dash: Eating on the Run 187
Learn the Art of Delegating 195

Conclusion: Thirty Steps to a Saner You
Running on Empty 205
Wanted: One Fairy Godmother 206
Thirty Steps to a Saner You 206

Appendix A: Directory of Organizations 211

Appendix B: Surfing with a Briefcase: The Best Web Sites for Working Women 217

Appendix C: Bibliography 223

Index 237

Acknowledgments

In addition to my editors at McGraw-Hill Ryerson, I would like to thank the following people who assisted me during the writing of this book: Sophie Cousins, president, Sophie's Maid Services; Cathy Fountain, president, Buy Design; Tracy Keleher, founder, Canadian Parents Online; Janice Kent, research assistant; Cindy Mount, president, Traicor International; Linda Omichinski, president, Hugs International; and Brenda Wines-Moher, Registered Dietician, Peterborough County — City Health Unit.

I also owe a sincere thank you to the following individuals, who shared their best tips on juggling work and family with me when I posted to various online groups:

Martha Bailey, Karen Beattie, Susan Blystone, Peter Boisseau, Suzanne Boles, Pauline Clift, Carolyn Dobel, Dorothy Farish, Barbara Florio, John Gallagher, Nancy Garcia, Rachel Goldsworthy, Kathleen Hamilton, Anne Harvey, Shirley Horne, Chrisina Zahakos Hovis, Carol Johnstone, Mark Kearney, Guenther Krueger, Jason Kurylo, Kate Langan, Ellen Lee, Veronica Leonard, Kathe Lieber, Esther Massimini, Sandra McKenzie, Kay Nelson, Denyse O'Leary, Lori Oliwenstein, Doreen Pengracs, Sandra Phinney, Holly Quan, Lesley Remington, Deborah Schoen, Ambre Ying.

I would also like to thank the members of the *Sanity Savers* panel, who contributed so much to this book: Margaret Allan, Victoria Austin, Debbie Babbitt, Kelly Bagapor, Jennie Baird, Sarah Jordan Beimers, Diane Bishop, Leslie Bissegger, Danielle Bombala, Elizabeth M. Bradstock, Rose Bright, Laura Buren, Charlene Busselaar, Cathi Callahan, Laurie Caloren, Gail Carrozzino, Anne Cavicchi, Stacy Chrest, Holly Clawson, Sandy Coffey, Danielle Cohen, Suzanne Colquitt, Sharon Coverley, Helen Coxon, Michelle Creasey, Kathe Cronin, Mary Burnham Curtis, Lori-Ann D'Antonio, Nikki Dalton, Andrea Dick, Anne duPlessis, Cindy Durrett, Janis Elspas, Susan Erhardt, Shannon Fairfield, Irene Figari, Cyndie Forget, Maureen Fox, Suzanne Fuente, Cindy Fuhrman, Cathy Gaudet, LaRee Goddu, Angela Gonzalez, Karen Gorirossi, Stephanie Griffin, Phaedra Hise Hargis, Jill Haussler, Rina Hawkins, Laura Hays, Marilyn Hilton, Anne Hoover, Marie Hughes, Amber Jackson, Cheryl Jadykin, Aina Johnsen, Joan Jones, Tricia Jones, Tina Keeley, Tracy Keleher, Sherisse Koberinski, Cyndi Kollath, Julie Kremer, Grace Lacson, Laura Larsen, LeeAnne Lavender, Jessica Leonardis, Ann Lewis, Marcia Lewis, Lou Ann Liebman, Tanya Lutz, Beth Macauley, Christina McCarthy, Tina McConnell, Jennifer McDowell, Mina McGean, Heather McGee, Heather McKinnon, Deb McLaren, Gayle McWeeney, Tammy Melanson, Lisa Mullen, Debbie Myers, Sima Nadler, Jennifer Ogle, Jackie Patrick, Jane Pendergast, Carrie Petersen, Suzi Prokell, Judy Quinn, Melony Marteen Robinson, Karen Rolfe, Donna Greenberg Root, Amie

Rossini, Jill Roush, Debbie Saltrick, Heather Santamaria, Sheila Schaffer, Karen Scherzinger, Sharon Scott, Marcia Shavlik, Nicola Shute, Rene Siegel, Phyllis Smith, Silke Smith, Robin Smothers, Lauren Snellgrove, Kirste Spencer, Beth Starks, Lisa Stone, Lisa Stratton, Natalie Sweeney, Jennifer Tibbetts, Lori Umiamaka, Janice Ungar, Angela Walberg, Ruth Ann Wallace, Donna Walters, Dana Williams, Eileen Winrock, Stephanie Wright, Debra Young Krizman, Pilaar Yule, Stacie Zamperini.

Last but not least, I would like to thank my family for putting up with me while I put in an insane number of hours researching and writing this book.

Ann Douglas

Operation Overload – Why a Woman's Work is Never Done

It's 12:30 am. You should have been in bed hours ago, but you've been busy paying bills, making out your grocery list and preparing a casserole for tomorrow night's dinner. You're about to stumble up the stairs to bed when it suddenly dawns on you that you don't have a clean bra to wear to work in the morning. You momentarily weigh the career fallout of going braless and decide you'd better play it safe. It would be a shame to see that promotion disappear just because of a laundry crisis.

You head down to the laundry room and throw a load of whites in the washer. You're tempted to use the short wash cycle to speed the process along so that you can get to bed a few minutes earlier, but then you remember what your son's sweat socks smelled like when you dug them out of the laundry hamper. Better give them the full wash cycle and throw in a bit of bleach to kill off whatever mutant strain of bacteria happens to be growing in his gym bag this week.

Come to think of it, it's time to buy him some more socks — to buy everyone some more socks, for that matter. That would mean you wouldn't have to do laundry nearly so often. Better add "buy socks" to your To Do List for tomorrow's lunch hour. You can pick up the socks while you're shopping for a present for your sister-in-law's baby shower and ordering the cake for your mother's birthday. Of course, you'll have to miss your lunch

> ## "Worth Quoting"
>
> "I had a work life. I had a personal life. Together, however, they made not one but two separate lives. Each wanted a hundred percent of me."
> - Elizabeth Perle McKenna,
>   *When Work Doesn't Work Anymore*

hour fitness class again. There's no possible way to fit that in, too ...

How often do you find yourself acting out scenes like this in your own life? Once a month? Once a week? Everyday? Are there times when you feel like someone has cranked up the speed on your treadmill and there's no possible way you can keep up?

If you find yourself feeling exhausted and overwhelmed on a regular basis, you're certainly in good company. According to Statistics Canada, stress has become a way of life for many working women. Here are just a few of the highlights from the *1992 General Social Survey on Time Use*:

➤ Forty-three percent of women admit to cutting back on sleep when they need to find more hours in their day.

➤ Thirty-five percent of women report that they are under constant stress because there are more demands on them than they can possibly meet.

➤ Thirty-two percent of women worry that they don't spend enough time with their family or friends.

➤ Thirty-one percent say that they don't have time for fun any more.

➤ Twenty-six percent would like to have more time for themselves.

➤ Twenty-two percent of women intend to slow down in the coming year.

Life in the Fast Lane

Part of the problem, of course, is the fact that we're leading incredibly fast-paced lives. We're running at breakneck speed from the time we step out of bed in the morning until we hit the sack again some 18 hours later.

No one has a lot of time on their hands these days: not men, not women, not children. But while we are all living life in the fast lane, some of us — working women in particular — are driving fast enough to break our speedometers. Here's what the Vanier Institute of the Family has to say about the time crunch that most working women face:

Retired people, couples without children, and singles have more time to call their own. Men, in general, feel less time pressure than women. Employed women with young children feel exceptionally pressured. Full-time employment and the addition of children to the family increase the pressure, especially for women.

It's not hard to figure out where the pressure comes from. We're trying to keep an incredible number of balls in the air.

We hold down full-time jobs in organizations that are a lot leaner and meaner than they were even five to ten years ago. That means that we're working a lot harder and putting in more hours than we were before downsizing mania hit the Canadian workforce. While some of us don't mind putting in the extra time and effort that today's employers are demanding, many of us feel like we don't have much choice. After all, if you're not putting in as many hours or achieving the same results as the person in the next cubicle, your boss might assume you're less committed to your job than the next person — a conclusion that could put your pay cheque on the endangered species list.

We're under incredible pressure to play Martha Stewart at the end of a long day at work. Apparently, it's no longer enough to keep your house sufficiently clean to keep the health unit at bay: you're also somehow supposed to make every room in your house look like something out of *Canadian House and Home* magazine. (Don't believe me? Just flip on the Home and Garden channel and you'll see what I'm talking about. Clearly this channel is aimed at people who have a lot more time on their hands than I do. I mean why on earth would you take the time to hand stencil your walls when you can find a commercially-manufactured wallpaper that will create the same effect in just a fraction of the time? I just don't get it.)

Those of us who have children are expected to play Supermom when we get home from work. Because our schedules won't allow us to have lots of time with our children, we're expected to deliver on the quality front instead. This means dragging yourself to your son's hockey game and feigning enthusiasm when you'd rather be camped out on the couch with a TV remote in your hand. Or explaining to your boss that you're going to be late in the morning because you have to drive your daughter and her science fair project to school.

Those of us who are involved in relationships are also expected to find time at the end of the day to spend with our significant others. Many of us are perpetually in the doghouse because sheer exhaustion causes us to fall asleep at an inappropriate point on "date night." (I know it's hard on the male ego if you doze off in what should be a particularly romantic moment, but there are times when sleep wins hands down over sex. Heck, there are times when sleep is even more appealing than chocolate. That just goes to prove how chronically sleep-deprived many of us have become, now doesn't it?)

Those of us with sick or aging relatives often find ourselves under intense pressure to deliver on this front as well. We need to find time to visit our relatives in person, to send cards and to act as advocates on their behalf by dealing with a never-ending parade of doctors and government bureaucrats.

Many of us are active in our communities. Whether we coach soccer once a week, serve on the board of directors for a church or non-profit organization once a month, or canvas for a local charity once a year, we may find it difficult to squeeze these volunteer activities into our already overloaded lives.

Given all of the conflicting demands on our time and energy, it's no wonder that many of us end up going weeks — even years — without attending to our own needs. What tends to get lost in the day-to-day shuffle are the chunks of time required to hit the gym on a regular basis, to sign up for a night course with a friend, or to get away for the weekend with our partners — the very things we need in order to take care of ourselves, body and soul.

Working Woman's SOS

Ready to hit the panic button? To rip up your To Do List and wave a white flag of surrender? You don't have to go to those sort of extremes to get your life back. What you do need to do, however, is to rethink every area of your life and

FACTS & FIGURES

Almost two-thirds of Canadian employees are responsible for caring for a child, an aging relative, or both.

come up with ways of making your life less stressful, more enjoyable, saner. That's what this book is all about: showing you how to save your sanity despite the many conflicting demands on your time.

As you read the book, you'll discover that *Sanity Savers* is packed with valuable information, including:

➢ proven secrets for reducing stress on the job

➢ practical tips on keeping up with laundry, housework and other domestic chores

➢ helpful advice on finding time for your partner, children and/or ageing parents no matter how zany your schedule may be

➢ innovative methods of streamlining your life so that you have time to do the things that matter most to you

➢ lively anecdotes from real working women who've juggled their work and personal lives — and lived to tell

➢ summaries of the latest research about the joys and challenges of being a working woman

➢ a comprehensive directory of organizations (Appendix A), web sites (Appendix B), and resources (Appendix C) that every working woman who is serious about restoring sanity to her life needs to know about.

What You Won't Find in this Book

What you won't find in this book are a lot of gimmicks: things like time management charts and useless checklists that seem to imply that if you just worked a little harder or were a little more organized, you truly could *Have It All*. Frankly, I find that kind of approach insulting. What's more, I don't believe for a minute that an activity log or a *Cosmo*-style quiz is going to make a heck of a lot of difference to your life or mine.

That's not to say that the situation is hopeless. (Do you honestly think my publisher would allow me to write a 250 page book that basically says, "Throw in the towel. Accept your life as it is. Nothing's going to change after all!") There is plenty we can do to restore sanity to our lives.

Just one small *caveat* before you read any further: the last thing I'm trying to do in this book is to pretend that you can achieve perfect balance every single day of your life. People who know me personally would laugh hysterically and call a press conference to expose me as a fraud if I wrote a book that tried to make that kind of argument.

So What Makes Me So Perfect?

Nothing, actually.

While I do my best to keep as many balls as possible in the air at any one time, I'm probably the least perfect person you'll ever have the privilege of meeting. Consider the evidence for yourself.

My working life is the stuff of which nightmares are made. I'm usually busy juggling a half-dozen magazine articles, a book or two and a handful of corporate communications projects. (At one point, my computer was covered with so many Post-it notes that it started to resemble Big Bird.)

➤ My idea of a home-cooked meal usually involved using at least one canned ingredient — and sometimes three or four. (Bet you didn't know, for example, that you can whip up an amazing batch of fudge in fifteen minutes or less by using just three ingredients! All you need are a 300 ml can of evaporated milk, four cups of chocolate chips and a tablespoon of vanilla extract. You just melt everything together in a saucepan, pour it into a wax-paper lined baking dish, and — voilà! — you have a candy creation that would do even Laura Secord proud.)

➤ My children have learned to be suspicious when there's a flurry of house-cleaning activity at our place: "Are Grandma and Grandpa coming to visit?" (What does this tell you about the usual state of cleanliness in the Douglas household?)

➤ I'm still carrying around far too many pounds of pregnancy fat because I've been too busy to hit the gym since my daughter was born — back in 1988! I'm inching my way toward my fitness goals, however, as I'm regularly showing my face there at least once a week — but I'll be darned if I can figure out how some of the other women at the gym manage to make it there three to five times each week.

➤ I am a pitifully easy mark for anyone who needs a volunteer. (Smart idea to make that kind of admission in print, now isn't it? My phone should starting ringing any second.)

Despite the fact that my track record on the balance front is somewhat less than stellar, I would humbly argue that I am, in fact, the perfect person to write this book. Not convinced? Let me explain.

Like you, I'm a genuine work-in-progress — someone who's trying to find ways to keep all the essential balls in the air and to let the non-essential ones fall to the ground. I don't always succeed. In fact, I can think of a couple of examples when I've dropped the wrong balls this week and it's only Wednesday!

I think my lack of perfection is a good thing — maybe not for my family, but certainly for you, the reader. If anything, my failures (which you'll be hearing a lot about in this book) will help you to feel good about your own successes on the juggling front. I'm gambling that you'd rather read a book that's written by a real human being than a so-called efficiency expert. After all, who wants to read a book that's written by some late-twentieth century Superwoman who has miraculously managed to achieve perfect balance — someone who's never had to miss a day of work because of a sick child, broken furnace, or other unexpected curve ball.

Survey Says ...

Because I live with these kinds of catastrophes on a daily basis, I understand what it's like to have too many balls in the air. I've also been fortunate enough to receive input from a panel of more than 150 working women who have achieved varying degrees of success in their own battles to achieve balance. Some were married, others were recently separated or single. Many had children. They worked in a variety of fields, at entry level and managerial positions and everything in between and a few were self-employed. These women — who agreed to be interviewed a dozen times over a three-month period — shared their strategies for coping with office politics, taming the laundry monster, staying connected with far-flung relatives and contending with countless other challenges that working women face on a regular basis. You'll find their words of wisdom sprinkled throughout the text.

Genuine One-of-a-Kind

You've probably gathered by now that *Sanity Savers* isn't like most other books of its type. In fact, it's hard to even say what type of book it is. It's not a bossy time-management tome that will have you feeling guilty for wasting five minutes of your day to flip through the morning paper, nor is it a warm-and-fuzzy new age title that will leave you feeling vaguely better about your life, but still unsure of what changes you need to make. I guess you could say that *Sanity Savers* falls somewhere in the middle. It offers up a smorgasbord of facts designed to enlighten, inform and entertain, and yet has the confessional tone of a late-night phone call to your best friend.

Hope you enjoy the book!

Chapter 1

Post-it Notes
from the Edge

If you're like most working women, you probably have a bit of a love-hate relationship with your job. When things are going well, you can't imagine doing anything else for a living, but when they're not, it's all you can do to stop yourself from climbing on top of your desk, tossing your jar of pencils in the air, and shouting, "I quit!"

As with anything else in life, it's generally the little things that push you over the edge: watching your To Do List take on a life of its own, getting caught up in a particularly nasty bout of office politics, or watching the promotion of your dreams get handed over to a woefully underqualified yet shamelessly self-promoting co-worker.

Situations like these could try the patience of a saint, and saintliness is likely not one of your better qualities. So what should you do when you're hit with one of these frustrating work-related curve balls? Pick up your marbles and go home? Put on your gloves and prepare to fight back? Perhaps a little of both!

As you have no doubt gathered by now, the focus of this chapter is staying sane on the job. With any luck, by the time you're finished reading this chapter, you'll have picked up some new ideas about reducing stress, the benefits of which will have an impact on work and other areas of your life.

Earning Less, Doing More

When was the last time you felt like you were on top of all your responsibilities at work? Last month? Last year? The day you first started your job?

If there are days when you'd gladly take a sledgehammer to your electronic calendar or tear your To Do List into a million pieces, you're certainly in good company. Stress is a major problem for a growing number of working women.

The next time you're having the day from hell, consider the fact that putting in long hours is fast becoming the norm. A recent study by Harvard University economist Juliet Schor revealed that employees are putting in the equivalent of an extra month of work each year as compared to the hours that were put in by workers in the 1970s. A similar study conducted by Aon Consulting, a Chicago-based human resources consulting firm, revealed that the percentage of workers who are regularly putting in 50-hour weeks has nearly doubled since 1995 — rising from 13 percent to 23 percent.

Stress is becoming a way of life for many workers. The Aon Consulting study revealed that 53 percent of employees now report feeling burned out on the job, up dramatically from 39 percent in 1995. As well, information overload is becoming an increasing problem. There are 150,000 books and 10,000 periodicals published in the US each year alone. Add to that the amount of information you're exposed to while surfing the Net, flipping through your morning paper, listening to the radio on your way into work, and you can see why many of us find it almost impossible to find time to deal with the mountains of information we encounter each day.

Is it any wonder that so many of us feel like we're coming unglued?

Of course, we're not the only culture that seems to have become obsessed with work. In fact, the time crunch that workers experience in North America seems insignificant in comparison to the pressures shouldered by many Japanese workers. Each year, more than 10,000 Japanese workers die as a result of karoshi — death by overwork.

What's Wrong with this Picture?

At first glance, it's hard to understand why we're chronically short of time. I mean, think about it. We are living in an age in which there are entire industries devoted to saving us time and energy.

Consider the modern office, for example. Walk into any office building in the country and you'll encounter a variety of high-tech wonder toys: computers, fax machines and other space-age gizmos that are designed to send our productivity through the roof. With all these powerful tools at our command, we should be sitting at our desks, idly filing our nails, letting the flotilla of office machines take care of the drudgery for us, right?

Well, maybe not. Despite all the futurists' predictions about what a wonderful place the workplace would be by the time the new millennium arrived, today's workers face just as much job-related stress as their low-tech predecessors — and perhaps a little more.

In today's lean-and-mean workforce, the pressure to perform can be overwhelming. Most of us experience a constant nagging fear that our jobs could disappear if we don't prove ourselves sufficiently valuable to the organization. For many of us, that means surpassing — not merely meeting — the expectations that our employers have set out for us.

Here's what Marcia, a 36 year old paralegal, has to say about the importance of doing more than what is expected at work — in her case, clocking additional billable hours. "I would love to not have to worry about billable hours, but in a private firm, that's how we make money. I have a quota of 1600 billable hours a year to meet. That is the minimum. I generally bill 1900, and that is more or less what is expected. It's kind of an unwritten expectation or you're history."

Facts & Figures

Studies have shown that there's a gender gap when it comes to coping with the symptoms of stress. While men tend to suffer from migraines and depression, women are more likely to develop back problems and carpal tunnel syndrome.

The Times — They are A-changin'

Twenty years ago, the only way your boss could monitor your productivity was to glance at your desk every now and again, checking up on the size of the piles in your "in" and "out" trays. If he was really obnoxious, he'd find an excuse to walk by your desk every couple of hours, pausing to read over your shoulder. More than likely, how-ever, he was a little more subtle: he'd sneak a peak inside your desk drawer before you arrived at work in the morning or flip through the piles of paper on your desk after you'd headed home for the day.

Today, of course, it's a whole lot eas-ier for your boss to keep tabs on what you are — or aren't — accomplishing over the course of a day. Employers have far more sinister tools at their disposal than they ever did before, whether they choose to use them or not. A perfect example is the aptly-named Desktop Surveillance program — a software package that is designed to give Big Brother (a.k.a. your boss) all kinds of fas-cinating statistics about you: your keystroke speed and accuracy, your transaction speed and how often your computer ended up sitting idle (gasp!) over the course of the working day.

What these electronic gizmos and the real-live human beings who choose to use them tend to forget is that most of us are work-ing as hard — and as fast — as we can. While most employers are relying on smaller workforces than ever before, they aren't low-ering their expectations of their employees. It's simply accepted that the seven survivors in a newly-downsized department will find ways to accomplish as much as 10 people did before. Is it any wonder that so many of us feel like we're working inside a pressure cooker that's just waiting to blow?

Is Your Job Making You Sick?

You know that all work and no play makes Jane a dull gal. What you might not realize is that it can also make her sick.

So many of us are putting in long hours these days that overwork is fast becoming the norm. The fact that everyone else is coming into work early, skipping lunch and taking a briefcase full of work home doesn't necessarily mean that it's the right thing to do. There's a price to be paid for working too hard.

At first, you might not even realize that there's a problem. You may honestly believe that you can do it all. Unfortunately, that's simply not the case. While it's possible to work at a punishing pace and to put in an superhuman number of hours at work for months — even years — at some point you're going to hit the stress wall.

Perhaps you're already starting to experience some of the classic symptoms of stress:

➤ tiredness

➤ irritability

➤ nervousness

➤ an inability to concentrate on your work

➤ a sense of hopelessness about your life

➤ changes in your sleeping or eating habits

➤ stomach problems

➤ headaches

➤ muscle aches

➤ conflicts at home or work

➤ increased absenteeism

➤ increased use of cigarettes, alcohol or drugs.

While a certain amount of stress can be healthy — studies have shown that it helps to keep you on your toes — it's important to be able to differentiate between stress that is life-enhancing and stress that is potentially debilitating. The medical evidence about the evils of stress is, after all, pretty damning: if you subject your body to high levels of stress on an ongoing basis, you put yourself at risk of developing hypertension (high blood pressure), musculoskeletal problems (e.g. tension in your neck), diabetes, ulcers, mental illness and cardiovascular disease. Check out Appendix B for the dirt on a few web sites where you can determine just how high-risk your life is.

And don't think you're going to miss out on heart disease just because you're a woman, by the way. A recent study by the Heart and Stroke Foundation gave Canadian women a failing grade when it comes to leading a heart-friendly lifestyle. The study concluded that women are too busy working and caring for children and elderly relatives to take proper care of themselves. Despite the fact that nearly half of the 79,000 Canadians who die of heart disease each year are women, most women continue to underestimate the significance of this threat to their health.

Lifestyle 101

If stress is becoming a problem for you, it's time to make some changes to your life — both on and off the job.

You may feel that your situation is hopeless — that you'll never manage to bring your stress level down at work. That's probably not the case. No matter how stressful your job may be or how difficult it may be to get the support you need to make the necessary changes, in most cases, it can be done.

That's not to say it will be easy, however. You may be forced to make some significant lifestyle changes (e.g. stop eating takeout food at your desk and start exercising more!) and to find creative ways of managing stress both on and off the job.

That's what we're going to talk about next.

You'll be well on your way to reducing the amount of stress you experience if you can take steps to ensure that you're eating properly, exercising enough and getting the sleep you need. Just in case you dozed off in high school health class, here's a crash course in Lifestyle 101.

FACTS & FIGURES

Here's something to think about the next time you feel your blood pressure shooting sky-high at work. According to the American National Institute for Occupational Safety and Health (NIOSH), stress is a contributing factor to eight of the 10 leading causes of death in the United States.

What's Eating You?

If your typical breakfast consists of a coffee and muffin, you might want to give some thought to pulling up your nutritional socks. Studies have shown that your body needs healthy foods to help ward off the potentially harmful effects of stress.

Let me explain.

When you are stressed, your body quickly runs through its stores of glucose, its major fuel. Once the glucose stores have been depleted, your body has to look for an alternative source of fuel. Because it's more difficult for your body to break down its stores of body fat than the protein in your muscles, you start to lose muscle rather than fat. By eating a balanced diet that includes ample quantities of fruits, vegetables and whole grain products, you are able to provide your body with a steady source of fuel. You'll also be ensuring that your body gets sufficient quantities of vitamins A and C as well as thiamine, riboflavin and other B vitamins — your body's key artillery in the battle against stress.

Now, before you accuse me of being a nutrition nut, please hear me out. I'm not about to suggest that you get up an hour earlier so that you can whip up a breakfast of whole wheat pancakes with homemade jam on the side. Nor am I about to suggest that you give up such "vices" as sugar and fat and take out a lifetime membership in the Lentil of the Month Club. That would only add to your stress level — unless, of course, you already have the eating habits of a saint. What I am suggesting, however, is that you look for little ways to make healthy eating a part of your daily routine. Try the following tips.

Get your day off to the best possible start
If you don't have time for a sit-down breakfast, make yourself a healthy breakfast to enjoy in the car. Believe it or not, it takes less time to make yourself a fruit and yoghurt smoothie than what you'll spend waiting in line at the donut store drive-thru.

Try eating four or five small meals a day rather than three large meals
Eating more often will help to keep your blood sugar on an even kilter — something that will definitely leave you feeling more

sane. You'll also be less likely to munch on high-fat foods — something that far too many of us tend to do when we're feeling particularly stressed. So rather than listening to your stomach growl while you wait until lunch hour rolls around, enjoy a piece of fruit during your mid-morning break. You'll feel a lot better for it!

Make sure that you're eating a variety of foods

This will help ensure that your body is getting all the nutrients it needs to function properly. (This may be a good time to hang that copy of Canada's Food Guide to Healthy Eating on your fridge again!) If you're too busy to cook during the week, whip up a couple of healthy casseroles on the weekend and pop them in the freezer. Or see if you can buy some healthy prepared meals from a frozen food store or a catering company.

Don't get hooked on sugar

If you find yourself craving donuts and other sweets whenever you're feeling stressed, it could be because you've learned to depend on sugar highs. When you eat foods that are high in sugar, your blood sugar goes through the roof, giving you a sudden boost of energy. Unfortunately, the effect is short-lived. Your pancreas starts to produce insulin to combat the high levels of sugar in your blood, something that causes your blood sugar level to tumble rapidly. This drop in blood sugar can leave you feeling dizzy, irritable, depressed, jittery, nauseated and hungry enough to crave another sweet snack. That's why it's better to reach for complex carbohydrates like whole grain breads — foods that take longer to break down in your body than simple carbohydrates like candy bars and chips.

ETC.

If you've misplaced your copy of Canada's Food Guide to Healthy Eating, you can either call your local health unit and ask them to mail you a copy or download your own copy from cyberspace. Here's the URL: *http://www.hcsc.gc.ca/hppb/nutrition/pube/foodguid/food8guide.htm*. A vegetarian-friendly alternative to Canada's Food Guide is "The New Four Food Groups," promoted by the American-based Physicians' Committee for Responsible Medicine. Check out *http://www.pcrm.org/health/vsk/vsk9.html* for more information on this increasingly popular lifestyle.

Watch your intake of caffeine

While you might be tempted to refuel at the office coffee pot when you're having a particularly hard day at work, head for the water cooler instead. Studies have shown that the caffeine found in coffee, tea, soft drinks and chocolate triggers a "fight or flight" response in your body which only adds to your stress level. As if that weren't bad enough, your tolerance for caffeine decreases as you get older. Perhaps it's time to find something other than a bottle of Coke or a pot of coffee to jump start your brain in the morning!

Be your own liquor control board

While you might think that unwinding at the end of the day with a drink in your hand is the perfect way to combat stress, you could be setting yourself up for a night of insomnia if you enjoy that night cap too late in the evening. Besides, there are far healthier ways of reducing your stress level than turning to alcohol, like the points we've just mentioned above.

Sweat the Stress Away

What's the first thing that gets dropped from your schedule when you get too busy at work? It's probably your trip to the gym.

While it's easy to convince yourself that you're too busy to work out, there are few things that can deliver up the same stress-releasing benefits as exercise — unless, of course, you count sex! Exercise allows you to work off the adrenaline rush that you get when you're under stress and helps to return your body to a state of balance. You might even get to enjoy a so-called "runner's high," a burst of endorphins that leaves you feeling terrific. Exercise has even been shown to help improve concentration — a point you should use to your advantage if you're trying to convince your boss to pick up the tab for your health club membership!

The hardest part about exercising, of course, is actually making yourself do it. It's easy to convince yourself that you're too tired or too busy to exercise — or to come up with even more

Figure 1.1: **The Top Eight Reasons Why People Don't Exercise**

Reason	Percentage*
1. I don't have time to exercise	69%
2. I don't have the energy to become more active.	59%
3. I'm just not motivated enough to get involved.	52%
4. It costs too much to take up an activity.	37%
5. I'm not healthy enough to exercise or might get hurt.	36%
6. There are no exercise facilities in my neighbourhood	30%
7. I feel uncomfortable when I exercise.	29%
8. I don't have the right skills to get involved in an activity.	29%

* percentage of Canadians offering excuse not to exercise

Source: The Canadian Fitness and Lifestyle Research Institute, 1995

creative excuses. (See Figure 1.1 if you're looking for inspiration.) Of course, as your mother always told you, where there's a will, there's a way. Here are some tips on finding the will!

Exercise for the right reasons
Don't exercise because you feel you should: exercise because you want to enjoy the benefits of physical fitness including less fatigue, reduced stress, greater mental and physical stamina and increased productivity at home and at school.

Find the activity that's right for you
Can't get the hang of the fancy footwork in aerobics class? Hate the idea of plunging into an icy-cold swimming pool in the middle of winter? Look for a fitness activity that's right for you — perhaps rollerblading, martial arts or something else entirely.

Make an appointment with yourself to exercise
It doesn't matter if you're planning to head across town, take a walk around

FACTS & FIGURES

The top four health improvement measures that women intend to make, according to Statistics Canada:
1. Exercise more.
2. Improve eating habits.
3. Lose weight.
4. Quit smoking.

the block, or hop on the exercise bike while you watch the episode of *Oprah* that you videotaped while you were at work. If you don't schedule the time to exercise, you're never going to get around to doing it.

Commit to your exercise program for at least six weeks
Studies have shown that it takes your body at least six weeks to start reaping the physical and psychological benefits of exercise.

Choose the right time of day
If you exercise too late in the day, you could find yourself having trouble sleeping — the last thing you want to deal with if you're trying to combat stress!

Find an exercise buddy
This could be a friend, co-worker or family member who will meet you at the gym or keep you company while you take a walk around the block. Make a point of finding someone who's at roughly the same level of physical fitness as you — unless, of course, you don't mind being left in the dust by someone who makes Jane Fonda look like a couch potato.

Aim for variety
It's easy to get bored if you stick with the same exercise routine week after week. Take a different route if you're walking. Or have someone show you how to use that new piece of exercise equipment at the gym. Remember: variety is the spice of life!

Set fitness goals
It's easy to lose your enthusiasm for your exercise program if you're not working toward a specific goal. Perhaps you want to improve your cardiovascular fitness, increase your strength, or increase your flexibility. You don't have to aspire to run the New York Marathon in order to set a fitness goal!

Finding it difficult to make it to the gym? Here are some tips on making exercise part of your daily routine:

➤ Don't bend over when you have to pick something up off the floor. Bend your knees and sink into a squatting position. Then push with your thighs as you stand up. This is an excellent way to keep those thighs in shape and, what's more, this lifting technique is back-friendly, too.

➤ Keep canned goods and other essentials in the basement. That way, you'll have an excuse to run up and down stairs a little more often.

➤ Do isometric abdominal exercises when you're talking on the phone. (Just in case you flunked out of gym class, this involves tightening and releasing your abdominal muscles.)

➤ Fill gallon milk jugs with various amounts of water and use them as free weights.

➤ Turn your infant or toddler into a free weight when you're playing together. Your child will think it's a riot and your arms will get a vigorous workout.

➤ If you're getting into a rut when it comes to doing your in-home aerobic workout, swap exercise videos with a friend or tape a bunch of TV exercise shows. Or use the "picture in picture" feature on your TV set so that you can watch your favourite TV show and your exercise tape at the same time!

➤ Exercise in the kitchen while your kids are eating dinner. (You and your partner can sit down to your own meal later on.)

➤ Throw your baby in the stroller and run around the block. (Note: if you're going to be doing this on a regular basis, you might want to pick up a jogging stroller. They're sturdier and more stable than regular strollers and designed to go over rugged terrain. Just think of them as the ATVs of the stroller world!)

➤ Do some interval training while you're folding laundry. Fold ten items and then run upstairs to put the items away. Fold ten more items and then run upstairs to put those items away, too.

➤ Don't make exercise into another chore. Keep it short and sweet — 40 minutes or less from start to finish. That way, you'll be less likely to convince yourself that you couldn't possibly find time to exercise.

Get Some Zzzzzs

Have you ever noticed that at the very times when you need it most, you can't settle down for a good night's sleep? Perhaps your mind is working overtime while you obsess about that conflict you had with a customer or you are worrying about the presentation you have to give to that really important client first thing in the morning.

Whether you realize it or not, one of the keys to reducing your overall stress level is to ensure that you're getting plenty of good quality sleep — something that only makes sense. After all, how are you going to have the stamina to deal with a problem at work if you're surviving on four hours' sleep?

While you might assume that you're the only one in your office who's chronically sleep deprived, that's probably not the case. There are more people pacing the floor at 3:00 am than you might think — and a lot of them are women. Here are the highlights from some recent studies from south of the border:

➢ A 1993 report published by the National Commission on Sleep Disorders Research in the US revealed that as many as 35 percent of Americans aren't getting enough sleep.

➢ A similar study by scientists at Pennsylvania State University revealed that there's a gender gap when it comes to sleep problems: only 8 percent of men as compared to 33 percent of women report feeling excessively sleepy at least one day per month.

➢ Sleep problems get worse for women as they grow older. According to that National Commission on Sleep Disorders Research, as many as 40 percent of women over the age of 40 struggle with insomnia.

➢ According to the National Sleep Foundation in the US, 52 percent of women as opposed to 45 percent of men report having sleep problems.

We live in a pill-popping society — where the cure to what ails you is just one drugstore shelf away. Rather than opening a pill jar the next time insomnia rears its ugly head, try some of these natural cures for insomnia instead.

Practice good "sleep hygiene"

Go to bed at a regular time and get up at a regular time. Resist the temptation to sleep in on weekends or to take hour-long afternoon naps or you'll be less able to go to sleep that night — a habit that can cause you major grief come Sunday night.

Skip that third cup of coffee

If you're having trouble sleeping, you shouldn't be having more than two cups of coffee a day and you shouldn't be drinking your second cup any time later than noon hour. Caffeine doesn't merely make it difficult for you to dose off; it can cause you to wake up more often and leave you tossing and turning all night.

Reach for warm milk or herbal tea when craving a warm, late-night beverage

Milk contains an amino acid that can actually help to relax you, and herbal teas such as camomile tea can also help you to wind down. A lavender oil based bath will help too.

Exercise too late at night and you'll still be staring at the ceiling at 1:00 am

But do find ways to make exercise a part of your weekday routine. Sleep experts have found that 20 to 30 minutes of exercise five days a week can make a huge difference to people struggling with insomnia.

Don't rely on alcohol to make you sleepy

While the initial drowsiness may help you to fall asleep, it will reduce the quality of your sleep and cause you to wake up frequently during the night. It's also not a healthy habit to get into.

Over-the-counter drugs tend to chase the sandman away

Common offenders include painkillers, decongestants, diuretics and diet pills.

Don't light up

Smokers experience sleeping problems more frequently than non-smokers. The reason is obvious. Nicotine is a stimulant. It raises your blood pressure, causes your heart to pump faster and stimulates your brain.

Don't consume large quantities of liquids within two hours before going to bed

If midnight treks to the bathroom are becoming a problem for you, reduce your late-night intake of fluids. If you want to be really sure that your bladder will have a chance to empty itself before you hit the sack, walk around the house for five to ten minutes before you head to bed. This mild exercise will help to circulate fluids through your kidneys, thereby helping to trigger the urge to urinate before you call it a night!

Skip that late-night snack

The last thing you want is to have your digestive system going into overdrive at the very moment that you're trying to drift off to sleep. Besides, it's easy to get in the habit of over-eating when you're tired. Over time, those calorie-laden "pick me up" snacks can add up to a lot of extra pounds.

Take time to relax and unwind before bed

Meditate, listen to soothing music, read a book, or take a warm bath. In other words, do whatever it takes to set the stage for sleep.

Use white noise to block out noise that might disrupt your sleep

If that doesn't work, wear earplugs to bed.

Check the temperature of your bedroom

You're more likely to wake up in the middle of the night if you're too hot or too cold.

If you're having trouble sleeping, get out of bed

You don't want to begin to think of your bed as a chamber of horrors or you'll just be adding to your sleep problems. Instead of lying there staring at the clock and thinking about how tired you will be in the morning, get up and do something.

"Worth Quoting"

Wondering how much sleep you actually need? Throw away your alarm clock and you'll find out. "The amount of sleep your body needs is the amount of sleep you get on vacation or on a week when you don't have to wake up on any schedule," says sleep expert Donald W. Greenblat.

• Source: *Ladies Home Journal*

Empty your brain

If a particular problem is causing you to toss and turn, get up and grab a pad of paper and a pen. Write down everything that you're worrying about and promise yourself that you won't think about any of it again until the morning. Better yet, save yourself some grief and force yourself to get into the habit of downloading your worries onto a piece of paper before you turn in at night.

Learn How to Relax

Sometimes the best sanity saver of all is to just slow down and take a deep breath. Here are some tips on finding time for relaxation during even the craziest of days!

➤ Be the first one out of bed at your house so that you can have your shower and enjoy your breakfast in peace before other people start demanding your time and attention.

➤ Use the time you spend on the commuter train or in traffic to relax and unwind. Listen to a tape that you find particularly soothing or read sections of a book that is sheer indulgence (i.e. nothing to do with work!)

➤ Once a week, hire a massage therapist to come to your office and give you a 15 minute massage during your lunch hour. It's surprisingly affordable and you'll feel like a million bucks.

➤ Use the time when your child is playing in the tub to give yourself a facial treatment or to read a novel. As long as you're sitting there keeping him company, he's likely to play happily for 20 minutes or longer.

➤ Put on your favourite music when you're making dinner. Your hands may be busy, but the rest of your body can dance and unwind.

➤ Wind up your day by sipping a cup of camomile, lemon or peppermint tea. Studies have shown that the scent of these teas alone can help you to relax.

➤ Pamper yourself when you're travelling on business. Take a long bubble bath, read a novel and sleep in later than usual.

➤ Remember that while multitasking is great most of the time, there are times when it's best to do nothing.

One More Thing

You've started eating properly, you're exercising regularly and you're making a point of skipping the late night newscast so that you can get to bed at a decent hour. You're well on your way to bringing your stress level down into the sanity zone — but you're not quite finished stress-busting yet. You still need to give yourself an attitude adjustment.

As you know, it's easy to get into the habit of obsessing over every little thing — a habit that can keep your stress levels hovering at dangerously high levels much of the time. While some folks are born with the ability to manage stress, others of us have to be taught. Time for another crash course, this time in the art of not getting stressed at work. Here are a few quick points.

Don't sweat the small stuff
Best-selling author Richard Carlson's got it right: if you allow yourself to get strung out about every little thing, you'll drive yourself crazy in no time at all. We all encounter a lot of annoying situations and downright irritating people over the course of a given day. The secret is to know when it's worthwhile getting upset — and when it's simply not worth the effort.

Take a look at the big picture and remember what matters most
Here are a few words of wisdom from Gayle, a 28 year old graphic designer and mother of one: "If working is an important part of your life, that's okay. But remember that you have another business to attend to: home. And the investors there are much more important."

Learn how to choose your battles
Know when it's time to walk away and when it's time to stand your ground. There are some issues on which you won't want to compromise, so save your energy for them.

"WORTH QUOTING"

"Management is getting a lot for its dime these days. When it's too much, you have to say so."

• psychologist Kathleen V. Shea, quoted in an article by Russel Wild in the *Dallas Morning News*

Arm yourself with the facts

If you're determined to do battle with someone at work, make sure you arm yourself with the facts. Take the time to do your homework first so that you'll be able to make the most convincing argument possible.

Look at what your stress level is costing you

If you're chronically stressed and unhappy, you're not enjoying life as much as you could be. You're also probably not a lot of fun to be around, something that can cause stress in your relationships both at work and at home.

Take a new look at an old problem

If there's something about your job — or your boss — that's been driving you crazy for months, find a new way to tackle the situation. If you're bored to tears with your daily routine, see if you can take on some new responsibilities or swap jobs with someone else in your department. If you resent the fact that your boss doesn't seem to value your work, write her daily memos touting your own achievements!

If at first you don't succeed, don't allow yourself to get too stressed

Remember that it can take time to resolve problems at work. They didn't crop up overnight — nor are they likely to disappear overnight.

Train yourself to leave work-related problems at work

"I've learned how to turn off my work brain on my way home," says Suzanne, a 29 year old attorney. "It's a hard thing to do at first, but it gets easier as you 'practice' not allowing yourself to stress over work when you're not actually there."

Make a list

Don't like your job? Try making a list of the things about your job that you do enjoy. (Hint: if you can't think of a single thing to write down, start working on your résumé instead!)

As you can see, there are plenty of steps you can take to bring your stress level down to a saner level — eating better, exercising more, getting the sleep you need and developing a more upbeat outlook. In the next chapter, we'll talk about another sure-fire way to zap stress — taming your To Do List.

Chapter 2

Juggling on the Job

While there are times when changing jobs is the only solution, there's a lot you can do before you hand in your letter of resignation. Up until now, we've been focusing on all the big-picture changes you can make to your life to reduce your stress level at work. Now we're going to zero in on the real nitty-gritty: little changes you can make that will help you to feel less stressed and to enjoy your job more.

Here are some proven strategies for regaining control over your working life.

Allow Yourself to Drop Some Balls

There are a million and one tasks competing for your attention on any given day. There are phone calls to make, e-mail messages to write, reports to read, orders to fill and there is always filing to be done. That's why one of the biggest secrets to staying sane on the job is to learn which balls you can drop — and which ones you have to keep in the air.

Certain balls are obvious: if you don't get around to processing customers' orders or you neglect to return their phone calls, you could find yourself out of a job. Others are less obvious: do you honestly know whether, from the organization's perspective, it's more important for you to fill out your expense report or to catch up with your filing?

"Worth Quoting"

According to a recent Statistics Canada study, the more decision-making power you have at work, the less stress you are likely to experience. "Psychological stress (tends) to be high in jobs with high demands, but little latitude for decision making,"

• researcher Kathryn Wilkins recently told *The Globe and Mail*

Obviously, if you're self-employed or you work in a very small office, you will probably have a pretty good idea about where your priorities should lie. If you work for a particularly large organization, however, you may need some bona fide detective skills to determine the organization's priorities: some companies engage in so much bureaucratic doublespeak that it's almost impossible to get at the truth. You could also run into difficulty trying to figure out whose work gets priority when there is more than one set of players involved.

If you work in the shipping department of a large manufacturing operation, for example, the manufacturing line supervisor may tell you that incoming raw materials need to receive top priority, while the sales supervisor may tell you that outgoing goods need to be given your full attention. You're only one person. Which balls do you allow to hit the floor?

Sometimes the best thing to do is to ask for clarification. If you're less than 100 percent sure about where your day-to-day priorities should lie, sit down with your supervisor and ask her to provide you with some direction. Show her your To Do List and ask her to help you to determine which items are top priorities and which ones aren't. You might be surprised to find out that items which you thought were important — like writing detailed weekly shipping reports, for example — really aren't all that important to the organization after all, and that your supervisor would prefer that you spend your time on other more pressing tasks instead.

You might even reap an unanticipated benefit from having this sort of conversation with your boss. She'll get to see how many demands are placed on you and just how much you actually do manage to accomplish in a day — the very information you want her to have at her fingertips come salary review time.

Take a Good, Hard Look at Your Priorities

Once you and/or your supervisor have identified your priorities, take a good hard look at how you actually end up using your time on a day-to-day basis. You may be shocked to discover, for example, that those activities which are most important to you and/or the company (e.g. building relationships with your clients, communicating with your co-workers and engaging in long-term planning) tend to get shoved to the side while you deal with far more trivial matters (e.g. answering unnecessary e-mails, attending meetings that don't seem to accomplish much and reading lengthy reports just because someone sent you a copy).

If you find that you're devoting the majority of your time to insignificant matters, it's time to rethink the way you organize your day. Sometimes it helps to come up with a daily schedule for yourself, perhaps something like this: handle urgent e-mail messages between 9:00 a.m. and 9:30 am; work on major projects between 9:30 am and 12:00 pm; take lunch from 12:00 pm to 1:00 pm; return phone calls from 1:00 pm to 1:30 pm; work on major projects from 1:30 pm to 4:30 pm; and clear off your desk and plan your next day from 4:30 pm until 5:00 pm. Obviously, there will be days when you have to deviate from your schedule in order to meet a particularly tight deadline, but you should stick with it more often than not. If you're constantly deviating from your schedule, it's time to come up with a more realistic game plan instead.

Tame Your To Do List

To Do Lists are great — provided you let them know who's boss. Here are three easy steps to making them work for — not against — you.

Step One: Empty your Brain
Write down every task that's been floating around in your head, no matter how insignificant or mundane. You'll probably end up with a huge list of items in more-or-less the same order in which they tumbled out of your brain: call that disgruntled customer who left you that angry voice mail message yesterday; order a new cartridge for the photocopier; read the instructions for the new software package that the resident technology guru just installed on your computer; fill out your vacation request; order a new cartridge for the printer; call accounting to follow up on a missing credit note; and so on.

Step Two: Prioritize

Rank each item on your To Do List in order of importance. Rather than trying to rank all 20 items in order — something that can be mind-boggling, to say the least — try breaking them down into three groups: A, B and C. You might decide, for example, that "A" tasks are top priority; "B" tasks are slightly less important; and "C" tasks can be put on the back burner until you have more time. If you find yourself with more than a handful of "A" tasks, you may want to take time to rank these items in order of priority too, using a series of numbers. Your top priority would be "A1", your next priority would be "A2", and so on. (Hint: don't bother ranking the B items until you have time to get to them. Your To Do List may change substantially between now and then.)

Are you tempted to skip this stage because you already have a pretty good feel for which items on your To Do List are most important? Watch out. You could be setting yourself up for failure. If you don't take the time to assign a priority to each of the items on your To Do List, you could be tempted to tackle the easiest or most interesting projects first rather than the ones that are in most urgent need of doing. (Hey, I don't know about you, but I can always tell that I'm trying to avoid working on a particular project if every other item on the list, no matter how boring or trivial, suddenly starts to look a whole lot more appealing. I mean, if I start answering e-mail, cleaning off my desk, catching up on filing and reconciling my bank statements, you can pretty much bet that I'm doing whatever I can to avoid sitting down in front of my computer to write!)

Step Three: Planning

Once you've wrestled with your Dark Side and forced yourself to assign priorities to all the items on your To Do List, you're ready to proceed to the final stage. For whatever reason, this is the stage that most people tend to skip. Rather than re-reading their To Do Lists and deciding that they don't have a hope of accomplishing even half of what they've set out for themselves, they blindly forge ahead and then beat themselves up at the end of the day for not managing to accomplish everything on their list.

A more sensible approach, of course, is to be realistic about what you actually commit to doing. If you've got 10 items on your To Do List for tomorrow and there's no way that you're even going to be able to accomplish half that many tasks, you need to decide whether to downgrade some of those items to "B" status, to delegate them to someone else, to postpone them until a time when you're less busy, or to scratch them off your To Do List entirely. There's no point setting yourself up for failure by committing to do more than what you can reasonably accomplish in a day. Your To Do List should be an action plan, not a work of science fiction!

Now that we've talked about the importance of streamlining your To Do List, let's talk about other strategies for making this useful tool work for — not against — you on the job.

Make your To Do List at the end of each working day
That way, from the moment you arrive at work the next morning, you'll know exactly what you hope to accomplish that day.

Set aside blocks of time to work on priority tasks
Shut your office door, turn off the phone, ignore the fax and resist the temptation to look at your e-mail. You'll be amazed by what you can accomplish in just an hour without interruptions.

Don't forget to block off time for career advancement opportunities
This might mean signing up for workshops and courses that will improve your skills or joining a networking association that will allow you to make contacts in your field.

> ## SANITY SAVERS
>
> Is someone in your workplace wreaking havoc on your To Do List? If a disorganized co-worker is relying on you to save her skin on a regular basis, you may have to put your foot down and let her know that you're busy enough with your own job without assuming responsibility for hers, too. Likewise, if your boss seems to have an unrealistic idea about what you can and can't accomplish in a day, perhaps you should take him aside and gently remind him that you're no superhero.

Build a time cushion into your schedule
That way, if you get caught in traffic and you're 15 minutes late getting to work, your schedule for the day won't have been blown even before you step foot in the office. Take a similar approach when setting deadlines: give yourself a bit of breathing room rather than committing to a project deadline that you don't have a fighting chance of meeting.

Clear your desk so you can focus on one task at a time
Otherwise, you'll end up wasting a lot of time flipping from project to project and looking for misplaced papers. It's also easy to get sidetracked if you happen to glance at a stack of unpaid bills when you're supposed to be engaged in some heavy-duty creative thinking.

Break it down
If you're daunted by the idea of starting work on a major project, break it down into a series of more manageable tasks. Rather than thinking of this book as a 75,000 word project, I chose to think of it as 11 7,000-word chapters instead.

Admit to yourself that perfectionism is a form of procrastination
Don't spend hours and hours rephrasing a simple sentence. Spit out your thought and move on!

Don't become a slave to e-mail
While you may *feel* like you're working when you're answering e-mail, you could be just wasting time. Resist the temptation to read each e-mail as it arrives. You'll simply get sidetracked from the more important tasks upon which you should be focusing. Of course, e-mail is more likely to be a temptation if you get a steady stream of personal e-mails — material that would best be directed to your home computer.

Don't throw away your To Do List when you finish with it!
File it away in the back of your filing cabinet. To Do Lists can provide you with valuable ammunition when it comes time to argue for a raise, ask the company to hire you an assistant, or document the amount of overtime you've clocked in a particular month.

Declutter Your Desk

Clutter doesn't just take over your office. It also takes over your brain. Here's what anti-clutter guru Michelle Passoff, author of *Lighten Up! Free Yourself From Clutter*, has to say about it: "Clutter is like a fungus growing on areas of life that you wish were not there in the first place but that will not disappear, regardless of how far down the pile they are put. Usually, at the core of such a mess is something you are avoiding, knowingly or unknowingly."

Here are some tips on minimizing clutter at work.

Give some thought to how you organize your desk
Items that you need a number of times over the course of your business day should be on top of your desk on in your desk drawers. Items that you use less frequently — say once a week or once a month — belong on the credenza behind your desk. Items that you use less frequently than that haven't earned the privilege of being stashed anywhere near your desk: they can find a home in the communal office supply cupboard down the hall.

Keep your desk clutter-free throughout your working day
Make a point of clearing your desk each time you finish work on a particular project suggests Jeff Davidson, author of *The Complete Idiot's Guide to Managing Your Time*: "Your desk ... is like the top of an aircraft carrier deck. If you take the next pile of stuff you get and simply park it in the corner of your desk with some vague notion that an organizing fairy will come by and do something with it, good luck when the next thing lands!"

Don't waste time repeatedly leafing through the same pile of paper
Rely on a series of clearly-labelled file folders instead.

File on a regular basis — daily if you can swing it
You won't just dramatically reduce clutter. You'll also minimize the number of hours you waste digging for papers that have been lampooned in the dreaded "to be filed" pile.

FACTS & FIGURES

A paperless office? A likely story! According to a recent article in PC Week, only 59 percent of the 5.5 billion paper documents produced in the US each year are actually used over the subsequent 12 months.

Be picky when deciding what to keep and what to throw away

If you're unlikely to need the information again or if you can get your hands on another copy quite easily, don't bother holding onto that piece of paper after all. If you do decide to keep it, mark a discard date on the document before you file it away. That'll make it easier to decide what you can pitch the next time you clean out your filing cabinet.

Is your filing cabinet overflowing?

Don't go out and buy yourself a new filing cabinet! Clear out the one you already own. Get rid of as much material as you can. Toss out anything that you aren't likely to need again and move important but dormant documents into file archive boxes that can be stored elsewhere in the building.

Open your mail next to your recycling bin

That way, you can immediately get rid of any unnecessary paper once and for all. Remember, the secret to leading a clutter-free life is to handle each piece of paper just once!

Be discriminating in your reading material

Get your name off as many routing lists as possible and cancel subscriptions to trade publications and other business-related material that you don't have time to read. Time management guru Jeff Davidson suggests that you allow subscriptions to lapse for two to three months instead of renewing them automatically every year so that you can determine if you actually miss them.

Don't keep entire issues of magazines, journals and newsletters

Either photocopy or clip the relevant articles and then get rid of the rest of the publication. (If enviroguilt won't allow you recycle something you haven't had time to read, pass it on to someone else and let them decide what to do with it.)

Don't forget you're also faced with electronic clutter

More often than not, the in-box in your e-mail program is filled with messages from the moment you arrive at work in the morning. To minimize clutter, get in the habit of treating your "in" box as a temporary resting spot for messages rather than a permanent home. If it's worth keeping, file it in a subject-specific folder. Otherwise, hit the delete key. If you find that you're getting bombarded with electronic junk mail (a.k.a. SPAM) or low-priority messages from e-mail-happy colleagues, use your e-mail program to your advantage: set up your software so that junk mail is tossed in the trash can before you even see it and the less-than-urgent missives from your co-workers are automatically transferred to folders that you won't have to handle until you're ready. (This is done by setting your filters so that mail from certain addresses or with particular subject lines are handled in a particular way.)

Avoid Meetings like the Plague

How often do you attend a meeting that turns out to be a total waste of time? Probably a lot more often than either you or your boss would care to admit! Here are some tips on minimizing the amount of time you spend in meetings.

Don't agree to attend a meeting unless there's an agenda
A clearly defined agenda and time frame should be required, otherwise, you'll be wasting your time.

Try to get out of as many meetings as possible
Get in the habit of asking the person organizing the meeting if you could "meet" via a conference call or e-mail, or if you could send some written comments instead. If she's determined to forge ahead with the meeting despite your obvious lack of interest, ask if you can skip all but the portion of the meeting that directly relates to you.

If you're the organizer, limit the number of participants
As any veteran committee member can tell you, the more people who attend a meeting, the longer it takes to reach consensus on even the most trivial of matters.

Meet when you're less productive anyway
When you're scheduling an appointment with someone, try to set it for the least productive part of your day — usually the mid- to

late afternoon. If you've got more than one meeting to arrange, try to schedule them back-to-back so you won't end up fragmenting your day into a series of useless chunks of time.

Leave yourself an out

Need to meet with a long-winded colleague? Agree to meet in his office. That way, you can get up and excuse yourself if the meeting ends up running overtime.

Bring reading material

Find ways to minimize the amount of time wasted meeting with clients outside of the office. Carry reading material with you at all times so that you can put your time to good use if the person you're waiting to see happens to be running late.

Watch Out for Other Time Wasters

Think you've got your time management problems licked because you've mastered the meeting monster? Think again. There are plenty of other time wasters lurking in your office: colleagues who can't wait to invite themselves into your office so that they can spend 15 minutes telling you what they had for dinner last night; e-mail messages that cry out for attention, distracting you from more important work; and a phone that has a knack for ringing at the most inopportune times. Here are some tips on wrestling with these perennial offenders.

Make it difficult for people to interrupt you

Position your desk so that your back is to the door — colleagues with time to burn won't be able to catch your eye and invite themselves in. If someone is gutsy enough to ignore the hint and invite himself in nonetheless, don't offer him a chair. Instead, greet him warmly and then stand up and walk out of your office. When he follows you, thank him for dropping by, excuse yourself, and then get back to work!

SANITY SAVERS

Don't store useful reference materials in your office or you'll be inviting colleagues to drop by each time they need to look up a postal code, use a business directory, or find a product in a catalogue. Instead, set up a work station away from your desk for these materials.

Come up with systems that make repetitive tasks
more efficient
Use forms and form letters as much as possible, and design
checklists to follow each time you have to work through a complex process (for example, a month-end accounting checklist, an
annual meeting checklist, and so on).

Don't let routine correspondence eat up too much
of your day
Remember that some e-mail messages and interoffice memos
don't warrant a reply.

Don't spend too much time on the phone
Stand up when you're on the phone so that you'll be less comfortable — and consequently less likely to yak! If you have difficulty getting off the phone with a particularly long-winded customer, try to time your calls so that you'll hit that person's voice
mail system instead.

Don't archive voice messages
Write down the essential information instead. Otherwise, you'll
waste a lot of time listening to the messages over and over again
in an attempt to glean the essential information.

As you're not going to be able to add more hours to your working day — and, frankly, who would want
to — it's important to learn how to
make the most of the time you have.
Then, as your To Do List shrinks to
more manageable proportions, your
stress level will start to nose dive as
well.

The time crunch isn't the only
source of work place stress, of course.
In the next chapter, we're going to be
zeroing in on one of the scariest topics
of all — office politics!

SANITY SAVERS

Don't waste time waiting in line at the
ticket desk at the airport if your flight
is cancelled. Head for a phone booth
instead. Nine times out of ten, your
problem will be resolved more quickly
if you make contact by phone rather
than face to face!

Chapter 3

Winning at Office Politics

Up until now, we've been talking about ways of managing stress and coping with the time crunch. Now let's zero in on another all-too-common source of workplace grief: office politics.

Tales from the Trenches

James Cameron really missed the boat when he chose to make the movie *Titanic*. I mean, if he was looking to make a movie about human drama and personal tragedy, he should have set his opus in an office building. The scenery might not have been quite so pretty — Kate Winslet and Leonardo DiCaprio would have had to hang out an eighteenth story window rather than off the end of a ship — but what would have been lost in ambiance could have been more than made up for in terms of plot.

Don't quite follow my logic? Let me explain.

Just think about what goes on in a typical office setting. You take a large number of workers who've had their entire adult lives to get set in their ways and then you shove them into individual, closet-sized cubicles. (Actually, you don't shove everyone into a cubicle: you give a few of the people mini-van-sized offices so that they can feel morally superior to the others.) You give a handful of these folks preferential treatment and treat the majority of them with total disdain. I don't know about you, but I see the makings of a blockbuster movie here!

FACTS & FIGURES

A recent study by INFOcheck Ltd. revealed that men are twice as likely to experience personality conflicts at work as their female co-workers; twice as likely to be late for work; and eight times as likely to experience problems with their work performance. Kind of makes you wonder why so many men end up in the executive suite, now doesn't it?

While the particular issues vary from workplace to workplace, you can expect to deal with office politics no matter where you work. In some workplaces, face time — the number of hours you spend on the job — is the major issue. In others, it's gossip or gender politics. Here's what you need to know about each.

Face Time

You know that face time is a big deal in your particular workplace if it's not what you manage to produce over the course of a day that counts: it's how many hours it takes you to do it! In this particular game of office politics, it's the person who logs in the greatest number of overtime hours who wins. It doesn't matter if he wastes hours each day playing Duke Nukem or surfing the Net while he's camped out in front of his computer terminal. What gets him in the good books of the powers that be is the fact that he doesn't log out of the computer system until long after everyone else has gone home.

You don't have to be a rocket scientist to figure out that face time is a major issue for many working women — particularly those who have other demands on time that make it difficult to put in as much overtime as their employers would like. If, for example, a particular employee has to leave the office at 5:00 pm sharp to pick up a child at day care or to rush an aging parent to a doctor's appointment, she could be viewed as less committed to the company than a co-worker who routinely clocks 60-hour weeks.

Here's how Sunil Babbar and David J. Aspelin describe the whole face time phenomenon in a recent article in *The Academy of Management Executive*:

> Not all overtime is mandatory. Many workers, particularly white-collar employees, put in long hours of overtime as an expression of dedication to their companies. Others feel it is expected of them and is a criterion for promotion.

There are certain professions which place particular value on face time, such as the legal profession. Marcia, a 36 year old paralegal, was disgusted to discover, for example, just how important it is to put in long hours at the law firm where she is employed. "Face time is number one here. End of story. They don't care how many trials you win or how many clients you bring in — the bottom line is billable hours and money generated."

The software industry is also known for worshipping workers who are prepared to burn the candle at both

ends. Sima, a 34 year old software manager, became so frustrated by the value placed on face time in her workplace that she confronted her boss about the issue: "I once asked my boss which is better: an excellent employee who gets everything done in eight hours and then goes home or a horrible employee who gets very little done, but works 15 hours a day. The answer was that the first employee must not be very dedicated because otherwise she would stay and do even more."

Marie, a 41 year old software engineer, has encountered similar attitudes: "Clock-punchers aren't thought of particularly highly around here. It doesn't matter if you work at home at night after your kids are asleep: if you are always seen leaving at 5:00 pm on the dot, you will not be seen as a team player."

Face time can be a particular problem for women who work irregular hours or who spend a lot of time outside of the office. They can become almost invisible — something that's not exactly good news when their annual salary review rolls around. Here's what Kathe, a 43 year old human resources manager, has to say about the problem: "People in my workplace presume that you're 'off' if you're not visibly in the office. I do a lot of work outside the office, so this does affect me and concern me."

Don't underestimate the career fallout of turning down an invitation for some after-hours schmoozing with your co-workers, by the way. According to California-based office etiquette consultant Susan Osborn, who was interviewed for a recent Canadian Press article, being a no-show at these types of events is often interpreted as evidence that you're not as much of a team player as you should be. The moral of the story? Schmooz or you lose!

Some women, like Mary, a 35 year old research biologist, decide early on in their careers that they're not prepared to play the whole face time game — career fallout be damned: "The most productive people in our department are married to their jobs. One guy we work with is close to 50 and single. He spends about 16 hours a day at work. He produces three to five papers a year, but has no life and is one of the most unpleasant people I know. If he's a role model, count me out."

Gossip

"Gossip is mischievous, light, and easy to raise, but grievous to bear and hard to get rid of." While this statement sounds like it could have been written by a twentieth century essayist, it was was, in fact, penned in 700 BC by the philosopher Hesiod. Given that gossip has been a problem for a very long time, it's probably naive to assume that we're ever going to be able to irradicate it completely from our working lives — assuming, of course, we even want to.

Consider for a moment what your working life would be like if no one ever shared a juicy rumour at the office: it would be deadly boring. Here's what Walter Kiechel III had to say about life in a gossip-free office in an article in *Fortune* magazine:

> Just try to imagine what a corporation devoid of office gossip would be like. ... No one knows anything about anyone else beyond a bare minimum strictly related to work. Zombie Corp., in other words, and about as likely to materialize as the *Night of the Living Dead*.

While no one likes to be at the heart of a nasty rumour, it's hard to argue that gossip is entirely a bad thing. There's nothing like good old fashioned gripe session at the water cooler, after all, to cement friendships with your co-workers.

Some writers, including Kiechel, have also argued that gossip serves other valuable functions within an organization. He writes:

> As an early warning system, gossip allows people to think through in advance what they will do if the rumours become the awful truth. Subordinates may get an inkling of what the boss is wrestling with, and this long before he can make a formal announcement; the boss may hear whispers of bad news that no one has the guts to break to him straightaway.

Ronna Lichtenberg agrees. In her book *Work Would Be Great If It Weren't For The People*, she argues that gossip is a powerful communication tool:

> Everyone says that gossip is a bad thing. Not true. It's the octane on which organizations run. It's also very efficient, because it's targeted. Only those people who really want to know, and are meant to know, are included. And gossip spreads quickly and is always brief and interesting — there's no such thing as three pages of dull gossip.

Because gossip can be a source of very valuable information, most experts argue that it's not good to cut yourself off from the rumour mill entirely. "I keep my ear to the ground, but I try to stay out of the gossip loop," says Mary, a 35 year old research biologist. "I find that I'm better off if I know what's being passed around in the wind, but I don't allow myself to react to the rumours until something official comes out."

Gender Politics

According to a recent article in *Maclean's* magazine, women account for 2 percent of CEOs in the top 500 Canadian companies; 9 percent of corporate directors; 34 percent of managers and administrators; and 45 percent of the labour force.

We've come a long way, baby, but nowhere near far enough. Despite all the talk about equal opportunity in the workplace, one of the first lessons learned by most working women is that the old boys' network is alive and well and thriving in their own backyard.

Let me give you an example.

A few years ago, Royal Trust commissioned Environics Communications to conduct a survey of more than 650 affluent Canadian women — women who lived in households which boasted annual incomes in excess of $137,000. You'd think that these women would have a rosy view of women's place in the economy, given their income brackets, but actually quite the opposite was the case. The results of the study were nothing short of damning, according to an article in *Maclean's*. Sixty-nine percent of those responding to the survey said that the opportunities offered to women were more limited than those offered to men. What's more, 68 percent of the women who participated in the study insisted that taking a maternity leave could prevent a woman from being promoted.

The Royal Trust study isn't the only one to demonstrate that the glass ceiling is still intact in a large number of workplaces. A 1996 study conducted by Catalyst, a New York research firm, confirmed that there's not an even playing field where men and women are concerned:

➤ Seventy-five percent of the women who participated in the study said that women had to be better than men in order to be considered equal.

➤ Sixty-one percent said that it was important to develop a style with which male managers felt comfortable.

➤ Fifty-two percent said that male stereotyping and preconceptions of women prevented women from climbing the corporate ladder to the top.

➤ Forty-nine percent said that being excluded from the old boys' network also harmed women's careers.

The survey's findings are hardly news to women like Mary, a 35 year old research biologist. "Our field has typically been a good old boys' field," she confides. "Attrition so far has been the most helpful means to change those attitudes. It seems that the most supportive males in our organization are the younger married men, most of whom have working wives."

While waiting for some of the bona fide dinosaurs to die off is one strategy for dealing with gender politics, it's not the only thing you can do, says Cathi, a 33 year old health actuary: "The best weapon is excellence."

How to Win at Office Politics

Some of us are born politicians, able to turn into a John F. Kennedy or Niccolo Machiavelli in the blink of an eye. Others of us don't have a political bone in our bodies and are consequently blindsided by office politics on a regular basis. In this section of the chapter, I'm going to share some proven strategies for winning at work. I'm not about to pretend that they'll work everyday, in every situation and with every person. (After all, you may work for a genuine, authentic, 100 percent Boss From Hell!) What they will do, however, is reduce your chances of becoming a casualty in the latest round of office politics.

That said, here is a smorgasbord of sanity savers for dealing with office politics.

Radiate confidence and competence
Some women inadvertently short-circuit their own careers because they don't

---

"WORTH QUOTING"

Thanks, but no thanks. Here's what one Saskatchewan government member had to say to working women at the end of World War II: "Well, girls, you have done a nice job; you looked very cute in your overalls and we appreciate what you have done for us; but just run along; go home, we can get along without you very easily." While the government member in question, Saskatchewan Co-operative Commonwealth Federation member Dorise Nielsen, may sound like a dinosaur today, he was truly a man of the times. By the time the war ended, 75 percent of Canadian men and 64 percent of Canadian women believed that women who had helped to staff factories during the war should swap their overalls for aprons once again, leaving the paid jobs open for the returning war veterans.

come across as winners. If your body language says, "I'm really not all that important," and you're quick to shoot down any compliment, it'll only be a matter of time before you manage to convince people that you're less than star material.

Dress for the job you want, not the job you have

According to office politics guru Ronna Lichtenberg, personal taste rarely comes into the equation when it comes to shopping for that power suit: "If you're working at a company where everyone's wearing blue polyester leisure suits, and you want to advance in the company, you'd better start shopping for blue polyester, too."

Cultivate relationships with people throughout the organization.

A recent study at Bell Laboratories in New Jersey confirmed what the experts have known for years: getting ahead has nothing to do with brain-power. The researchers discovered that successful people have a knack for cultivating relationships with people in all levels of the organization. Then, when they need information or assistance in a hurry, they've got a number of people to call.

Master the art of networking

There's no doubt about it: networking is good for your career.

Unfortunately, not enough people know how to do it properly. There's more to networking than handing out business cards and shaking hands. In fact, that's probably the worst way to network. Rather than trying to meet as many people as you can in the shortest time possible, focus on cultivating more in-depth relationships with a smaller number of people. Then, once you've established contact, focus on what you can do to help that person, rather than vice versa. People tend to get their backs up if you start asking for help right away. If you turn the tables and help them out first, they'll be only too happy to return the favour.

FACTS & FIGURES

According to a recent study, the majority of working women have given high heels the boot. Only 25 percent of women wear shoes with a heel greater than one inch to work, says the American Orthopaedic Foot and Ankle Society, a significant drop from the 34 percent who wore high-heeled shoes a decade ago.

Create your own external support team

You can never have too many friends — particularly if those friends are knowledgeable, well-placed in your industry or profession and eager to do whatever they can to help you! Put together an ad hoc advisory team of six to eight people who will provide you with helpful, honest feedback about any work-related problems. You can either meet face-to-face with your team members or touch base with them regularly by phone or e-mail.

Be your own publicist

It's not enough to do a good job. You have to make sure that the right people notice. If you think that all your hard work is going unappreciated, write a memo to your supervisor summarizing your latest achievements and copy the memo to others within the organization. If you'd like to reach an even wider audience, write an article for a newsletter or trade publication or offer to talk about your current project at the next divisional meeting. If you feel uncomfortable blathering on and on about how wonderful you are — and, frankly, most women do — pretend that you've just been given the job of spreading the word about the achievements of an up-and-coming star: someone who just happens to be you. (Note: if you've put your support team in place, you should have another half-dozen cheerleaders ready to jump in and start singing your praises.)

Keep extra copies of really important documentation off-site

Without compromising confidentiality issues, keep back-up copies of important documents and other measures of your success at home. You never know when you might need them!

Blow other people's horns, too
Be the first to give credit when credit is due. If a co-worker helps you out on a particular project, make sure that other people know about it. You'll win her loyalty and respect and prove to others in the office that you're a real team player.

Don't be afraid to ask for what you want
Whether it's a promotion, a raise, or something else entirely that you're after, let your boss know what you want. "Women tend to view negotiating as lowbrow haggling or sleazy bargaining. Men negotiate more aggressively even for starting salaries and, as a result, continue to earn more through their careers," says Jennifer Chatman, professor of organizational behaviour at the University of California at Berkeley, quoted in a recent article in *Cosmopolitan* magazine.

Don't be an ostrich
While you might not want to get involved with office politics, it's important to realize that it's going on around you and respond accordingly. "I try not to get involved in office politics at all," says Marcia, a 36 year old paralegal. "The younger, more imma-ture employees play it and I simply don't go there if I can help it. It is hard not to and sometimes it is necessary to respond to it, but I simply do my job and do it well. I try to be a team player even if others don't want to. And I document my files and cover my behind when I know others are playing those games. With my billable hour quota, I simply don't have time for it."

Don't let office politics drive you crazy
If you're the victim of an unjust rumour, do your best to correct the misinformation, but then move on. Whatever you do, try not to lose too much sleep about the situation. "I try not to get too emotional about office politics," says Margaret, a 36 year old engineer. "After 13 years in the workplace, I have finally figured out that stupid rumours don't survive very long anyway, so there's no point wasting much effort trying to abolish them. Just let them die a slow, painful death."

Choose your battles
Compromise on minor issues that aren't worth fighting about and save your energy for the times that really count. Here's what

Sandy, a 32 year old project manager, has to say about this issue: "I used to fight every battle and every argument to win. Now I pick and choose my battles because I don't have the time or energy to address all of them. This is very important if you want to reduce your stress levels. I constantly remind myself that I am only building computer systems for people with cushy jobs to use; I am not curing cancer or feeding starving children. My job is not that important in the big scheme of things."

Don't reveal personal info that could be used against you

While you might be tempted to confide in your boss about your debt problems or marital difficulties, be very careful about what you say. If your boss thinks that your personal life is out of control, he'll be less likely to recommend you for a promotion. The moral of the story? Don't say anything that could be used against you later on.

Take risks and seize opportunities

Remember what your grandmother used to say: "Nothing ventured, nothing gained." It's true. Some of the most successful people in the world are risk-takers. You do have to be prepared to take calculated risks if you want to take yourself to the top. The key word, of course, is calculated. Don't take any risk unless you're prepared to live with the consequences if you happen to lose.

Don't let a misdirected e-mail message blow up in your face

While it may be darn right therapeutic to dash off an e-mail to a co-worker venting about what a rotten s.o.b. your boss is being today, imagine what would happen if your boss ended up getting her hands on a copy of the message. Even if you didn't make a Freudian slip in cyberspace and accidentally send the e-mail directly to her, there's always the possibility that she could get her hands on a copy. Here are some cautionary words from Karen Coyle, regional director of Computer Professionals for Social Responsibility, from a recent article in

SANITY SAVERS

"If you're a secretary or at a junior level, don't bake cookies or cakes for the office. People may appreciate your baking skills, but they won't visualize you as management material."

• Susan Loveira, human resources expert quoted in a recent article in *Cosmopolitan* magazine

FACTS & FIGURES

Here's something to think about before you click on the send button: a 1998 study by the American Management Association revealed that as many as 20 percent of U.S. employers routinely read their employees' e-mail. And don't think you're being smart by deleting that e-mail the moment you've finished reading it, by the way. It may still be sitting on your company's main server or on your computer's hard drive just waiting to be retrieved by an evil genius!

the *New York Times*: "Many people are unaware that an employer can and often does monitor e-mail. Most people see it as water-cooler communication, when in fact they should see it as posting a memo on the bulletin board."

Get inside your boss' brain

Find out what issues your boss is most likely to melt down over and take action to avoid pushing those particular buttons. If she can't stand it when people are late in the morning, do your best to be prompt. If she can't stand it when something is misplaced, dazzle her with your ability to put your hand on any document in the entire filing cabinet in 10 seconds or less! Finding out what she likes and doesn't like will make it easier to stay on your boss' good side — something that can save you a whole lot of grief.

Make yourself indispensable

You know you're wonderful. Make sure your boss knows, too. Find a million and one ways to convince your boss that the smartest thing she ever did was hiring you and to remind her that you've since become totally indispensable. (Hint: If you're off sick for a day, you want her to notice a difference!) Of course, you'll want to use the opposite strategy when you're getting ready to go on maternity leave — you want to prove to your boss that the department will function as usual while you're off caring for Junior.

Put yourself in charge of your own career

"Career self-reliance means approaching your career as if you are self-employed, regardless of who you work for," insists career consultant Betsy Collard, who is quoted in Pamela Boucher Gilberd's book *The Eleven Commandments of Wildly Successful Women*. Rather than letting someone else determine the path of your career for you, take on that role yourself. Find out how trends in the job market are affecting your industry and profession and be prepared to respond to those trends.

Hit the books on a regular basis
The moment you stop learning you stop being marketable. As you're unlikely to hold down a single job for your entire working career, it's important to keep your skills current. That means constantly upgrading your skills in what human resources experts consider to be the six hottest areas: communication, team building, cross-training (learning other jobs), computers, foreign languages and negotiating.

Be thankful that you're Canadian!
A recent study by Chicago-based consultant John Stanek of International Survey Research revealed that Canadian workers are far happier with their jobs than their American counterparts. "I think Canadian employees feel more in control," he recently told a reporter from *The Globe and Mail*. "It's a more Darwinian environment in the US."

Accentuate the positive ...
It's hard to believe that something as simple as being upbeat about life can impact on your job performance, but studies have shown that it can. One study conducted by the Metropolitan Life Insurance Company revealed that optimists tend to outperform pessimists by a significant margin: 21 percent the first year and 57 percent the second year. So smile: it's good for your career!

So far, we've been focusing on strategies for staying sane from nine-to-five. Now we're going to move on and start talking about what you can do to carry your newfound sanity over into other areas of your life.

Chapter 4

When Worlds Collide – Easing the Friction between Your Personal and Working Life

A recent study confirmed what many of us have long suspected: the most stressful day of the week for working women is Friday. Instead of shouting "Thank God it's Friday," many of us find ourselves shouting "Oh, no, it's Friday!" The reason is obvious. While weekends are supposed to be a time to rest and rejuvenate, most of us find ourselves in catch-up mode instead. We're forced to tackle all those boring-but-necessary chores that got shoved to the back burner during the working week — things like grocery shopping, banking and laundry.

Perhaps you've experienced this phenomenon in your own life: crazy weeks followed by crazier weekends. Whether you spend your weekends running kids to hockey practices or taking your mother grocery shopping, the fact remains that the To Do List that greets you at the end of your working week is likely to be even longer than the one that you left behind at the office. And that's a scary thought.

In this chapter, we're going to examine the ways in which working lives spill over into our personal lives — and vice versa. Along the way, we'll be looking at the latest research on work-and-family programs — facts and figures that should provide you with enough ammunition to convince your boss to make your workplace a little more family-friendly.

"WORTH QUOTING"

"Women are combining work and family and they're not succeeding. Something has to give."

- Statistics Canada economist Ernest Akyeampong, quoted in *The Globe and Mail*

The Work-Family Crunch

Think you're the only woman at work who's trying to get by on three hours sleep? The only one who gets called out of important meetings to pick up a child who's thrown up at day care? Think again. While you may feel like you're the only one who's struggling to balance work and family, you're certainly in good company. The work-family crunch is a problem for huge numbers of working women (check out a few of the working women's chat rooms referenced in Appendix B if you don't believe me). And with government cutbacks shooting holes in social and health care services such as child care and home care for the elderly, it's only going to get worse.

Consider the facts for yourself:

According to a 1993 study by the Canadian Aging Research Network (CARNET), almost two-thirds of Canadian workers are responsible for caring for a child, an older relative or both.

➤ Health care consultants estimate that 80 percent of the health care received by older Canadians is provided by members of their own family — many of whom work outside the home.

➤ Nearly 75 percent of Canadian women with children under the age of 16 work outside the home.

➤ According to a recent report in *Fortune* magazine, 25 percent of employees with children under the age of 12 experience breakdowns in child care two to five times over a three-month period.

Facts & Figures

In the 1960s, 65 percent of women returned to work after the birth of their first child, but only 1 percent did so within two years of their child's birth. Today, 78 percent of new mothers return to work after the birth of their first child — 56 percent within a two-year period.

What the numbers don't tell you, of course, is how it feels to be scrambling to keep too many balls in the air at any one time — something that far too many of us do on a daily basis.

Here's what Tina, a 33 year old editorial assistant and mother of two, has to say about the work-family crunch:

I think our whole social structure needs a good slap in the head. Why does everything crucial to our lives have to be critical at the same time? Look at your thirties. At this stage of your life, you're establishing your career; starting a family; buying a home for this family; and supporting ailing, aging parents. All of this has happened to me since I turned 30. Just how thin does a person have to spread herself? Who created this rat race and why do we perpetuate it?

Tina isn't the only person asking these questions, of course. Over the past 20 years or so, the work-family crunch has been the subject of countless newspaper and magazine articles and a number of private and public sector studies. In fact, our fascination with these issues has spawned a whole new area of human resources consulting: work-life consulting.

Get a Life

You've no doubt heard the buzz words that are used to describe family-friendly programs and policies in the workplace. In some companies, they're called work-life programs; in others, they're referred to as work-family programs or alternative work options. Regardless of what people choose to call them, however, these words all mean basically the same thing: programs that are designed to take some of the stress out of balancing work and family.

The whole work-life field has come up with a language of its own: words like flextime, job sharing and tele-working have been coined to describe the work-life policies that increasing numbers of employers are choosing to put into place.

While these programs have been getting a lot of press, one message that seems to get lost along the way is that these programs are not merely designed to help families with young children to juggle their competing commitments — a misconception that has caused a mini-backlash against

Facts & Figures

Canadian women missed an average of 13.3 days of work in 1995 — more than twice as many days as their male co-workers missed, according to a recent Statistics Canada study.

FACTS & FIGURES

According to a recent article in the *Academy of Management Executive*, the number of US employers offering some sort of child care assistance has grown by 5,000 percent since 1980.

some policies amongst disgruntled and childfree co-workers. These types of policies also have a lot to offer employees who have ageing parents, disabled siblings or similar commitments. Even more importantly, they open up a whole world of opportunities for employees who believe that there's more to life than working — and who are prepared to walk the walk. In other words, work-life programs aren't just for a selected few: they're there for everyone's benefit.

If there's any bad news on the work-life front, it's the fact that there are far more employees interested in taking advantage of work-life programs than employers who are making them available. Still, growing numbers of employers are giving these programs serious consideration — and not just because they're nice guys. They're finally clueing into the fact that if they want to attract and keep top-notch employees, they're going to have to give them what they they're asking for — family-friendly work policies. Consequently, the hot benefits area is work/family opportunities.

Let's quickly run through the pros and cons of some of the most popular family-friendly work policies.

Job Sharing

Job sharing is just what it sounds like: a policy that allows two or more part-time workers to share one full-time job. It's a powerful solution to the work-family crunch, but one that gets overlooked by far too many employers and employees.

Here's how it works. You and your job sharing partner sit down and figure out how you're going to share a full-time job. You might decide to divide everything right down the middle so that you each work half the hours. Or you might decide to go with a slightly different split — 40/60 for example.

Once you settle on the split, you then have to agree upon a schedule. You may choose to work fixed hours that remain constant from week-to-week (e.g. you each work half-days from

Monday to Friday or to divide the week in the middle, doing the "changing of the guard" at noon on Wednesday). You may choose to work alternate working days (e.g. you work Monday, Wednesday, and Friday one week and Tuesday and Thursday the next). Or you may choose to come up with a floating schedule (e.g. a schedule in which you vary your days of work from week to week in order to accommodate one another's ever-changing family commitments).

The Pros of Job Sharing

➤ Job sharing allows you to enjoy the best of both worlds: you have a chance to enjoy the satisfaction that comes from working, and yet you still have time for family and other non-working commitments.

➤ Job sharing is a great stress-reliever because it reduces the number of hours of paid labour that you perform over the course of a week. You can choose to spend your days off catching up on household chores or doing something special for yourself like taking a course, working out at the gym, or spending time with family and friends.

The Cons of Job Sharing

➤ Your hours aren't the only thing that gets cut in half. Your pay cheque gets chopped too. What's more, your benefits packages could either be trimmed considerably or eliminated altogether — something you need to think about before making a commitment to job share.

➤ You could be forced to take on full-time hours or start looking for a new job if your job sharing partner decides to quit or go on maternity leave and a suitable replacement can't be found.

➤ Your employer may expect you to fill in at the last minute if your job sharing partner calls in sick. (This may pose a particular problem for you if you have family members who are depending on you to provide care or assistance on those days when you are not scheduled to work.)

> If you choose the wrong job sharing partner, you could find yourself stuck trying to pick up the pieces for someone who is disorganized, error-prone or just plain lazy.

> You might have a hard time finding child care since it's usually more difficult and frequently more expensive on a per hour basis to find part-time as opposed to full-time child care.

> You might be viewed by your employer or your co-workers as being less committed to the organization than you were when you were working full-time hours. Like it or not, there continues to be a stigma — however slight against part-time employees.

Flextime

If you can barely drag your weary bones into the office by 9:00 am, but you'd gladly camp out there half the night, flextime could be the answer to your prayers.

Flextime is an arrangement that allows you to set your own working hours (although there are usually a few ground rules). It allows you to work around the thousand-and-one commitments in your life while still holding down a full-time job. You can get your daughter on the school bus in the morning, meet your partner for lunch and make it to your son's track and field meet in the afternoon. (Okay, you can't do them all on the same day, but you get the general idea!)

Studies have shown that flextime continues to be the most popular type of work-life program with working women. According to Nora Spinks, president of Work-Life Harmony Enterprises, a Toronto-based consulting firm, even allowing working women to have as little as 15 minutes of leeway with regard to the times that they arrive at or leave work each day can dramatically reduce the amount of stress that they experience.

What Spinks has to say makes a lot of sense. Having the free-dom to start your working day at 9:30 am rather than 8:30 am may make it possible for you to enrol your daughter in a preschool program that doesn't start until 9:00 am — something that could solve your child care woes. Similarly, leaving work at 4:45 pm may allow you to catch the 5:00 pm train — something that may make it possible for you to get home in time to make dinner for your family. When it comes to workplace flexibility, a little means a lot.

Of course, there's no such thing as a perfect work-family pol-icy. There are always both pluses and minuses. Here are some points to consider.

The Pros of Flextime

➢ You can adjust your work schedule to accommodate some of the other demands in your life: the fact that you need to take an aging relative to a doctor's appointment at 9:00 am or pick up your child before the day care closes its doors at 5:30 pm.

➢ You may be able to cut down on your commuting time by tim-ing your trips to and from work so that you miss the worst traf-fic jams.

➢ Your employer may be willing to let you bank any extra hours which you end up working. In other words, if you choose to work from 7:30 am to 5:30 pm once or twice a week, you may be able to accumulate enough extra time to allow yourself to schedule an extra week of vacation or to take an extended weekend every now and again.

The Cons of Flextime

➢ Flextime usually doesn't mean "come to work whenever you feel like it" although there are a few employers who are willing to give their employees total freedom when

SANITY SAVERS

If you have young children, ask your employer if you can bank any over-time that you end up working so that you'll be able to take a day off the next time your toddler comes down with the flu.

it comes to setting their own working hours. In most cases, you will still be expected to be at work during certain core hours (for example, from 10:00 am to 2:00 pm daily). To avoid any flare-ups over the issue, be sure to have a heart-to-heart with your employer about the flextime ground rules.

➤ Your customers, suppliers and colleagues may have a hard time keeping track of when you're supposed to be in the office, even if you do your best to make them aware of your schedule. This may lead to misunderstandings and conflict.

➤ You might be in for a bit of a rough ride career-wise. A 1992 study by Catalyst in New York revealed that approximately 50 percent of women who work flexible hours encounter some sort of resentment from their co-workers and approximately 25 percent end up taking a demotion in order to switch to a position where it's possible to work flexible hours.

The Compressed Work Week

Imagine what it would be like to have Fridays off. You could spend the day running around getting caught up on all those errands that take valuable chunks of time from your weekend. Then, by the time Friday night rolled around, you'd be ready for some serious rest and relaxation. Such is the magic of the compressed work week: by choosing to put in four ten-hour days, you could have Fridays off for the rest of your life — and take home a 40 hour pay cheque to boot.

Here's a quick summary of the pros and cons of working a compressed work week.

The Pros of a Compressed Work Week

➤ If you work four ten-hour days, you can spend Fridays hitting the dry cleaners, the bank, the grocery store and the post office — leaving your weekend free for other activities.

➤ Your productivity could go through the roof, particularly if you're someone who is just getting into the groove of things when it's time to go home or if you work better after everyone else has gone home. Those extra couple of hours you put in on days when you choose to work late could end up being the most productive ones in your entire week.

➤ You will reduce the number of days you spend commuting to and from work and consequently the number of hours you waste battling rush-hour traffic.

➤ If you and your partner formerly worked nine-to-five, some of the extra day care hours can be picked up by your partner, thereby saving money on that expense.

The Cons of a Compressed Work Week

➤ You may find it exhausting to put in a ten-hour day at the office and then come home to deal with a full slate of responsibilities on the home front. A recent Statistics Canada study revealed that working compressed hours can actually increase the amount of stress experienced by working women.

➤ You might not be able to work a compressed work week at all if your children are cared for in a child care centre or home day care. It's difficult to find a child care program that is designed to care for children for ten or more hours each day.

Tele-working

Tele-working is the 1990s buzz word for working from home — one of the hottest employment trends around. It's different from starting your own business: it simply means that you're continuing to work for someone else, but that you're doing some — or all — of your work from home.

Tele-workers keep in touch with colleagues at work via phone, fax and

> ## Facts & Figures
>
> A study conducted by Hilton Hotels revealed that more than three-quarters of employees were more interested in having time off to spend with their families than in earning more money.
> • Source: *Academy of Management Executive*

e-mail — as well as the odd face-to-face meeting. While some employers are willing to allow their employees to tele-work on a full-time basis, most prefer arrangements in which the employee is required to put in appearances at the office on a weekly or at least monthly basis. Still, there are exceptions: the managing director of the Vancouver-based Internet company Suite101.com Inc., for example, tele-works from her home office on the Greek island of Santorini for nine months of the year. (Now there's a job I could learn to love!)

Here are some quick facts on tele-working:

➤ Approximately one million Canadians work from home at least a couple of days each month, according to a recent article in *The Globe and Mail*.

➤ The number of tele-workers in Canada increased by approximately 40 percent between 1994 and 1999 and is expected to grow by another 50 percent by the year 2001, according to the Canadian Teleport Association.

➤ At least half of Canadian employees believe that all or a portion of their jobs could be done from home, according to a recent study by the Egos Research Associates Inc. of Ottawa.

➤ The most prevalent industries for virtual work, according to a recent article in the *Sloan Management Review*, are information technology, consumer products and professional services.

Now let's consider what's good, bad and ugly about working from home — a subject we'll return to in greater detail in the chapter on self-employment.

The Pros of Tele-working

➤ Tele-working can help to reduce the amount of time you spend in

---

"Worth Quoting"

"In the 1950s, people maybe had this sense of this 'Ozzie and Harriet' life. You work 9 to 5 you come home, and that's family time. That's really not the reality of the '90s. Work can be at 9 o'clock at night after you've put your children to bed and you suddenly have to do a few more things."

• Sara Horowitz, executive director of Working Today, a New York-based worker advocacy and service group, quoted in a recent article in the *Los Angeles Times*

---

the car (unless, of course, you have a preschooler who still needs to be shuttled to day care before you can start your working day).

➤ It can help to ease the stress of juggling work and family commitments by allowing you to adjust your working hours to accommodate your family's schedule. If you have school-aged children, for example, you might decide to work from 9:00 am to 3:30 pm, switch into family mode from 3:30 pm to 8:30 pm, and then hit your home office again for another hour or two once you've tucked your kids into bed.

➤ If you work more effectively on your own, your productivity will increase without the daily distractions of co-workers, office politics and the like.

The Cons of Tele-working

➤ You may be required to purchase the equipment required to set up your home office — something that could easily set you back a few thousand dollars. A study by Kensington Technology Group of San Mateo, California, revealed, for example, that the majority of US tele-workers are not reimbursed for any equipment they purchase for use at home.

➤ It's easy to get left out of the loop at work — something Marilyn, a 43 year old technical writer, learned the hard way when she started working from home. "It became obvious that I wasn't getting all the information about the office by working at home," she laments. "And I began to think that I'd become invisible to everyone except those I worked with directly on my current project."

➤ It's hard to keep your family away from your business — and your business away from your family. You'll need to make a conscious effort to keep your children from making paper dolls out of your sales reports and to train customers not to call you at home on a Sunday afternoon. You'll also have to find ways to cope with business calls that intrude on dinner and family obligations that cut into your working day.

➤ If you have a young family, you will still need to find child care. As tempted as you may be to attempt to work with your children underfoot, don't kid yourself into believing that you can spend quality time with your children and meet your responsibilities to your employer at the same time.

➤ Working from home is not a good idea if you've already got workaholic tendencies. Rather than helping you to get your work and family life more in balance, your decision to work from home could end up turning your home into an office!

➤ Some managers aren't prepared to alter their management style in order to accommodate the needs of tele-workers. According to the authors of a recent article in the *Sloan Management Review*, "successful virtual offices require radical new approaches to evaluating, educating, organizing and informing workers. The changes in store for managers of remote workers are perhaps more profound than those for the remote workers themselves."

Child Care-related Benefits

> **SANITY SAVERS**
>
> "I think it's very important to stay visible at the office, keep in touch by phone or e-mail when working at home, maintain professionalism all the time, please your manager above all (okay, I'm still political!), do excellent work all the time, continue to contribute great ideas, innovate, be flexible if assignments or situations change, and get along with everyone."
> • Marilyn, 43, technical writer and part-time tele-worker

Flexible working hours aren't the only hot item on the work-life menu these days. Child care-related benefits are also attracting a lot of attention. And for good reason. It's hard to imagine an issue that's more important to the large number of working women who have young children at home. As the 1984 Royal Commission on Equality of Employment noted, child care is "the ramp that provides equal access to the work force for mothers."

While there's still a tremendous shortage of child care, employers are finally starting to take the Royal Commission's message to heart by offering their employees access to onsite or emergency child care services, subsidizing their employees' child care expenses, or providing their employees with access to child care referral services.

Just a quick aside before we plunge into a discussion of the pros and cons of child care-related benefits. Elder care is becoming a major issue for working women, too, but it hasn't got quite the same profile as the child care issue — yet. While a handful of working women have access to elder care referral programs and other work-life programs designed to meet the needs of employees with aging parents, that continues to be the exception rather than the norm. With any luck, by the time this book is revised, I'll be able to add to the section of this book which deals with elder care support in the workplace!

Onsite Day Care Services

Picture this: you arrive at work with a briefcase in one hand and a diaper bag in the other. You drop off your toddler on the main floor of the building and then take the elevator up to your office. Sound like the stuff of which a working mother's dreams are made? It's actually a fact of life for a handful of Canadian workers.

While onsite child care is anything but widely available — mainly because of the cost — it's one of the most sought-after work-life benefits. Don't believe me? Whisper the words "company child care centre" in a crowd of working mothers and watch how much attention you attract!

Let's quickly run through the pros and cons.

The Pros of Onsite Day Care Services

➤ You don't have to make a pitstop (and find parking!) at a child care centre on your way to work. You simply show up with a briefcase, a diaper bag and one or more children in tow.

➤ It's reassuring to have your children close by. You can pop in over your lunch hour to check on your baby and you're just a few steps away if your toddler develops a fever.

➤ The child care centre may feel like a warm, homey place because you know so many of the families whose children use the centre.

➤ Your employer may pick up all or part of the tab for your child care expenses.

➤ You may get first dibs on any child care spaces that open up simply because you're employed by the company that operates the centre.

➤ The quality of care that your child receives is likely to be of higher-than-average quality. The reason is obvious: your company's reputation is on the line. What employer would want to be associated with a child care centre that was notorious for its health and safety violations?

The Cons of Onsite Day Care Services

➤ If your baby arrives in the midst of a corporate baby boom, there might not be a space for you after all — something that can be extremely disappointing if you have your heart set on obtaining a space in the company child care centre.

➤ If you decide to switch jobs, you could be asked to pull your child from the company-run child care centre, depending on what your company's policy is about accepting children of non-employees.

➤ The value of any child care services provided by your employer are taxable to you, the employee.

SANITY SAVERS

Is your company too small to offer onsite child care facilities? Why not suggest that your employer team up with a group of area employers to underwrite the costs of a jointly-operated child care facility? According to the Centre for Work and Family at Boston College, these types of partnerships are becoming increasingly more common.

Emergency Child Care Services

A more affordable option for employers who are eager to help employees with their child care-related woes is to provide employees with access to emergency child care services. This can work in one of two ways: employers can purchase home care services from a nursing agency or child care agency or they can arrange for their employee to take their child to a so-called sick child day care centre (more of an option in the US than in Canada).

Here are the pros and cons of this type of child care benefit.

The Pros of Emergency Child Care Services

➤ You can still make it to work if your child care arrangement falls apart at the last minute because your child or his caregiver is ill.

➤ You don't have to pay for child care twice in order to make it to the office. (Most child care centres, home day cares, and in-home caregivers require that you pay for days when your child is ill, so if you have to pay for your regular space plus an emergency child care space, you're paying for two spaces that day, even though you can only use one.)

The Cons of Emergency Child Care Services

➤ You may feel uncomfortable leaving your child in the care of someone she has never met before.

➤ You may prefer to stay at home with your child if he is feeling sick, but may feel pressured to make it into the office because your employer provides emergency child care services.

➤ This benefit is taxable to you, the employee.

Child Care Subsidy Programs

Some companies offer to subsidize their employees' child care costs — either reimbursing them for a portion of their child care expenses or reserving a block of spaces at an area child care centre and then subsidizing the cost so that they can make them available to their employees for less than the going rate.

The Pros of Child Care Subsidies

➤ Your out-of-pocket child care costs are less if your employer is picking up part of the tab.

> **FACTS & FIGURES**
>
> The five top-performing firms from 1972 to 1992 — Southwest Airlines, Wal-Mart, Tyson Foods, Circuit City and Plenum Publishing — all have family-friendly work policies, according to a recent article in the *Academy of Management Executive*.

The Cons of Child Care Subsities

➤ Your employer might require you to enrol your child in a particular child care centre if you want to take advantage of this program.

➤ There may be a cap on the amount of subsidy that is available to you as an employee. In other words, child care for your first child may be covered, but it might not be covered for your second or subsequent children.

➤ If your employer has a cafeteria-style benefits package (e.g. you pick and choose the benefits that are of greatest value to you), you may lose out on another type of benefit if you choose to participate in your employer's child care subsidy program.

Child Care Referral Services

Child care referral services are designed to take some of the stress out of being a working parent. Typically, a company will contract the services of a work and family consulting firm which can provide leads on child care vacancies in a particular community.

The Pros of Referral Services

➤ Shopping around for child care is a big job. It's a relief to have someone else doing some of the legwork for you.

The Cons of Referral Services

➤ It's hard to convey your parenting philosophies and personal preferences when arranging child care. Consequently, some of the leads that the service provides may not be suitable at all.

➤ There is no guarantee that the child care referral service will find a suitable child care arrangement for your child. As with anything else, it's a matter of supply and demand.

➤ You're still the one who has to visit child care centres and home day cares, check references and make the final decision. You can't hand over your responsibilities as a parent — nor would you want to, of course.

Other Family-friendly Benefits

There are a number of other types of family-friendly workplace programs that make it easier for employees to juggle their work and family commitments. Here are a few items that you might want to add to your own wish list:

➤ extended maternity or parental leave (paid or unpaid)

➤ partial or full reimbursement of adoption costs

➤ relocation assistance

➤ an intergenerational care centre (providing care to both aging relatives and young children)

➤ facilities for nursing mothers (a refrigerator, an electric breast pump and a comfortable and private place to pump)

➤ a parking spot near the door for women in their third trimesters of pregnancy

➤ noon hour workshops on pregnancy, parenting, elder care, stress management and other health-related issues

➤ an onsite lending library of family and health-related videos and other materials

➤ bereavement leave

➤ credit counselling services

➤ home repair referral services (to help employees find a plumber in a hurry!)

➤ social or athletic club dues and fees

➤ onsite recreational facilities.

Dream of spending a year getting away from it all? You can make it happen if you start planning now. Here are a few tips:

➤ Speak to human resources department to find out whether sabbaticals are encouraged at your particular place of work. If they are, find out what criteria are used to determine eligibility.

➤ Determine whether sabbaticals at your company are paid or unpaid. If you're responsible for paying your own wages while you're off work, start saving for your sabbatical right away. If you sock away 15 percent of your take-home pay today, you'll have a healthy nest egg built up in five years' time.

➤ Start thinking about what you would do with your sabbatical: go back to school? travel abroad? or something else entirely?

➤ Talk to other people who've taken sabbaticals to find out what advice they would offer to anyone who is thinking of following in their footsteps.

➤ Start making a checklist of all the things that you will have to do if you're serious about taking a sabbatical: e.g. rent out your home, sell or store your car and so on. If you're not sure what all is involved, you might want to pick up a copy of *Six Months Off* by Hope Dlugozima.

➤ Talk to your partner and your kids and find how they would feel about dropping out for a year. Then, run the idea by your boss so you'll have a sense of how much resistance you might encounter.

➤ Once you've done your homework, sit down and make a list of the pros and cons of taking a sabbatical and decide whether it's feasible for you to start working toward one.

Other Types of Benefits

Some companies have decided to take the concept of family-friendly workplace policies and really run with it. For example, employees in the Toronto office of Canada Life Assurance Company are able to use the services of registered massage therapists two days each month. California-based Netscape Communication Corp. provides its employees with access to the services of two full-time onsite concierges who perform such services as planning employees' personal vacations, organizing their children's birthday parties and shopping for gifts. According to a recent article in *The Globe and Mail*, concierge Daniele Bennion has "tracked down discontinued Harley-Davidson motorcycle parts, organized a yoga vacation in India, supplied a list of West Coast universities that teach aerospace engineering and found a basketball league for someone's ten-year-old daughter." The company factored in the cost of having staff members perform these tasks themselves and concluded that it was getting a 175 percent return on the cost of providing the service. The US-based Cigna Corporation brings a chef into its workplace every other month to teach employees how to prepare healthy and delicious meals for their families. John Nuveen and Company, a Chicago-based investment bank, picks up a large portion of college tuition costs for children of employees who have been with the company for at least five years.

What Work-life Programs Have to Offer

> ## FACTS & FIGURES
>
> According to a recent article in *The Globe and Mail*, a growing number of companies are using sabbaticals as the carrot to attract and retain employees. "Bigger companies are most likely to offer such leaves," the article noted. "Among those with over 5,000 employees, 10 percent offer paid sabbaticals and 27 percent unpaid. Among businesses with fewer than 100 employees, 3 percent offered paid leaves and 15 percent unpaid."

Wondering what you can do to convince your employer to introduce family-friendly innovations to your workplace? The best way, of course, is to convince her that going this route isn't merely good for the people who work there: it's also good for the company's bottom line.

Here's some ammunition to help you with your pitch — a brief run-through of the major benefits of introducing family-friendly programs to the workplace.

Increased loyalty
Studies have shown that companies that introduce family-friendly policies are more likely to attract and retain top calibre workers. Here's what three leading work-family consultants had to say about the whole loyalty issue in a recent article in the *Harvard Business Review*: "When a manager helps employees balance their work lives with the rest of their lives, they feel a stronger commitment to the organization."

Reduced turnover
A study by the Marriott corporation found that 20 percent of its corporate and field workers had left previous jobs because of work-family conflicts. Given the high cost of retraining workers who choose to move on — one estimate pegs the total at a half-year's salary — companies stand to save a lot of money if they can stop employees from walking out the door.

Reduced absenteeism

Studies have shown that work-family programs can help to reduce the amount of time that employees miss from work. According to the American Management Association, flextime alone allows companies to slash their absenteeism rates in half.

Reduced office costs

Allowing employees to work from home cuts down on the number of square feet of office space that are required to house them — good news for a company's bottom line.

Improved productivity

Family-friendly work policies have been proven to boost employee productivity. Consider what Levis Strauss Chairman, Robert Haas, had to say about this issue in a report produced by the Minnesota Centre for Corporate Responsibility:

> We used to think you could separate the soft stuff from the hard stuff. The soft stuff was our commitment to the workforce and the hard stuff — what really mattered — was getting pants out the door. No more. Now we know that you can't get stuff out the door unless your employees are 100 percent committed and free of home life distractions. And the way you get them there is simple. You do everything you can to help them handle those home life issues.

How to Approach Your Employer

You've armed yourself with the facts and come up with some pretty persuasive arguments. Now it's time to state your case to your boss. Here are a few pointers on how to proceed.

Have a frank discussion about your career goals

Your employer may mistakenly interpret your desire to cut down the number of hours you work in a week as evidence that you are no longer as committed to your job as you once were. That's why it's important to let him know that your job is still extremely important to you and that your desire to job share doesn't mean that you're any less excited or motivated than before.

Read her mind

Anticipate your employer's concerns about any policies you plan to suggest and then find ways to address her concerns. If she's worried, for example, that you'll be less productive if she allows you to work from home, offer to submit a daily or weekly activity report to prove that you're as productive as ever.

Speak in a language that he understands: dollars and cents

Point out that not all family-friendly programs cost the earth: some can be implemented for next to no money at all. You'll also want to point out that the return on family-friendly programs tends to be extremely high: in other words, while the company may end up forking out some cash up front to establish the programs, the programs are likely to pay for themselves many times over because of increased productivity and reduced absenteeism and turnover. If he's still not convinced of the benefits of going along with your idea, point out that there are some tax write-offs involved. That should catch his attention! (Here's the fine print, in case he wants to know more: if your employer provides you with such benefits as courses on wellness and stress management, mental or physical health counselling, the use of onsite recreational facilities, or onsite child care, those benefits can be deducted from the amount of tax the company owes the government.)

Prove that there's widespread support for the idea

Survey your co-workers to find out how many employees would like to participate in programs such as flextime, tele-working, or job sharing. Don't forget to ask a second question: would you like to see this type of program available, even if you're not in a position to use it yourself? Many people may not choose to take advantage of the opportunity to work from home, but would be willing to see such programs available to their co-workers.

Suggest a trial run

Your employer might not be willing to commit to a permanent program until she sees how everything works out, so suggest that the company pilot a particular program. Then, if the response is as positive as you expect it to be, the company could consider offering the program on an ongoing basis.

Don't add to his workload

Reassure him that you're prepared to do the leg work to make this happen. If you're expecting him to do all the research required to establish family-friendly programs, he might balk at the idea simply because he's already got too much to do. That's why it's a good idea to offer to do this research for him — and to do it on your own time.

As you can see, work-life programs have a lot to offer. They make it easier for you to walk that precarious tightrope between work and family and they're good for your employer's bottom line. In the next chapter, we'll zero in on another possible solution to the work-family crunch that so many working women experience: self-employment.

Chapter 5

Flying Solo:
Is Self-employment the Answer?

You're sick and tired of the rat race — fed up with getting stuck in traffic jams with the thousands of other disgruntled commuters who make their way onto the highway at the same time each and every workday morning. On particularly bad days — those days when your toddler cries when you drop him off at day care and your boss gets on your case the moment you walk in the door at work — you may wonder if you should just quit your job and go into business for yourself.

Before you take the plunge and sign up for this roller coaster ride called self-employment, it's important to know what you're getting yourself into. That's what this chapter is all about!

According to Statistics Canada, approximately 1.8 million Canadians were self-employed in 1996. More than 34 percent of them were women. The key reason that Canadians turn to self-employment is because they wish to have greater independence than what they would enjoy if they were working for someone else. (See Figure 5.1 for a list of the top six reasons Canadians choose self-employment.)

Clearly self-employment is an increasingly popular option for working women. According to a 1995 study conducted by the Bank of Montreal's Institute for Small Business, there are more than 700,000 women-led firms in Canada and these firms provide jobs to 1.7 million Canadians. The number of women-led firms is growing at twice the national average rate of growth (19.7 percent vs. 8.7 percent). Women-led firms are creating jobs at four times the national average. Employment in women-led firms has increased by 13 percent as compared to the 3.1 percent growth rate for all firms.

Figure 5.1: **The Top Six Reasons Canadians Choose Self-employment**

1. To have more independence (42%)
2. To have the chance to work in a family business (19%)
3. Because no other work is available (12%)
4. To make more money (9%)
5. To have a more flexible schedule (7%)
6. Because they can work from home (6%)

Source: Statistics Canada, 1995 Survey of Work Arrangements

Those are encouraging statistics if you're seriously considering going into business for yourself, but you'll want to look beyond the numbers when deciding whether self-employment is the right choice for you. You need to find out what factors should be considered when determining whether you'd make a good entrepreneur. You need to uncover the truth about the 12 biggest myths about self-employment. And you need to learn how to avoid the most common pitfalls of self-employment. Those are the topics we'll be focusing on in the remaining pages of this chapter.

Do You Have What it Takes to Run Your Own Business?

It's one thing to flirt with the idea of starting your own business: it's quite another to have what it takes to turn your dreams into reality. While there are no guarantees in the world of entrepreneurship, you increase your odds of being successful if you've got "the right stuff" for self-employment. Here are some questions you should consider as you go about making this important decision.

"Worth Quoting"

"Despite the fluctuating income and other distractions, I'd do almost anything to avoid having to work in someone else's building under someone else's orders again."

• Elizabeth, 40, editor

Are you a self-starter?

This question may seem like a no-brainer, but it's amazing how many people enter the ranks of the self-employed only to learn the hard way that they don't have enough get up and go to run a business. If you rely on your boss or a co-worker to keep you enthused about projects or to prod you along, you're probably not ideally suited for self-employment. Successful entrepreneurs don't have any problem motivating themselves to work. If anything, they have trouble getting themselves to stop!

FACTS & FIGURES

According to the Business Development Bank of Canada, the survival rate for female-owned businesses (47 percent) is nearly twice as high as the survival rate for male-owned businesses (25 percent).

•Source: *Financing a Small Business: A Guide for Women Entrepreneurs*, published by the Business Development Bank of Canada.

Are you a dreamer or a doer?

Believe it or not, you have to be a bit of both. You need to have the ability to come up with great ideas but you also have to have the ability to map out the necessary steps to turn them into reality.

Are you confident about your ability to make this business venture pay off?

Insecurity can be a real barrier to success in business. If you're going to hang out your shingle, you have to feel confident that you've made the right choice about going into business for yourself and you have to be prepared to shout that message to the world.

Do you have a passion for the business you intend to launch?

It doesn't matter whether you're intending to offer bookkeeping services, to make children's clothing, or to start your own restaurant: whatever your business focus may be, it's important to choose a business about which you feel passionate. There's no point spending the majority of your working hours doing something that you absolutely despise! Besides, when you're working around the clock to meet a deadline for an important client, it's your passion — to say nothing of your adrenaline! — that kicks in to help you achieve your goals.

Are you willing to put in the number of hours required to start and grow a small business?
Running a business is rarely a nine-to-five proposition, particularly during the start-up phase. If you don't have 40 to 60 hours per week to devote to your business for the foreseeable future, you either need to rethink the timing of your launch, the type of business you're intending to start (some require more time than others) and/or the income you're hoping to bring in. (If you don't need to earn a full-time income, you can probably get away with working less-than-full-time hours.)

Are you a creative thinker?
The most successful entrepreneurs are those people who have learned to "think outside the box" — to spot solutions and opportunities where others only see barriers. If you've got this gift — and trust me, it is a gift — then consider yourself blessed: you've got a higher-than-average chance of succeeding in your own business.

Do you have good people skills?
You can have the best business idea in the world and the technical know-how to carry it off, but your business will be doomed to failure if you don't have the people skills required to land contracts and keep your customers happy. Bottom line? If you've made a career out of hiding away from the public and using voice mail as a shield to avoid communicating with people in person, you should probably rethink the whole idea of going into business for yourself.

Are you a leader?
Some people are natural-born leaders; others are natural-born followers. It's obvious who is most suited to self-employment. (Hint: if you're a follower, just who do you plan to be following?)

Are you well organized?
If you're the type of person who forgets to pay bills, double-books appointments and walks into meetings 15 minutes late, you're

probably not a good candidate for self-employment. If, on the other hand, you're one of those amazingly well-organized individuals, you could be staring a solid business opportunity in the face: there's a growing demand for professional organizers to help entrepreneurs restore order to chaos!

Are you hard-working?

The job description for an entrepreneur might read something like this: "slackers need not apply." If you fritter away hours of your workday by sending personal e-mail messages or surfing the Net, you probably lack the self-discipline required to be your own boss. Remember, when you're self-employed, you can't hide behind the accomplishments of other people: the buck stops with you, period.

Are you decisive?

Do you find it relatively easy to make important decisions or do you prefer to allow other people to make them on your behalf? Once you've committed to a particular path of action, do you second-guess your decision for days? If you're someone who has a difficult time making decisions, you might want to forego the opportunity to run your own business. After all, you'll be faced with decisions on a daily basis — everything from what brand of paper clips to purchase to which bank to approach for financing — and you can't afford to paralyze your business with indecision.

Are you reliable?

Are you the kind of person that people know they can count on, or someone who is infamous for leaving people in the lurch? The quickest way to kill a business is to fail to honour commitments to customers. If they can't trust you to keep your promises, they won't bother doing business with you again. What's more, they'll tell two friends, and so on, and so on ...

Are you persistent?

Are you the type of person who won't take no for an answer or someone who is easily frustrated and ready to call it quits as soon as the first black cloud appears? There's no point hanging up your shingle if you're going to be tempted to pull it down again in a week or two!

Are you a risk taker?
All entrepreneurial ventures involve a certain element of risk. Will you be able to cope with that entrepreneurial wild card or will you drive yourself crazy playing a 3:00 am game of "What if?"

Are you in good health?
It may seem like an odd question to ask, but it's surprisingly important. Even if you intend to spend your days sitting at a desk, talking on the phone, you need to have the physical and mental stamina required to run your own business. Trust me, 18-hour days are a lot more demanding than you might think!

Do you have a nest egg?
Even the most promising small business ventures take time to start turning a profit — sometimes a year or more. Do you have sufficient savings in the bank to tide you over until you can actually start paying yourself?

Do you have a supportive family?
Behind every great entrepreneur is a long-suffering family! That's why it's important to be sure that your family is on board before you commit to launching your own business. Your partner needs to be willing to accept the fact that there will be nights when you'll be cuddled up with your computer rather than with him. And your kids need to understand that there will be times when you will be tied up with the business and unavailable to them.

Is this a good time for you to start your business?
While there's no perfect time to launch a new business, some times are more perfect than others. If you're pregnant with triplets, you might want to postpone your business launch until the babies are sleeping through the night — or perhaps even toilet-trained!

Do you have a solid concept for a business?
It's easy to come up with creative ideas; it's far more challenging to find ones that are worth pursuing. Before you sink your life

savings into some poorly thought out concept, you need to be confident that there's a sufficient market for your product or service. That means sitting down and writing a detailed business plan and then taking your rose-coloured glasses off long enough to look at the numbers.

Do you have the skills and experience to make this business fly?

It's possible to come up with the perfect concept for a business, only to discover that you're not the person to run it. There may be a real need for a snowboarding store in your community, but if your idea of a high risk winter sport is walking across slippery parking lots, you're obviously not the person to run it. (Hey dude, let's talk credibility for a moment!)

Are you tapped into the industry as well as the business community?

No matter what type of business you decide to launch, it's helpful to have an "in" with the key customers and suppliers. If you're launching a catering company, for example, it's helpful to know which suppliers can provide you with the best produce at the best cost and which local businesses are most likely to be in need of your services. If you've been working in the industry or the business community for a number of years, you've probably already got your customer and supplier networks in place — a major stepping-stone for any would-be entrepreneur.

Do you have access to experts who can steer you in the right direction?

You don't have to go and hire the most expensive accountant and lawyer in town, but you do need to get some good advice. Fortunately, a lot of this information is free for the asking. Start out by contacting your local small business office or by contacting one of the many provincial and national business organizations that are listed in Appendix A. Then fill in any remaining knowledge blanks by paying someone to do things right. (Hint:

> ## "WORTH QUOTING"
>
> "The business graveyard is full of managers who invested heavily in 'sure-fire' innovations that flopped."
> • consultant Jim Clemmer, *Pathways to Performance*

Etc.

The Business Development Bank of Canada runs two programs of interest to women who run their own businesses. Step In is a training and mentoring program for women who are starting their own businesses while Step Up is designed for women entrepreneurs who have been in business for approximately two years and who are ready to take their business to the next level. You can find out more about these two highly-respected programs by calling the Business Development Bank of Canada at 1-888-INFO-BDC or visiting the Bank's web site at *www.bdc.ca.*

you don't want to discover two years down the road that your business incorporation is null and void!)

Do you know how to get your business off the ground?
There's so much to think about when you're launching a business: registering your business as either a sole proprietorship, partnership or a corporation; opening up a bank account; filling out the paperwork that will allow you to collect federal and/or provincial taxes; shopping around for suitable business insurance, and so on. If you have the opportunity, you should plan to take a course in small business management from your local community college or university. If you can't swing that, then pick up an armful of books on entrepreneurship the next time you hit the library.

Do you know what is really involved in running a small business?
If this is your first shot at being your own boss, you're going to have to do a little homework. Don't just rely on what the government consultants have to say: talk to real live entrepreneurs about the highs and lows — financial and otherwise — of running a small business. Join your local entrepreneurs association or take a self-employed friend out to lunch and ask her to tell you the truth about running a business: how often she ends up heading back to work after her kids are in bed, how long it took her business to run a profit and whether she has any regrets about going into business for herself.

Now that you've got a sense of whether or not you're cut out for this whole self-employment thing, let's look at the truth behind some of the biggest myths you'll encounter about being your own boss.

The Nine Biggest Myths about Self-employment

I don't know whether to blame the TV cameras, the glossy magazines or the folks who write those glitzy government entrepreneurship brochures, but someone is doing a snow job on those of us who are self-employed. There's so much misinformation about self-employment that it's extremely difficult to get at the truth. Here's my attempt to set the record straight: I'm going to tackle nine of the biggest myths out there about what it means to run your own business.

> **Myth 1: "If you're in business for yourself, you get to set your own hours. You can spend Wednesday afternoons enjoying a game of golf or head out of the city first thing Friday morning so that you can get a head start on the cottage country traffic."**

First of all, let me say that I don't know a lot of entrepreneurs who play golf or own cottages. That's not to say that they don't exist: they just don't happen to fall in my circle of friends! Even the most successful entrepreneurs I know would be hard-pressed to fit in a game of golf and take Fridays off on a regular basis — unless, of course, they were schmoozing with a client while they made their way around the links or looking into the possibility of opening a franchise office in cottage country! So if your main motivation for starting your own business is the freedom that comes from working when you want, let me clarify things for you: you'll probably have less time for play during your work week than you did when you were an employee of the Acme Widget Factory.

> **Myth 2: "You get to enjoy total freedom. After all, you're your own boss!"**

The only people who get to enjoy total freedom are those who are independently wealthy. (In most cases, that excludes the self-employed!) If you're self-employed, you don't just have one boss: you have as many bosses as you have clients. And all it takes to put a wrench in your plans for the evening is a 7:00 pm panic phone call from your biggest client. That's not exactly what I'd call freedom!

Myth 3: "All you need is a great business idea. The rest just falls into place."

This myth is just a minor variation of that old adage, "Build a better mousetrap and the world will be knocking at your door." It's not enough to have a good product or service. Heck, it's not even enough to have a *great* product or service! If you fail to market yourself properly or to devise suitable methods for getting your product into the hands of prospective customers, you're going to end up with a warehouse full of mousetraps.

Myth 4: "You'll make more money being in business for yourself than you could ever make as an employee."

Maybe yes, maybe no. It depends what salary you could be making as an employee and how much overhead you're carrying in your own business. If your gross sales are $50,000 a year but your overhead is 80 percent, you'd actually be further ahead taking a $11,000 a year job flipping hamburgers at McDonald's. Just one bit of fine print: there are some noteworthy tax deductions available to the self-employed that can help to make running your own business a little more lucrative.

Myth 5: "Running a home-based business allows you to be home with your children and make money at the same time."

Unless your child is a candidate for sainthood and/or has reached the age of majority, you're not going to be able to run your business with him underfoot. You're going to end up short-changing either your child or your clients (or both). Then there's the issue of the damage to your office that any self-respecting toddler can wreak in five minutes or less. (You do realize that the CD drive in your computer is a terrific spot to hide gum wrappers, now don't you?)

If you're seriously thinking of working from home and you have a young family, you need to find a way to keep your kids away from your business and vice versa. That might mean shifting your working hours (e.g. only working in the evenings while your children are in bed) or lining someone up to do child care if you prefer to do your work during the day.

If you decide to have your children cared for in your home while you work, you'll need to lay down some ground rules for your children in order to minimize the number of interruptions. (In our house, the rule is that you ask the child care provider for juice, but you can come and see mom if you have a big problem!) You'll also want to make sure that your office is as soundproof as possible if your children will be romping around with their caregiver while you're trying to work. While working from home no longer has the same stigma that it once did, you don't necessarily want to announce to prospective clients that there's a tribe of wild children roaming in the vicinity.

You should also make a point of minimizing the ways in which the business intrudes on the family. Teach clients that they need to call first if they have materials to drop off to you once your working day ends. Otherwise, you're likely to end up having to deal with a client when you're trying to host a birthday party for your child.

Myth 6: "If you want to go into business for yourself, you should buy a franchise."

Contrary to what many people believe, there's a world of difference between starting your own business and buying into a franchise. When you start your business, you get to call the shots; when you buy into someone else's business, you have to follow their lead. Bottom line? While you have to have an entrepreneurial slant to be a successful franchiser, you can't be so entrepreneurial that you find it difficult to go by the other guy's rules.

If you're seriously thinking of buying into a franchise, don't let the glossy prospectus dazzle you. You still have to evaluate the franchise opportunity as carefully as you would any other business opportunity. While some people have the impression that all franchises are healthy and successful, that's simply not the case. The five-year failure rate for franchises is approximately 20 percent. If you're interested in finding out more about

SANITY SAVERS

Once you've established working hours for your home-based business, get the word out to your clients as well as friends and family members. After all, if people don't know when your working day starts and ends, how can you blame them for dropping by at inopportune times?

franchising, get in touch with the Canadian Franchise Association. You'll find their contact information in Appendix A.

Myth 7: "There are fewer distractions when you work from home."

While you may not get waylaid at the water cooler quite as often, you're kidding yourself if you think that you'll be free of distractions if you choose to set up your business in your home. For one thing, there's the telephone: you can expect to have to field at least a call a day from a carpet cleaning company, a long distance telephone company, or a charity looking for a handout — reason enough to fork over the cash for call display so you can dodge these nuisance calls during your prime working hours. Then there's the doorbell: once your business gets up and running, you can expect a steady stream of couriers coming to and from your door.

If anything, there are more distractions at home than in a typical office. I mean, there's the TV set, the radio and even the refrigerator. While most of us manage to ignore these distractions the majority of the time, it's easy to look for distractions if you're interested in avoiding a particularly unpleasant work-related task. The moral of the story? If your house starts looking so immaculate that Martha Stewart starts calling you for advice, you're earning yourself the title of Procrastination Queen.

Myth 8: "Most people who start their own businesses do so because they don't have any other choice."

People tend to buy into one of two stereotypes of the self-employed: we're either Horatio Alger heros who have gone from rags to riches, thanks to our own hard work; or we're losers who had to turn to self-employment because no one else would hire us.

The truth, of course, falls somewhere in the middle. According to the most recent figures from Statistics

SANITY SAVERS

To minimize the number of times you have to abandon a project midstream in order to answer the doorbell, leave outgoing courier parcels on your front porch and sign the paperwork that the various courier companies require in order to leave a parcel on your doorstep without first obtaining your signature.

Canada, only about 12 percent of self-employed Canadians were "pushed" into business ownership because there was no other work available. That means that 88 percent of self-employed Canadians chose to go into business for themselves because of their desire for added independence, increased flexibility, the opportunity to run a family business, or the prospect of earning more money.

Myth 9: "You need a lot of money to start a small business."

Contrary to popular belief, you don't have to spend a fortune to set up a small business. According to the Business Development Bank of Canada, women who start their own businesses typically require less than $10,000 in start up capital; and 50 percent of those who start home-based businesses get up and running for less than $1,000. Obviously, the amount of money you have to invest in order to get your business off the ground will be determined by the industry you choose to work in: a jeweller is going to have a heftier startup bill than someone who launches a freelance writing business.

The Most Common Mistakes Small Business Owners Make — and How to Avoid Them

You've wound your way through all the government paper work and mastered all the high-tech features on your new fleet of office machines. Now comes the real test of your entrepreneurial mettle — surviving your first year!

Here is a list of the most common mistakes business owners make when they go into business for themselves and some tips on how to avoid them.

Failing to understand what kind of a commitment you're making
Until you're actually in the driver's seat, it's easy to underestimate the

> ## "WORTH QUOTING"
>
> "My intentions in leaving the corporate environment and working from home were to spend more time with my kids while they were young. But with so much business out there, I find myself taking on too much work, giving in to desperate, terribly overworked colleagues who begged me to help."
>
> • Rene, 35, high tech public relations company president

extent to which starting a business will change your life. It's not just the amount of time and energy that a new business demands. It's the way it moves into your brain. In the early days of your new venture, you may feel like your business is taking over your entire life — that you're eating, drinking and sleeping business. Know what? You're probably right!

Starting a business in a field outside your own area of expertise

There's enough of a learning curve associated with going into business for yourself without forcing yourself to venture into an unfamiliar industry at the same time. Instead of venturing into unchartered territory, stick with what you know best.

Allowing emotion to prevail over reason

You stayed up half the night thinking about all the wonderful ways you could promote your new widget. You can practically see yourself making a guest appearance on *Oprah* and seeing the grande dame of television plug your product herself. Time to do a quick reality check. While it's only natural to be excited about your business, it's important to keep your feet planted firmly on the ground and make decisions based on hard facts, not just your gut feeling.

Failing to write a business plan

Business plans can be rather boring to write, but they're an essential tool if you're serious about succeeding in business. Don't fool yourself by claiming that you don't need to put pen to paper because your business plan is all in your head. Take the time to do one up properly. You can obtain lots of free information on writing business plans from your local small business office (see Appendix A).

Having too much overhead

Until the income starts pouring in, you should try as much as possible to keep your initial costs down. Obviously you don't want to scrimp in areas that will reflect poorly on your business, but you do need to avoid any frills until your cash flow improves.

Failing to monitor your business' bottom line

The days of going to the accountant at the end of the year with a shoebox full of receipts are over — or at least they should be!

Smart entrepreneurs rely on software packages that tell them the good news or the ugly truth about their business' financial health with just a few simple clicks of the mouse. You can't afford to run your business in the dark for months at a time, so arm yourself with the tools you need to monitor your business' bottom line on a day-to-day basis. Hint: be sure to pay particular attention to your marketing costs: that $150/month Yellow Pages ad is actually costing you a mind-boggling $1,800 per year!

Failing to obtain proper advice from the experts

As much as you'd like to keep your costs down low, a $14.95 book on incorporation is no substitute for expert advice. That $200 consultation with your friendly neighbourhood accountant could pay for itself many times over!

Flirting with burnout

All work and no play makes Jane a dull — and possibly burned out — girl. While most entrepreneurs find that it is more difficult to discipline themselves to stay away from work than it is to discipline themselves to get to work, you've got to force yourself to take some down-time. Get into the habit of turning off your computer at a set time each day and force yourself to take weekends off. This regular investment in your physical and mental being will pay off for both you and your business.

Not charging enough for your services

It's easy to underprice yourself when you launch your business since you're "the new kid on the block" and you don't have the track record or customer base of your competitors. Unfortunately, if you forget to factor in your overhead when you're setting your prices, you could quickly find yourself working for nothing or next to nothing.

Marketing too aggressively — or not aggressively enough

It's hard to predict in advance how much return you're going to get for

> ## "WORTH QUOTING"
>
> "We who work at home never actually get to leave work, so when we get a bit of inspiration at 2:00 am, we don't simply make note of it and get to it in the morning; we go into the area designated as 'office,' take the Magic School Bus Dinosaur CD out of the CD drive, move the Duplo masterpiece off the chair, and get to work!"
>
> • Deb, 30, self-employed marketing consultant

each hour of marketing effort you invest in your business. You could find yourself sitting around waiting for the telephone to ring or you could find yourself scrambling to keep up with an overwhelming flood of orders from customers.

*Allowing your business to take over your family life —
and vice versa*
It's difficult to keep your business life and your family life separate, particularly if you work at home or your spouse is involved in your business, but you won't be doing your clients or your family any favours if you allow a lot of crossover. Establish clearly defined working hours and confine all business-related paraphernalia to the office.

Getting off track
It's easy to take your business off into exciting new directions without first pausing to think about the implications of these changes. While the adventure-loving part of you may welcome the opportunity to forge off in new directions, you've got to train yourself to slow down long enough to consider whether such new initiatives are good or bad for the business. That means pulling out your business plan and your calculator and deciding whether heading off in a new direction is, in fact, the best solution.

The Top Five Home Office Motivation Zappers — and How to Avoid Them

1. *Working against — not with — your peak energy times*
   If you're a night owl, you may find it hard to get motivated on a work-related project first thing in the morning. Similarly, if your most productive hours of the day come before noon, you may find it hard to motivate yourself to stay on task if you're working on a less-than-thrilling project in the afternoon. That's why it's a good idea to try to structure your working life around your high and low energy times: do priority tasks that require a lot of focus during your high energy times and leave filing and other drudgery for those times when your energy levels hit a low.

2. *Boredom*

No matter how much you enjoy being self-employed, there are going to be some tasks that you dread because they're just plain b-o-r-i-n-g. (In my case, it's keying transactions into my accounting software package. I managed to avoid keying in transactions for almost three months recently but then I had to spend a particularly hellish evening catching up so I could fill out my dreaded GST return.) If you can't hand the tasks over to someone else — always an excellent avoidance tactic! — then try to find ways to make the task more tolerable. Listen to music while you catch up on your filing or sip a cup of your favourite tea while you do the number-crunching required to fill out the latest batch of government paper work.

3. *Feeling overwhelmed by a particular task*

There are times when you'll do anything to avoid a particular task because it's just too much work to contemplate tackling. The way around this problem is to break the project down into a series of smaller tasks. If, for example, you have to research and write a proposal for a client, you might break that down into a series of smaller, more manageable steps: for example, assessing the client's needs, researching the various options, evaluating each alternative, deciding on a format for the report, writing the initial draft of the report and revising the report. (I'm going to let you in on a secret: I recently wrote an 818 page book. If I'd sat down and said, "I'm going to write an 818 page book, I would have been paralysed by the worst case of writer's block you've ever seen. Instead, I told myself that I needed to write 23 chapters that were 10,000 words a piece. That's how I tricked myself into writing the 230,000 words that went into the book!)

> ### SANITY SAVERS
>
> Finding it difficult to tackle a task you especially hate? Promise yourself that you'll work on it for half an hour and then switch gears. If you're immersed in the task by the time the half-hour mark rolls around, keep plugging away at it. If, on the other hand, you're having a miserable time and you can't wait to switch to something else, leave the rest of the task for another day.

4. *The fear of failure*

As excited as you may be about phoning a prospective customer to ask for her business, the one thing that can stop you dead in your tracks is the fear that she might say no. Rather than making that call, it's easier to procrastinate and find other tasks to occupy your day. The only way out of this particular conundrum is to tackle your fear head on. Make a list of the worst things that could happen if she said no: chances are the consequences aren't nearly as dire as you had imagined.

5. *Feeling burned out*

As I mentioned earlier in this chapter, most entrepreneurs occasionally flirt with burnout. You should suspect that burnout is at the heart of your motivation problem if you're forcing your body to put in an insane number of hours at work and you're not providing it with the raw materials it requires — exercise, healthy foods and sufficient amounts of sleep. I find that this happens to me if I've been in hermit mode for too long, trying to meet a book deadline. I start feeling less motivated and my productivity level crashes. The solution to this problem, of course, is to prevent yourself from burning out in the first place. Perhaps it's time to revisit those stress management techniques we talked about back the first chapter of this book!

Looking for ways to squeeze the maximum number of minutes out of your working day? Here are a few tips:

➤ Don't waste valuable time shopping for paper clips in person. Do business with an office supply store that delivers.

➤ Limit the number of suppliers you use. It's a lot more efficient to write one cheque to a courier company than to sit down and write a half-dozen to every company in the phone book.

➤ Carry a pad of paper and a pen in your car so that you can jot down brilliant business ideas whenever and wherever they strike.

➤ Hire a high school or university student to do no-brainer jobs like filing. Your time would be better spent marketing your products or services.

➤ Carry your laptop with you when you're getting your car repaired or if you have an hour to kill in between appointments. That way, you can put the time you would otherwise waste to good use.

There you have it in a nutshell: everything you ever wanted to know about the weird and wonderful world of self-employment — but were too overwhelmed to ask. As you can see, self-employment has its pros and cons, just like any other type of working arrangement. You are in charge of your own destiny — but you have no one to blame if you fail. You get to set your own hours — but sometimes that means giving yourself permission to work all the time. Self-employment isn't for everyone. Only you can decide if it's right for you. Good luck as you go about making this important decision.

Chapter 6

Mom's the Word

Faster than a speeding commuter train. More powerful than a high-speed modem. Able to leap small toddlers in a single bound. Look! Up in the sky! It's a bird. It's a plane. It's Supermom! Yes, it's Supermom, strange visitor from another planet who came to Earth with powers and abilities far beyond those of mortal women. Supermom — who can substitute ingredients in any gourmet recipe, bend grapevine wreaths with her bare hands, and fight the never-ending battle for Work, Home and the Canadian Way.

Wait a minute. There's something wrong with this picture. Do you truly know anyone like this? Could it be that Supermom isn't real after all?

Sorry, Virginia, I hate to burst your bubble, but there's no such thing as Supermom. While most of us have grown up believing that we can have it all — a loving partner, adoring children, a picture-perfect home and a job that we can't wait to get to in the morning — most of us are quite happy to settle for two or three out of four. Here's the ugly truth that the glossy magazines, soap operas and other contributors to the Supermom myth have been hiding from you for years: while you may be able to "have it all" over a lifetime, it's pretty hard to "have it all" at the same time.

Don't believe me? Consider these tales from the Mommy Files.

Statistics Canada recently conducted a study of federal government employers to find out what allowed some women to be more successful

> ## "Worth Quoting"
>
> "Supermom doesn't exist: never has, never will."
> • Anne, 33, executive secretary and mother of one

"WORTH QUOTING"

"If you're beginning to question your sanity, welcome to the world of working moms."

• Beth, 33, university professor and mother of three

than others. The most highly-placed women in the government ranks told them that what had allowed them to be successful was not having children. The researchers discovered that men didn't feel the same need to forego a family for the sake of having a career: 45 percent of women at the top of the career ladder were childless as opposed to only three percent of their male counterparts. "It still seems a requirement for women to make a choice if they really want to get ahead," principal researcher Linda Duxbury told *The Globe and Mail*.

In their book *Women and the Work/Family Dilemma*, Deborah Swiss and Judith Walker summarize the results of their study of female graduates of Harvard's law, medical, and business schools — women who should have a greater-than-average chance of "having it all." They discovered that even women at the top of the career ladder find it hard to balance their families and their careers: 53 percent of those surveyed said that they had changed jobs or specialties because of family obligations, and 25 percent had chosen to leave the workplace altogether. The women told of subtle and not-so-subtle pressures to put their careers before their families. One woman was told by her male mentor, "Don't take your whole maternity leave. Not if you want to keep your job."

In this chapter, we'll be talking about what it's like to be a working mother. We'll talk about how having a child may affect your career and how you may feel about committing to the ultimate of juggling acts. Then we'll zero in on solutions designed to take some of the stress out of being a working mother.

The Mommy Track: How Having Children can Affect Your Career

Here's something they forgot to teach you in school: having children can affect the path that your career takes. Depending on what type of career you choose and how high you set the bar for yourself, you could find yourself being switched to the Mommy Track by an employer who views you as less committed than your childless, workaholic co-workers.

The Choices We Make

Some women who know that they are planning to have families some day make a point of choosing careers that will be reasonably family-friendly. That was certainly the case for Marcia, a 36 year old paralegal and mother of two:

> If I had decided not to have children, I probably would have gone to law school. However, I always knew I wanted to have children and, if I went the lawyer route, I knew I would not have the kind of time I wanted to spend with my children. As a paralegal, I get to do the work and I get to go home at 5:00 pm.

Gayle, a 28 year old graphic designer and mother of one, made similar choices when mapping out her career path:

> There are a lot of ways to go when you're in the graphic design field. It can be very competitive, such as working at an advertising agency with long hours and tight deadlines, but top pay. It can also be mellower, such as working as an in-house artist where the hours are mostly regular, there are looser deadlines, but the pay is lower and there is less chance to be a star. If I hadn't had kids, I might have gone for that high-stress job in the city with better pay. Instead, I chose to go the more relaxed route.

That was Then, This is Now

Some women find that their feelings about their careers change dramatically after the birth of their first child.

"I never thought that having a child would affect me this way," confesses Jennifer, a 29 year old customer logistics expert and mother of one. "I was convinced that after the baby was born, everything would be the same. I didn't think that my focus would go from career to family overnight."

"Becoming a mother has made me put my career on the back burner," admits Tina, a 27 year old law clerk and mother of one. "Somehow, it just doesn't seem as important now to make more money or to get my own office as it did before I had Emily. She is my number one priority. Work isn't."

"Being a mother has turned my 'career' into a 'job,'" adds Lori, a 30 year old social worker and mother of one. "By that, I mean my future is not mapped out in terms of how I'll achieve my career goals, but rather how my work affects my family. Being a mom is my most important career, and anything after that needs to fall in line with, if not enhance, that commitment."

Many women discover that there are benefits to this change in focus — particularly women who have been extremely high achievers at work. It's almost as if becoming mothers allows them to give themselves permission to lower the bar a little at work.

Consider what Kelly, a 37 year old pricing manager and mother of one, has to say about the way the birth of her son has affected her life:

> My career may not have benefited from motherhood, but I sure have! I discovered that work is not the most important thing in my life: I love my husband and my child and they are the centre of my universe, not work. Before Teddy was born, I would work 10 to 12 hour days on a regular basis and I think the people at work grew to expect that and to some degree to take advantage of me. I drew the line in the sand after Teddy was born and I returned from maternity leave. I just started leaving at the end of my eight hour day.

Marilyn, a 43 year old technical writer and mother of three, has found that she has become far less career-minded since she started her family. "It might have bothered me at one time if another writer was vying with me for a plum project or position, but I really don't care anymore," she confides. "I

"WORTH QUOTING"

"My career path would have been completely different had I decided not to have children — but then I would have been completely different, too. The circumstances of our lives affect how we make decisions in general."

• Sharon, 36, community college instructor and mother of three

think that the responsibilities and concerns of taking care of my family are far more important to me now than what happens at work. This may sound terrible, but I have the attitude that as long as I get paid, I don't care what indignities I have to endure at the office."

Other women find it difficult to put their career goals on ice during their children's early years and consequently find that their dual loyalties to their families and their careers leave them feeling torn in two directions.

"I would love to be able to work full-time to further my career," says Phaedra, a 33 year old writer and mother of one. She continues:

> Unfortunately, I'm torn by the desire to also parent my child those few extra days a week before my daughter turns five and bops off to school. It's incredibly frustrating. It's like having two lovers — one is poor, emotional, fabulously handsome and great in bed. You're in love with him. The other is rich, sensible, even-tempered, but you don't love him. So which do you settle down with? The guy you love? Then you're doomed to a life of poverty and emotional turmoil. The rich guy? Then you're stuck in a loveless relationship. For me, working part-time is an awkward compromise. It's like marrying the sensible rich guy but carrying on an affair with the great lover.

Between a Rock and a Hard Place

Many women don't have the luxury of working anything other than full-time hours, of course. They may want nothing more than to stay at home with their children on a full-time or part-time basis, but they have no choice. If they don't work, there isn't enough money to pay the hydro bill.

Consider these facts for yourself:

➢ More than one-third of Canadian families in which both spouses work would be below the poverty line if they had to live on a single income, according to Statistics Canada.

➤ Since the mid-1960s, the cost of food, housing, education and other goods and services has risen more quickly than the average male breadwinner's income. According to Arlene Skolnick, author of *Embattled Paradise: The American Family in an Age of Uncertainty*, "Despite their lower pay, married women's contributions to the family income became critical to maintaining living standards in both middle- and working-class families (since the 1970s)."

➤ According to the authors of *Profiling Canada's Families*, a report prepared by the Vanier Institute of the Family, "To get ahead, having both spouses in the work force is not an option — it's a necessity."

Many women who would rather stay at home with their children find themselves forced to work for reasons of economic necessity — a situation that they find heartbreaking to say the least. Consider what Jennifer, a 21 year old customer service representative and mother of one, has to say about the fact that her family needs her pay cheque:

> I would much rather be home with my little girl, but we just can't afford that right now. Since I returned to work, I've become more comfortable with my role as a working mom, but as my little girl has grown and has learned to do more things, it has gotten harder to leave her. When I'm walking out the door and she is waving and saying, 'Bye mama,' it just makes me want to lock ourselves in our apartment and never leave.

"Worth Quoting"

"Contrary to the belief of many of the people I interact with on a daily basis, cathedral ceilings are not quality of life! Quality of life is loving your job, having time for your family and having time for yourself. It's not commuting three hours each way every day so that your family can live in a bigger house with cathedral ceilings that you're never around to enjoy."

• Marie, 41, software engineer and mother of two

No Easy Choices

Some women are fortunate enough to have the luxury of choice. They can decide what's best for themselves and their families and plan their working lives accordingly. For some women, the ideal solution is working full-time.

For others, it's working part-time. For still others, it's waving the white flag and disappearing from the workforce altogether.

Phyllis, a 37 year old information consultant and mother of two, says that no matter what you commit to career-wise, it's important not to bite off more than you can chew: "You need to have realistic expectations about what you can hope to accomplish at this stage in your career. I think it is too easy to set yourself up for failure by setting goals that require more than what you are able to give at this point in your life."

Phyllis decided to work part-time hours because it currently makes more sense for her family to invest in her husband's career. She explains:

> We take a business approach to our family life. We have a loose strategic plan in place. Right now, my husband's focus on his work benefits all of us by providing the bulk of our income and giving me the option of working part-time and from home. I have to adjust my expectations if I want him to provide all of that for us. That said, my husband makes some sacrifices whenever possible in order for me to pursue some of my goals, because it will impact on our future when our family situation changes. This strategic planning approach gives us each a focus and makes our contributions to the family clear. We know why we are doing things the way we are and why we are making the sacrifices we are. That helps us to keep things in perspective.

Marie, a 41 year old software engineer and mother of one, agrees that it's important for working women — and working men — to make sure that their career path is compatible with the family's goals: "People need to sit down and analyse what they want out of life, what the goals of the family are and what part each person in the family will play to meet those goals," she insists. "Otherwise, you may find yourself going to work every day resentful and unhappy and your family goals still might not be met. All too often, we kind of fall into things. We fall into a job, we fall into where we live, we fall into a routine. We don't question."

No matter how much time you spend trying to come up with the perfect solution to the work/family challenge, it's important to realize that the reality is going to fall somewhere short of perfection.

"It isn't perfect," admits Pilaar, a 38 year old bookkeeper and mother of two. "Perfect would be being independently wealthy and travelling the globe, exploring with our kids, but for us suburbia-bound folks with a mortgage, it works for us right now."

"There is no *right* way to be a parent," insists Debbie, a 39 year old sales development manager and mother of one. "I've tried it all — stay-at-home, part-time work and full-time work. They all have their pros and cons. I think the truth is that whatever makes you a happy person is ultimately what will be best for your kids."

Lisa, a 35 year old fitness instructor and mother of three, agrees: "I think it's important for moms to feel challenged and fulfilled. If you achieve those feelings by being a full-time, at-home mom, then that's what you should do; if you achieve those feelings by working outside the home, then that's what you should do. It's a very personal decision that needs to be re-evaluated from time to time to make sure that it's still working for everyone involved."

Don't be surprised if something as simple as the fact that your children are growing older necessitates a change in plans, adds Irene, a 41 year old regulatory affairs administrator and mother of two: "I think it was easier for me to be a working mother when my girls were little. Babies are so flexible: you can take them anywhere with you. They don't have any social plans of their own. Now that they are getting older, my daughters have so much more to do such as birthday parties, sports, playdates and so on, that I am actually thinking of requesting a reduced hours position with my company." Other mothers return to full-time hours once their children are in school full days.

Jane, a 38 year old architect and mother of two, has also found it necessary to revisit her goals on a regular basis: "As mothers, we have to re-invent ourselves at every turn. We have to redesign our lives and expectations constantly in order to meet the changing needs of our kids, husbands, community and our professions."

The Career Fall-out of Being a Working Mother

One factor that many working women fail to take into consideration when they're mapping out their career paths is the resistance they may encounter from co-workers and supervisors along the way.

Some of the resistance is subtle — like the comment that was made to Jane, a 38 year old architect and mother of two, during a job interview: "The fellow who was interviewing me pointed out that the company health insurance plan covered birth control pills."

At other times, it's anything but. A long-term employee of a law firm was horrified to see what happened when one of the firm's partners, a woman, asked the firm for a little flexibility in her schedule:

> A female lawyer here asked if she could cut back her hours slightly for about nine months of the year so she could pick her child up from kindergarten several days of the week. Initially, she was given permission, but then the day before kindergarten started, she was told that if she left work early on a regular basis, she would have to give up her partnership status, her raises for the next five years and all of her benefits. She ended up quitting the firm three months later.

Margaret, a 36 year old environmental engineer, feels that most working mothers find themselves facing a real double-bind: "If a woman takes a half-year of maternity leave, when she returns, she is viewed as being less committed to the company.

Alternatively, if a woman finds child care and returns to work as soon as she is physically able, she is looked down upon for being a bad mother. You just can't win, so there's no point trying to play the game."

Some working mothers, like Karen, a 34 year old technical writer-editor and mother of two, feel that it's inevitable that you'll lose at least a little career momentum when you're busy attending to the needs of your family: "I'm not as committed to my job as others who don't have young children or other family obligations," she admits. "It's not wrong to be less committed. (It took me a long time to learn this!) It's a personal choice on my part. This doesn't mean I'm not conscientious. I do take my work seriously and do it well, but family issues are a higher priority for me."

It's important to keep in mind that men who play an active role in child rearing can also face a similar backlash from colleagues, stresses Kirste, a 33 year old investment assistant and mother of two. "My husband is going through a lot of this, too," she explains. "He took some time off after the births of both our girls and was their main caregiver for a couple of months when I went back to work after my maternity leave. His job has definitely suffered — especially after the second leave. He's had to watch other people land some of the more interesting projects and/or move up the ladder past him. It's made him a real feminist when it comes to work/family issues!"

Kirste and her partner aren't the only working parents to notice that fathers are sometimes penalized at work because of their home situations. Here's what journalist Betsy Morris had to say in a recent article in *Fortune* magazine:

> Well-educated men with working wives are paid and promoted less than men with stay-at-home wives, probably because they can't clock as much face time. ... Corporate manuals would do well to carry a warning. 'Ambitious beware. If you want to have children, proceed at your own risk. You must be very talented, or on very solid ground, to overcome the damage a family can do to your career.'

Strategies for Dealing with Your Co-workers

Some working women feel that the best strategy for minimizing career fallout is to downplay your family commitments as much as possible: "Don't volunteer too much information about your home life and schedule," says Angela, a 29 year old interactive courseware developer and mother of one. "As much as you would like to share this information with your boss or your co-workers, it could work against you."

"Whatever you do, do not be a Kathie Lee Gifford with Cody Syndrome," warns Debbie, a 32 year old advertising and exhibits manager and mother of three. "I have never seen *Live With Regis and Kathie Lee* in its entirety, but every time I've seen it, she's been jawing on and on and on about Cody, her son."

Other working women, like Lisa, a 35 year old fitness consultant and mother of three, recommend a different approach. They suggest that you lay all of your family-related cards on the table: "I think it's important for working moms not to try to mask the fact that they have children at home who need them," she insists. "I have a friend who runs her own business. She's concerned about buying a car that looks like a 'mom mobile.' She doesn't want potential and existing clients to get the impression that her kids come first. I think that's the wrong attitude to take! I think it's okay for a working mom to look like a mom, as long as she is polished and knowledgeable and responsive to her clients' needs."

Reality Check: How You May Feel About Being a Working Mother

Like most working mothers, you probably have good days and bad days. On good days, you feel confident about your decision to juggle work and family. On bad days, you wonder how you ever could have been crazy enough to think you could do it all. You probably have experienced each of the following emotions on at least one occasion — and perhaps all simultaneously!

Guilt

Ahh, guilt. Every working mother's favourite emotion. If you're like most working mothers, you've probably earned a Ph.D. in guilt over the years.

Here are just a few of the many things you may be feeling guilty about:

➢ being away from your child

➢ leaving your child in someone else's care

➢ missing your child's "firsts" (e.g. the first step, the first word, etc.)

➢ being away from your child if he is ill or needs a hug

➢ being late picking up your child one day because you got caught up in an important meeting at work

➢ being the only mother at your daughter's child care centre who didn't have time to send in homemade chocolate chip cookies for the bake sale

➢ not being able to get time off work to attend your son's school play

➢ deciding to work if you choose to work for other than financial reasons.

"Worth Quoting"

"On the days when things go wrong, either at home or at the office, I feel that I have two full-time jobs and I am doing both of them badly."

• Karen, 36, university professor and mother of three

Obviously, this list could go on forever. In fact, given how good we mothers are at the whole guilt thing, the guilt list could fill the remaining pages of this book! I don't think there's any way you can ever make the guilt go away entirely: you just learn to make peace with it.

Worry

Worry is another popular emotion with working mothers. How many of these perennial favourites have made it on to your worry list?

➤ Is my child receiving good care from his caregiver? Or does the caregiver secretly abuse or mistreat him?

➤ Does my child cry the whole time she is away from me?

➤ Does my child like his caregiver and does his caregiver genuinely like him?

➤ Does the caregiver actually follow my instructions for feeding my child, changing her diaper, administering her medications and so on?

➤ Will my child be too sick to go to day care on a day when I absolutely have to be at work?

➤ Will the nanny or home day care provider suddenly quit, leaving me with the tortuous task of finding another child care arrangement?

Sadness

It's also quite common for working mothers to feel sad about being away from their children — particularly during their first few weeks back at work following a maternity leave — something Brenda Sisson and Heather McDowall Black point out in their book, *Choosing With Care*. "Even though you may have always planned to return to work, plans you made before the birth of your child don't seem quite as straightforward now that you have come to know and love your child," they write.

Here are some reasons why you may be feeling sad:

➤ you miss your child

➤ your child misses you

➤ you are missing out on some of your child's "firsts"

➤ you would rather be able to stay home with your child.

Anger

You may feel angry about being a working mother because:

➤ you would rather be able to stay home with your child, but have to work for financial reasons

➤ you are frustrated by the shortage of quality, affordable child care in your community

➤ you feel that your career is taking a larger hit than your partner's because of your parenting responsibilities.

Jealousy

You may feel jealous of:

➤ women in your office who don't have as many balls in the air, and who actually manage to spend time taking care of their own needs

➤ women who are able to stay at home with their children or work part-time

➤ your child's caregiver — especially if your child cries and clings to her when it's time to go home (something that even the most confident parent can find positively heartrending).

Satisfaction

If you feel confident about your decision to work and you genuinely enjoy your job, you will probably find yourself experiencing a great deal of satisfaction despite the moment-to-moment highs and lows in the roller coaster ride called being a working parent! You're more likely to feel this way, of course, if you have a supportive family, a caring employer and a bullet-proof child care arrangement.

"I can still love my kids, be a good mother and have a career," says Marcia, a 36 year old paralegal and mother of two. "I am a better mother because I work."

A Smorgasbord of Emotions

Most working mothers experience a mix of emotions: some good, some bad and some ugly.

"I have pretty ambiguous feelings about being a working mother," admits Amber, a 33 year old public health nurse and mother of two. She continues:

> I like working because I love what I do and I can do it part-time. That really helps with my self-esteem: stay-at-home moms are not given the credit and esteem they deserve. I feel like I'm in touch with the rest of the world, and I like having intelligent, adult conversations once in a while. On the down side, I don't like leaving my kids with someone else (although my children have a wonderful caregiver), I don't like worrying about making a fast meal after I've been working. And I don't like the struggle to find time for myself for exercise or just peace and quiet.

"Having just spent six weeks at home with my kids during the summer holidays, I find myself uncertain as to whether it's a good thing to be a working mother or not," confesses Karen, a 36 year old university professor and mother of three. Karen elaborates:

> It was great to be with them all the time, but I was going nuts at home, caught up in that no-man's land of stress and boredom that comes from being home

all day. By the same token, while I am glad to be back at work and receiving the intellectual stimulation and adult time that it provides, I am confronted with different stresses and difficulties. But, certainly, over the years, coping with work and family has become easier: the children have accepted their routine, and I have learned some canny strategies for coping with the multiple personalities my life requires of me!

The Truth about Express-line Parenting

If there's one thing that causes working mothers no end of grief, it's those dreadful studies that attempt to blame working mothers for every type of societal evil imaginable. Here are two recent examples:

➤ Economist Victor Fuchs has gone on the record as saying that children today receive 10 to 12 fewer hours each week with their parents than the previous generation of children received from their parents.

➤ A 1991 article in *Policy Review*, a right-wing US publication, claimed that parents were spending 40 percent less time with their children than was the case 30 years ago: 17 hours a week today, as opposed to 30 hours per week back then.

As you can see, the panic meisters can't even agree on their figures!

Fortunately, there is currently another wave of research that offers much better news for working mothers:

➤ The trend to smaller families means that many children today receive more one-on-one attention from their parents than previous generations of children who came from large families, say researchers at Cornell University and the University of Utah.

➤ According to the latest figures from the US Bureau of Labour Statistics, working fathers spend an

> ## "Worth Quoting"
>
> "The way I look at it, I can chase down a career or promotion, or work on increasing my seniority whenever I want in the future. I can't ever get my children's childhood back."
>
> • Amber, 33, public health nurse and mother of two

average of 2.3 hours per day with their children — 30 minutes longer than the previous generation of fathers spent with their children.

Since the academics can't seem to get their numbers to agree, let's turn to the real experts instead — real life working moms.

Susan, a 34 year old librarian and mother of one, says that if you're away from your child all day, it's important to make the most of the time you do have together:

> Make the time you spend with your family count. I know it sounds cliché to say 'quality time, not quantity time' but as a working woman I don't have quantity time. That's why I choose to spend the time I do have with my daughter doing things she will enjoy going for walks, reading, playing — rather than passively watching TV or doing housework.
>
> Because we are thrilled to see one another when I pick her up from day care, Rhiannon and I have a pleasant evening every weeknight, playing together and reading until she goes to sleep. On the weekends, I devote my time to her entirely. I believe there is such a thing as quality time spent with one's children. As long as you strive to make your time with your kids happy, loving and fun, there's no reason to feel guilty about your desire or need to work.

Kelly, a 37 year old pricing manager and mother of one, agrees that it's important to make the time you spend with your child really count: "When I get home from work, I play with my son for hours before he has to go to bed. My husband takes care of dinner and I don't tend to household chores or pay the bills while my son is around. I wait until he is sleeping or do it on the weekend when he naps. That is how I choose to spend my time with him and I love it and he does, too."

Looking for ways to stay connected with your child when you're putting in an insane number of hours at the office? Here are a few ideas:

➤ Leave a note in your child's desk when you're visiting her classroom on parent-teacher night.

➤ Send him an e-mail message to tell him about the web site you discovered that's devoted to his favourite hockey team.

➤ Put a sticker or other inexpensive trinket in her lunch bag to let her know that you're always thinking about her.

➤ Spend an hour listening to his favourite music or watching his favourite TV show with him.

➤ Have fun with her on a regular basis: play video games, go rollerblading or pick up a comedy at the video store.

➤ Leave a message for him on the answering machine at home if he'll arrive home before you do.

➤ Fax her notes once a day if you're travelling on business.

➤ Take him to the office every once in a while and let him over-hear you bragging about him to your co-workers.

➤ Make her favourite dinner at least once a week.

➤ Find 1,001 other ways to say, "I love you" with actions rather than words.

Solutions Unlimited

Up until now, we've been talking about work and family issues in general — how your career path may change because you have children and how you may feel about being a working parent.

Now it's time to swap some sanity savers for dealing with sit-uations that most working mothers will encounter at some point in their careers.

Announcing Your Pregnancy at Work

The pregnancy test has just come back positive. You want to shout your big news to the four winds, but you're not sure how to go about announcing your pregnancy at work. While there's no magic wand you can wave to guarantee that your boss will be thrilled with your news, you can reduce the chances of him hav-ing a total meltdown over the issue if you plan your announce-ment carefully. Here are a few tips.

Tap into the company grapevine

Talk to new or expectant mothers to find out how your boss is likely to react to your announcement and what accommodations, if any, the company is willing to make for pregnant employees and employees who have recently given birth.

Time your announcement carefully

The experts say that you should hold off on sharing your news until your pregnancy is well established — around the end of the first trimester. It's a particularly good idea to postpone your announcement if you think your boss will react negatively to your announcement. That way, you won't end up causing waves at the office only to discover that you aren't going to need a maternity leave after all. (If you're suffering from severe morning sickness, you may have to spill the beans a little sooner than you would like. Either that, or you'll have to come up with a series of highly creative excuses to explain why you bolt from the room whenever someone pours a cup of coffee!)

Know when to bide your time

If you're due for a salary review, you might want to keep your news to yourself until after it's been conducted. That way, if the results of your review are less than you had hoped for, you won't have to wonder if you were the victim of pregnancy discrimination.

Anticipate employer's concerns and be prepared to address them

Go in with a game plan that specifies how long you intend to be off work, who might be able to replace you, what work modifications (if any) may be required and what you intend to do to help train your replacement, suggests work-family consultant Nora Spinks of Work-Life Harmony, a Toronto-based work and family consulting firm.

Don't make promises you can't keep

You don't have a crystal ball that tells you exactly when you'll be finishing work and how long you'll be off on maternity leave, so don't make promises that imply you do. Instead, merely express your willingness to sit down and talk about these issues when your pregnancy is a little further along.

Etc.

Wondering how Canada stacks up to the rest of the world when it comes to maternity leave? Not as well as you might believe. While we're miles ahead of the United States, we don't even come close to matching the benefits offered by such countries as Russia, Hungary, Brazil and Bulgaria which offer 24 or more weeks of fully-paid leave. You can read the details for yourself at *http://washingtonpost. com/wp-srv/inatl/longterm/woe/ archives/mom.htm*.

Be prepared for a lukewarm reaction

Even if your boss is genuinely happy for you, she may be worried about what your pregnancy is going to mean to the company. If yours is the first pregnancy she has had to deal with, she may initially react with panic!

Consider when to share your news with your clients

If your job requires that you work closely with a core group of clients, you'll also need to consider when to share your news with them. Suzi, a 26 year old publicist, learned the hard way that clients sometimes get spooked when you announce a pregnancy:

With my first baby, I told my clients right away. My thought was that if they had a problem with the fact that I was expecting, then I didn't need to be working with them. I also thought that it was the '90s and people didn't have a problem with a career woman having a baby. Unfortunately, I experienced a lot of problems by being so open about my pregnancy with my professional contacts. I found that if clients knew, they thought that I was falling off the planet or something. They worried about their accounts, and if I was unavailable for a meeting or something fell through, they blamed it on the pregnancy — even though that was never a problem for me.

Understand your rights as a pregnant employee

Your provincial Ministry of Labour can provide you with the facts about pregnancy discrimination and your local Human Resources Development Canada office can explain the eligibility requirements for maternity, parental and sickness benefits.

Basically, the *Canadian Labour Code* provides the following benefits. If you have worked at least 700 hours during the previous

52 weeks, you are eligible to receive 55 percent of your average weekly earnings (slightly more if your family is categorized as low income in the eyes of Revenue Canada) while you are on maternity or parental leave. You are entitled to 15 weeks of maternity leave and 10 weeks of parental leave (the latter of which either you or your partner are entitled to take). If you develop pregnancy-related complications and your doctor insists that you leave work early, you may also be eligible for up to an additional 15 weeks of sickness leave. You should also know that the *Canada Labour Code* guarantees your right to refuse to do work that could be considered dangerous to your unborn or nursing baby.

Working During Pregnancy

Gone are the days when women were supposed to do a disappearing act the moment they found out they were "with child." These days, pregnant women are as much a part of the office landscape as fax machines, computers and telephones.

Here are some tips on working during pregnancy. Check out some of the web sites mentioned in Appendix B for more great hints.

Know what makes for a safe working environment
While most women with low-risk pregnancies can work throughout their pregnancies, there are certain situations in which you might want to request a reassignment: if you are exposed to infectious diseases, chemicals or toxic substances at work; if your job requires that you stand for more than three hours per day; if your work is highly strenuous or physically demanding; if your work involves a lot of repetitive work that could increase your chances of developing carpal tunnel syndrome (repetitive stress syndrome); if your job involves a lot of bending, stooping, stair- or ladder-climbing or heavy lifting; if you work in an extremely hot, cold or noisy environment; or if you work long hours or rotating shifts.

Find ways to stay comfortable on the job
The experts suggest that you wear comfortable shoes and loose clothing; put your feet up on a stool in order to relieve pressure on your lower back; keep a jug of cold water on your desk to

remind yourself to drink frequently; take five- or ten-minute cat naps during your lunch hour and/or your breaks; and keep your stress level to a minimum. (You can brush up on your stress-busting techniques by flipping back to Chapter 1.)

Resist the temptation to skip lunch
Your growing baby needs food on a regular basis — ideally four to six mini-meals per day. If you're too busy to take a real lunch hour, make sure that whatever you end up eating at your desk scores an A+ in the nutrition department.

Negotiating the Best Possible Maternity Leave
Hoping to take an extended maternity leave so that you'll have more time to get to know your new baby? Here are some tips on convincing your boss to give you the most generous maternity leave package possible.

Do your homework
Tap into the company grapevine and find out what types of maternity leave arrangements other women in your company have made. Often, what's written in the company benefits manual is just a starting point for discussions. (Just think of it as the list price for a car — an initial figure that's open to negotiation.)

Offer to play a major role in selecting and training your replacement
After all, it's in your best interests to do whatever you can to ensure that things run smoothly in your absence. The last thing you need when you stumble back to work in a post-baby haze is to have to troubleshoot the 1,001 problems that arose in your absence.

Let your employer know how available you'll be during your leave
If you're willing to field weekly phone calls, but you don't want to be bothered with a dozen questions a day, say so. Work-family consultant Nora Spinks of

---

SANITY SAVERS

Don't go broke trying to fill your closet with maternity power suits. In many communities, it's possible to rent an entire maternity wardrobe for about what you'd expect to pay for one or two outfits you could wear to the office. Check in your Yellow Pages under "Women's Apparel — Retail."

Work Life Harmony suggests that you be as specific as possible: let your employer know what issues you're willing to be consulted on during your maternity leave and which meetings you're prepared to attend, for example.

Be creative
If your employer expects you to return to work sooner than you would like, ask if you can work part-time for the first few months. If he won't go for that, ask if you can tele-commute a couple of days each week or work flextime hours (see Chapter 4 for more information on these family-friendly options).

Don't plan to be at work when the labour contractions start!
There's something to be said for taking a week or two off before your baby arrives. Here's what Kim, one of the mothers I interviewed for my book *The Unofficial Guide to Having A Baby*, had to say about working until the last minute: "I wish someone had told me how unrealistic it was to work up until the baby was born. My thinking was that as long as I felt good, I should keep working so that I could spend my maternity leave with the baby. I worked up until the day I gave birth, went home from work, stopped at the store and my water broke. So it was off to the hospital. I wish I had taken a week off to rest."

Don't agree to come back too soon
It's easy to underestimate how tired you may feel and how much you may want to be with your baby. If anything, err on the side of caution: ask for a longer leave than you intend to take and come back early if you find that you're going stir-crazy at home.

Shoot for the stars
Ask for what you want in terms of the length of your maternity leave and the percentage of pay you would like to receive, and then be prepared to compromise. Keep in mind that it's in your employer's best interest to cut you a good deal: a recent study by Cigna Healthcare in the US revealed that working women are seven times more likely to return to their jobs after their maternity leave if their employers are willing to negotiate a fair maternity leave plan. Given the high cost of training someone to replace you, your employer may be willing to meet you halfway.

Returning to Work After Your Maternity Leave

The moment of truth has finally arrived: you're returning to work after the birth of your baby. Here are some tips on surviving those first few weeks back on the job.

Plan ahead for your first day back at work
Fill your freezer with healthy meals that can be popped in the microwave as soon as you arrive home from work. (Hint: don't wait until after your baby is born to make these meals or they'll never get done. Instead, put some of that third-trimester nesting instinct to good use in the kitchen. This is, by the way, the perfect make-work project if your due date comes and goes and there's still no baby!)

Get the heads up from someone at work
Take a co-worker out to lunch the week before you go back to work and ask her to bring you up to speed on what's going on at work. That way, you won't feel quite so overwhelmed and clued out on your first day back on the job.

Accept the fact that you're going to feel a bit crazy at first
It's hard enough being a working woman; it can be downright exhausting to be a working mother. You may find yourself feeling a little weepy the first week — particularly if you're not getting enough sleep. LaRee, a 28 year old bank teller and mother of one, is the first to admit that she was a bit of a mess during her first day back on the job: "I was in such a panic to get to see my son on my first day back at work that when I backed out of the parking lot, I drove into the garbage dumpster. I didn't even stop to survey the damage. In fact, I forgot all about it until my husband came into the house that evening, fuming about the large dent in my car."

Clear your To Do List of all but the necessities
This is no time to be taking on volunteer work, signing up for a night school class, or renovating your house. Your top priorities should be your baby and your job. Give yourself permission to let everything else go.

Dress the part
After months of living in maternity clothes or sweat-pants, it can

feel a bit odd to be wearing "real clothes" again, to say nothing of putting on makeup! It's definitely worth the effort, however. Even if you don't feel like you've got your act together yet, you'll do well convincing others if you manage to dress the part.

Reassure your co-workers and supervisor that it's business as usual again

While you may need to request certain concessions from time to time — for example, you may need to take an extra-long lunch hour in order to take your baby to a doctor's appointment — you want to let everyone know that you can be counted on to pull your weight at work once again.

Find someone to talk to — ideally another working mother who's been there, done that

It's important to have someone to confide in on those days when you feel like you were insane to think that you could juggle a baby and a job. If you don't want to spill your guts to your co-workers — something that could come back to haunt you — pick up the phone and call your best friend or your sister-in-law instead; or turn on the computer and visit one of the many working mothers' bulletin boards and web sites online. (You'll find some leads on the very best sites in Appendix B.)

Breast-feeding and Working

Breast-feeding isn't an all or nothing proposition. You don't have to wean your child just because you're returning to work. Here are some tips on making breast-feeding work for you if you decide to continue to nurse your baby once your maternity leave ends.

Think about what you need to do to make it work

Some situations are ideal — if you have access to on-site child

SANITY SAVERS

Your first week back at work is the perfect time to call in all those favours you've been accumulating. Let a friend make you dinner. See if your mother-in-law would mind helping you catch up on your laundry one evening. If you can't round up enough volunteers, pay someone to help you. High school, college and university students are quite capable of doing laundry, cooking, cleaning and running errands for you. What's more, they're a bargain. If you don't know any families with students, call the placement office of your local high school, college or university and ask them to post a "help wanted" ad for you.

care, for example. Others are not — if you work irregular hours and can't predict your schedule more than a few minutes in advance. If your working situation is particularly challenging, you may want to talk to other women in your workplace who successfully breast-fed their babies after returning to work so that you can pick up some tips from them.

Plan to take as long a maternity leave as you can

The longer you're off work, the more time you can spend establishing your milk supply, troubleshooting any difficulties you and your baby may be experiencing (e.g. poor positioning or incorrect latch) and recovering from the rigours of childbirth.

Find a breast-feeding-friendly child care provider for your baby

Look for someone who breast-fed her own babies or who has had previous experience caring for breast-fed babies. (They are, after all, a different breed!) Find out what techniques she uses to soothe breast-fed babies who are used to nursing when they are in need of comfort and what feeding methods she would use to get your baby to take breast milk (e.g. small cup, spoon, medicine dropper or oral syringe) if he refused to take a bottle.

Introduce a bottle early — but not too early

Don't wait until the week before you're returning to work to teach your baby how to use a bottle. She might refuse to have anything to do with it! The experts suggest that you introduce a bottle after breast-feeding is well established (around the six week mark, in most cases), but before your child gets too set in her ways to take to a bottle easily (around the three to four month mark, for most babies).

Rent or purchase the Cadillac of breast pumps

A hospital-grade breast pump most closely mimics the sucking action of breast-feeding babies, something that promotes an efficient letdown and helps to minimize any breast soreness. Many of these units come with double-pump kits, a timesaving feature that can allow you to pump from both breasts at once. (Now that's what I call multitasking!)

Master the art of pumping

Learn how to massage your breasts to get the milk flowing and how to relax while the breast pump is working its magic. (Hint: this may be the only time in your day when you can close your eyes or read for pleasure. Who knows? You just might get hooked on pumping!)

Wear breast-feeding-friendly clothes

The last thing you want is to have to remove your entire dress so that you can get at your breasts — or to discover that you've just leaked milk all over your $90 silk blouse. Look for garments that either button up the front, that pull up easily (e.g. oversized shirts), or that allow for easy access to your breasts (e.g. specially designed nursing shirts that have secret trap doors in all the right spots); choose brightly-patterned or dark colours (they help to hide breast-pads and to camouflage any leaks); and select only wash-and-wear fabrics (cottons and synthetics are ideal). You should also plan to keep a spare shirt at work in case you have a particularly leaky day — something that's most likely to happen during your first few weeks back at work as your breasts try to come to terms with your new nursing schedule.

Line up support at work

Ask your employer to support your decision to breast-feed your baby by ensuring that you have a private spot to use your breast pump or nurse your baby (assuming that your baby's caregiver is able to bring him to you for a midday feeding). You might even ask if the company would be willing to purchase a hospital-grade breast pump for the use of its employees and to provide a small refrigerator where breast milk can be stored. If your employer seems less than enthused about supporting your decision to breast-feed, remind her that breast-fed infants are generally only

SANITY SAVERS

Run out of breast pads at work? Hit the sanitary pad vending machine instead. As long as you don't mind having a slightly square-breasted look, you'll find that a sanitary pad cut in half makes a great emergency breast pad!

sick half as often as their bottle-fed counterparts, and that the fewer days your baby is ill, the fewer days you'll miss from work!

Don't let breast-feeding become just one more item on your To Do List

Give yourself permission to substitute formula for certain feedings or to wean your child entirely if you're starting to resent the time that you're spending hooked up to a breast pump. While breast-feeding is the ideal food for babies, formula makes a good second choice. Contrary to what some people would have you believe, offering your baby a bottle of formula does not constitute child abuse! Don't let anyone make you feel like you're a horrible mother if you decide to stop nursing your baby.

As you can see, there's a lot to think about when you're a working mother, particularly when your baby is still young. Don't be surprised if there are days when you feel like waving the proverbial white flag. We've all felt that way from time to time! One thing that will help to keep you sane is a top-notch child care arrangement — the subject of our next chapter.

Chapter 7

Mary Poppins, Where are You? Finding the Right Child Care

Want to know what working mothers are most worried about? You won't have to dig very deep. Keep your ears open the next time you walk through the cafeteria at work and you're likely to hear at least one working mother talking about the concerns she has about her son or daughter's child care arrangement. Is the child care provider abusing her child? Does the child care provider genuinely like her child? Will the child care provider quit without giving her any notice, leaving her with a major crisis to resolve overnight? These are just a few of the thoughts that go through the minds of many working mothers while they're trying to function on the job.

In a perfect world, we'd all have our own personal live-in Mary Poppins — someone who would provide our children with top-notch care during the hours while we are away. Unfortunately, most working families find themselves struggling to make their way through the child care jungle in a quest to find a safe and stimulating child care environment at a price they can afford.

Your Search for Child Care

It's something that's much easier said than done, given the chronic shortage of child care in this country, but it's by no means impossible. Here are a few tips designed to take some of the stress out of your search for child care.

Start your search early
Child care spaces are in chronically short supply, so it pays to start your child care search as soon as possible — especially if

you're looking for child care for an infant. While you may still luck out and find the child care arrangement of your dreams despite the fact that you have left your search until the last minute, you increase your odds of finding something suitable if you start looking a little sooner. As a rule of thumb, you should have your search well underway by the end of your second trimester of pregnancy. Of course, if you've got your heart set on finding a space for your child in a particular day care centre or if you live in a high-demand area or city, you will want to get your name on the waiting list even earlier than that — perhaps even as soon as you decide that you're ready to start a family!

Put the grapevine to work for you
Let everyone you come into contact with know that you're looking for child care: family members, friends, neighbours, your dentist, your child's paediatrician and so on. Not only will this help to speed up your search, it'll also increase your odds of finding a high quality child care setting.

Find out what makes for a good child care arrangement
Most parents spend more time researching car purchases than they do in educating themselves about what makes for a good child care arrangement. Before you start evaluating various child care arrangements, you'll want to arm yourself with the facts. Find out what caregiver-child ratios are appropriate for children of various ages; what training child care workers are required to have in your particular province; what health and safety features you should be looking for when you're evaluating a child care centre or home day care; and what makes for a fun and stimulating child care program. (You can find detailed checklists and other useful information in my book *The Unofficial Guide to Child care.*)

Look for an arrangement that will meet your family's needs for the next few years
Changing child care arrangements is hard on both you and your child. That's

why it's important to consider your family's long-term needs before settling on a particular arrangement. Will the quiet home day care environment that is ideal for your sleepy newborn be an equally suitable setting when she becomes a rambunctious toddler? Will your child's space in the company day care centre disappear if you decide to change jobs? Is the nanny you're thinking of hiring committed to your family for the long term or for just a year or two? These are the types of questions that you need to consider before settling on a particular child care arrangement.

Take the time to check the caregiver's references properly
It's tempting to rely on your gut instinct when you're evaluating a particular child care arrangement, but you owe it to your child to check things out a little more thoroughly. That means checking the references of the nanny, home day care provider, or day care centre staff person who will be caring for your child. Because many people are reluctant to badmouth a particular child care provider out of fear that they'll be sued for making slanderous remarks, you really have to read between the lines when you're conducting a reference check. Bottom line? If the person providing the reference is less than enthusiastic about the caregiver's ability to care for young children, start looking for another caregiver.

*Find out what your responsibilities are if you hire an
in-home caregiver*
The moment you hire a nanny or other in-home caregiver, you automatically become her employer — at least in the eyes of Revenue Canada. That means that you are responsible for finding out whether she's legally entitled to work in Canada; paying her the minimum wage (or more!) and complying with provincial and federal labour laws; and withholding her Canadian Pension Plan contributions, Employment Insurance contributions and income tax from her pay cheques. You can get more detailed information about the ins and outs of hiring a caregiver by contacting your local Human Resources Development Canada office (in the blue pages of your phone book) or by visiting the Human Resources Development Canada web site at *http://www.hrdc-drhc.gc.ca.*

Easing Your Child into a New Child Care Arrangement

Starting a new child care arrangement can be stressful for both you and your child. Here are some tips on making the transition a little smoother for the two of you.

If your child is old enough to understand, take some time to explain day care
You know that you're going to be coming back for him at the end of the day; he won't know unless you tell him. You may find it helpful to pick up a children's book about day care so that he can see the pictures of parents dropping children off at day care in the morning and then picking them up again in the afternoon.

Make a few dry runs
Visit the day care centre or home day care a few times before your child's first day — or invite your child's in-home caregiver over for dinner once or twice before she officially starts working for your family.

Take time to show the new child care provider the ropes
The more information you can tell her about your child, the easier the transition will be for all concerned. Describe your child's daily routine, her likes and dislikes, her food preferences, her sleeping habits, and your family situation in as much detail as possible. Rather than overwhelming the caregiver by providing this information verbally, give her some written notes. That way, she'll have something to refer back to if she can't remember what lullaby your child likes to listen to when she's drifting off to sleep.

Be there for your child
Make a point of spending at least a half day with your child when he starts a new child care arrangement. You can gradually allow the caregiver to assume more responsibility for your child's care as the two of them warm up to one another. It doesn't matter whether your child's being cared for in a child care centre, home day care, or by a nanny in his own home: he'll be more willing to give his new caregiver a chance if you're there to provide some initial reassurance.

Plan to spend some time at the caregiver's each morning
Get in the habit of arriving at the child care centre or home day care at least 15 minutes before you have to leave. That will give her caregiver a chance to get her involved in an activity before you have to make your exit. She will be less likely to protest if she's having fun.

Resist the temptation to sneak out when your child isn't looking
While it may seem like the perfect way to avoid tears upon your departure, you're really only setting yourself up for more problems in the long run. Your child may become constantly worried that you're about to leave him without warning — something that may cause him to wake up repeatedly in the night to check that you're still there!

When it's time, hand your child to the caregiver rather than allowing her to take him from you
It's a little thing, but your child will be reassured by the fact that it was your choice to hand him to the caregiver rather than vice versa.

If your child is having a difficult time being apart from you, leave an item of your clothing with his caregiver
A young baby may be comforted by being able to snuggle up to a sweater that smells like you. A toddler or preschooler may prefer to have a photo of you to carry around in his pocket.

Hold your tears until you get outside
You may find it very difficult to say goodbye to your child when you first return to work, but it's important to try to put on a happy face for the sake of your child. If you seem distraught, she'll pick up on your concern and start to get upset, too. Even if your child is too young to understand what you're saying, tell her that you love her and that you'll be back to pick her up

"Worth Quoting"

"I thought my heart was going to break the first day I had to leave my son at day care. I sobbed all the way to work and I kept tearing up every time someone asked me how I was doing. Now that my son is older, I see how much he enjoys playing with the other children, so that makes it easier. Most days when I tell him I'm leaving, he barely stops playing long enough to wave goodbye."

• Anne, 33, executive secretary and mother of one

in a few hours. She'll be reassured by your body language and the tone of your voice.

Expect a few tears upon your return

Researchers at Boston's Children's Hospital discovered that children tend to cry more when their parents *return* than when they *depart!* Apparently, this is because babies tend to express their strongest emotions when they're in the company of those they care about most. So if your baby starts wailing at the sight of you walking through the child care centre doors, take this as the ultimate compliment!

Work on your relationship with your child's caregiver

Find ways to communicate on a regular basis. If it's too crazy to try to talk when you're doing the daily pickup or drop off, send a notebook back and forth so that you can exchange both friendly messages and important information.

Make an effort to get to know your child's "other family"

Attend open houses or organize a potluck dinner or other social event so that you can get to know the child care providers as well as the other families who use the child care centre or home day care.

What to do When Your Child is Sick

You don't need to be a rocket scientist to figure out why every working parent needs a backup plan that's designed to handle every possible child care contingency. You need a plan that is detailed enough to put even the Y2K emergency preparedness folks to shame: a plan that covers what you will do if a broken water pipe forces your child's child care centre to close, your home day care provider comes down with the flu, your nanny's car breaks down, you remember at the last minute that it's a school holiday, or your child wakes up with a queasy stomach.

The most difficult scenario for any working parent to handle, of course, is

---

SANITY SAVERS

"I keep the same software programs that I use at work on my computer at home, so when I have a sick child, I can do some work while I'm off. My efficiency is reduced, but I can make up for lost time in the evening, later in the week, or on the weekend."

- Margaret, 36, environmental engineer and mother of two

dealing with a sick child. Here's what Lori, a 30 year old social worker and mother of two, has to say about this classic conundrum: "This is the area in which I feel most torn. In my mind, being a good mother means caring for my son, but being a good employee means going to work. I have not found a way to reconcile the two without feeling that I've abandoned my son when he most needs his mother's arms."

Part of the art of being a working mother — the part that requires 75 percent medical knowledge and 25 percent intuition — is figuring out when your child is well enough to go to day care or school and when he absolutely has to stay home. Figure 7.1 should help you to make up your mind about the medical portion of the equation.

If you decide that your child does need to stay home from child care, you'll find yourself left with three basic options:

➢ working from home for the day

➢ taking the day off entirely (either by using a personal day, a vacation day or some banked overtime) or

➢ seeing if your partner can stay at home with your child for all or part of the day so that you can make it into the office for at least a few hours.

Dealing with Other Child Care Problems

If, on the other hand, it's your nanny who's ill rather than your child, you may decide to find some sort of backup child care arrangement for your child so that you can still make it in to work. Here are a few tips on putting such a backup arrangement in place.

Shake your family tree
Find out if there's a family member who would be willing to help you out from time to time. While your mother-in-law might not be super-keen about caring for her beloved grandchild on a daily basis, she might not mind filling in once every couple of months or so.

Figure 7.1: When to Send Them to Day Care and When to Keep Them Home

Disease	Symptoms	Mode of Transmission	Infectious Period	Child can Return to School or Day Care	Siblings can Return to School or Day Care
Chickenpox	Fever and headache; rash within 24 hrs. Itching for four days. Blisters appear in crops over three to four days, turning to crusty scabs. Symptoms appear 11 to 21 days after exposure.	Spread through the air and by direct contact with blister fluid, saliva, phlegm, or articles freshly soiled by the sick child.	Up to five days before the onset of the rash, and not more than five days after the spots appear.	When all lesions are dry (at least five days after the first crop of lesions appeared).	Should only be attending school or day care if they have already had chicken pox.
Common Cold	Runny nose, sore throat, cough, decreased appetite.	Spread through the air and via contaminated hands and objects.	From one day before to seven days after onset of symptoms.	Child can attend school or day care unless too ill to take part in activities.	No need for siblings to stay home.
Conjunctivitis (Pink Eye)	Red swollen eye(s); then thick, yellow discharge and crusting. Eyes itch and smart; no pain. Symptoms appear 24 to 72 hours after exposure.	Spread by touching the eye or through contact with articles soiled with discharge or phlegm.	Contagious until treated.	When whites of eyes are clear and crusting is gone.	No need for siblings to stay home unless they are also infected.
Ear Infection	Earache; irritability, fever and cold symptoms.	Not infectious.	Not infectious.	No need for child to stay home unless he/she is not feeling well enough to go.	No need for siblings to stay home.
Fever	Temperature over 38.5° C. A child with a temperature of 40° C and higher will look and feel sick.	Not infectious.	Not infectious.	Keep child away from school or day care until he/she is feeling well enough to return.	
Gastroenteritis (i.e. infection due to campylobacter, E.coli, Shigella, Yersinia, or viral)	Poor appetite, vomiting, stomach cramps, watery or bloody diarrhea. Symptoms usually appear 24 to 72 hours after exposure.	Spread through contact with stool or through contaminated food, milk, or water. Also spread by people with poor hygiene habits.	Contagious while symptoms are present.	When diarrhea stops and stool tests are negative.	No need for siblings to stay home unless they are also infected.
Impetigo	Blisters, then honey-coloured crusts on red base; often located around mouth, nose and diaper area. Symptoms take four to 10 days to appear.	Spread through contact with sores. Infection can be spread to other parts of the body by the child's fingers.	Contagious until sores are dry.	When sores are dry.	No need for siblings to stay home unless they are also infected.
Red Measles	Fever, cough, red eyes, runny nose, red spots in mouth, swollen neck glands. Blotchy red rash	Spread through direct or airborne contact with saliva, phlegm, or articles soiled by the sick child.	Contagious from four days before to four days after rash appears.	Child can return to school or day care anytime after the fourth day after the rash starts, if he/she feels well enough.	Siblings may continue to attend school or day care as long as they are immunized or immune. If

Figure 7.1: **When to Send Them to Day Care and When to Keep Them Home,** *continued*

Red Measles (*cont.*)	spreads from face to neck to body over three days. Symptoms appear seven to 18 days after exposure, with rash appearing on or about the fourteenth day.				they have not been immunized, they may need a measles vaccine or immune globulin.
Pediculosis (Head Lice)	Itchy scalp. Live lice are tiny wingless insects that crawl into the hair. Nits are tiny egg-shaped deposits which are firmly attached to the hair. Symptoms appear eight to 10 days after exposure.	Spread by direct head-to-head contact or by sharing clothing, hats, combs and brushes.	Contagious until treated and nits are gone.	After treatment.	Siblings may continue to go to school or day care as long as they are not infected.
Pertussis (Whooping Cough)	Cold-like symptoms with irritating cough. Coughing is prolonged and severe, and it may be characterized by a high-pitched whoop or crowing. Symptoms appear seven to 10 days after exposure.	Spread through direct or airborne contact with saliva, phlegm, or articles soiled by the sick child.	Contagious for up to three weeks after start of cough or up to five days after antibiotics are started.	After at least five days of antibiotic treatment, assuming child feels well.	Siblings may continue to attend school or day care as long as they are immunized or immune. If they have not been immunized, they may need a booster shot and antibiotic.
Rubella	Mild fever, headache, cough, red eyes, runny nose. Swollen glands at back of neck. May not feel ill. Rash consists of mottled or raised spots spreading from face to neck to body over 12 to 24 hours. Symptoms appear 14 to 23 days after exposure.	Spread through direct contact with phlegm, saliva, or articles soiled by the sick child. People without symptoms can spread the infection.	Contagious from seven days before to four days after rash appears.	Child should stay home for seven days after rash appears and should avoid contact with non-immune pregnant women.	Siblings may continue to attend school or day care as long as they are uninfected and have been immunized against the disease.
Scarlet Fever	Sore throat and fever; fine red rash which feels like sandpaper and fades on pressure. Most often appears on neck, chest, folds of armpits, elbow, groin, and inner parts of thighs. Symptoms appear one to three days after exposure.	Spread through direct contact with phlegm, saliva, or articles soiled by the sick child. Limited spread through the air. People without symptoms can spread the infection.	Contagious for 10 to 21 days after exposure, or 24 to 48 hours after antibiotics have been started.	Child can return to school 48 hours after the start of antibiotics if he/she is feeling well.	Siblings may continue to attend school as long as they are not infected.
Strep Throat	Fever; sore throat.	Spread person to person.	Contagious until 24 hours after the start of treatment	Child can return to school 24 hours after the start of treatment.	Siblings may continue to attend school as long as they are not infected.

Sources: Canadian Pediatric Society, Peterborough County — City Health Unit, 1995.

Start banging on doors
See if there's another family in your neighbourhood who would be willing to share their nanny if you find yourself in a pinch. You could offer to return the favour the next time their nanny calls in sick.

Pick up the phone
Find out if there's an organization in your community that specializes in providing emergency child care services for working families (e.g. in-home care from a registered nursing assistant). These services don't come cheap, but your employer may be willing to pick up all or a portion of the tab if it's critically important that you make it in to work.

Finding an After-school Program for Your School-aged Child

If you think it's difficult finding a suitable child care arrangement for an infant, toddler, or preschooler, wait till you try to find a program that can accommodate your school-aged child. While studies have shown that children who are left on their own for a few hours each afternoon are more likely to skip school, do poorly on tests, and engage in substance abuse and other risky behaviours, there continues to be a chronic shortage of after-school programs for school-aged children. It's almost as if the powers that be have forgotten that the Ozzie and Harriet family structure is a thing of the past: in many cases, mom's at work at 3:30 pm — not standing on the porch with a plate of freshly-baked chocolate chip cookies!

When after-school child care programs are available, they tend to be offered by the following types of groups:

➢ child care centres

➢ home day cares

➢ public and private schools

➢ community centres

➢ recreational facilities

➤ park and recreation departments

➤ religious institutions

➤ youth groups (e.g. Boys and Girls Clubs)

➤ tutoring services

➤ sports clubs

➤ theatres, art galleries and other arts-related organizations.

If you're not able to find a suitable after-school program for your child, you might want to hook up with a group of parents and try to organize your own program or ask your employer if you can shift your working hours so that you'll be at home when your child arrives home from school.

Is Your Child Old Enough to be a "Latchkey Kid?"

As your child gets older, you may be willing to allow him to take care of himself until you get home from work. You can assess how ready he is for such an arrangement by considering:

➤ whether or not he knows his full name, address and phone number (including area code) and whether he'd be able to provide this information reliably to emergency personnel

➤ whether he knows what numbers to call in the event of an emergency

➤ whether he is mature enough to carry his house key without losing it

➤ whether he could be trusted to answer the telephone and door appropriately

➤ whether he would remember to keep the doors locked at all times

➤ whether he would be able to follow some basic ground rules when you're not there to supervise him (e.g. not having friends over, remembering to turn off the stove if

SANITY SAVERS

See if you can arrange to share after-school child care responsibilities with another family in your neighbourhood. Shift your working hours so that one family is responsible for supervising the children before school and the other is responsible for supervising them after school — perhaps alternating weeks would make it easier.

he makes himself a snack, remembering to check in with you at work to let you know that he has arrived home safely)

➤ how he feels about being responsible for caring for himself.

With your child's assistance, compile a list of all possible emergency numbers, as well as friends and family members she could contact. Keep the list accessible and up-to-date. Bottom line? There are no easy answers to the whole latchkey kid issue. Only you can come up with the solution that's right for your family. Good luck.

Chapter 8

The Parental Ties that Bind

Looking forward to having more time for your own needs when your children grow up and leave home? Don't bank on it. You could find yourself caring for an aging relative, probably one or both of your parents or those of your spouse.

The experts say that elder care is shaping up to be an even bigger problem for working women than child care has been. "Elder care is a national crisis. Since 80 percent of caregivers are women, it's a women's issue," warns elder care consultant Karen Henderson who was quoted in an article in the *Toronto Star*. "There are huge numbers of us in middle age with parents still alive. This has never happened before in history."

Andrew Scharlach, a professor of aging at the University of California at Berkeley, predicts that one in three workers will be providing some sort of care for an aging parent or other relative by the year 2020. "This is a major issue in people's lives, one that will affect virtually all of us at one point in our careers," he told *USA Today*. "When it hits, it can clearly make a difference in whether we're able to work productively, or whether we're able to work at all."

The findings of some recent studies echo Scharlach and Henderson's warnings:

➤ A 1992 study by The Canadian Aging Research Network (CARNET) — a research group based at the University of Guelph — revealed that 46 percent of Canadian workers provide care to one or more aging relatives for three or more hours each week. What's more, half of these caregivers are also responsible for caring for children.

➤ Approximately 44 percent of Canadians live 100 kilometres or more from their parents — something that can cause tremendous stress and strain when it comes time to make elder care arrangements for an out-of-town relative.

➤ The number of Americans caring for aging parents has tripled over the past 10 years, according to a recent article in *Newsday*. This means that there are now 22 million US households caring for an aging parent — and three-quarters of those doing the care are women. (Figure 8.1 gives a few details on the living arrangements of older Canadian seniors.)

➤ Canadians are living longer and having fewer children. This means that many women will typically spend a greater number of years caring for aging relatives than they spend raising their own children: "It is estimated that today's woman will spend 17 years of adult life as a mother of a dependent child and 18 years more as daughter of an elderly parent," notes demographer Teresa M. Cooney in a report issued by the *Vanier Institute of the Family*.

➤ Despite Canadians' belief that the social safety net is there to help families with aging parents, in far too many cases, that net is full of holes. Consider what reporter André Picard had to say in a recent article in *The Globe and Mail*: "At present the homecare system in Canada is not a system at all. The country's health ministers cannot even agree an a common definition of the term. Homecare today is an idiosyncratic patchwork of $1.1 billion worth of programs, rife with unfairness, as illustrated by the fact that there are threefold variations in per-capita spending among provinces."

FACTS & FIGURES

In 1950, just 8 percent of the world's population was age 60 or over; by 2025, the elderly will represent approximately 14 percent of the world's population.

Figure 8.1   **Living Arrangements of Seniors Aged 75 and Over, 1991**

	Men	**Women**
With spouse	8%	15%
In institution	11%	19%
Living alone	18%	26%
Living with person other than spouse	63%	40%

Sources: Statistics Canada and The Vanier Institute of the Family

➤ It is projected by Statistics Canada that the number of seniors aged 65 and over could increase to 5.9 million by the year 2016 — a 64 percent increase over the 3.6 million seniors in Canada today.

➤ A 1993 study conducted by the Families and Work Institute revealed that 23 percent of caregivers are responsible for the care of more than one elderly person — a weekly commitment that averages 20 hours per week for women and 12 hours per week for men.

➤ There is a chronic shortage of nursing home beds for people who need long-term care. In February of 1997, there were 16,000 people waiting for long-term care beds in Ontario. These types of shortages only add to the burdens of working women who are struggling to balance the needs of aging relatives with the demands of their own careers.

What the numbers don't tell you, of course, is what it feels like to be responsible for caring for an aging relative. Consider what these women have to say.

At one point in her life, Tina, a 33 year old editorial assistant and mother of two, found herself "sandwiched" between the needs of her newborn baby and the health care needs of her aging father-in-law:

> Five years ago, Brian's mom died and six weeks later his father had an abdominal aneurysm from which he wasn't supposed to survive. I was pregnant with our first child while he was in the hospital. When I

was eight months pregnant, we rented out our home and moved in with him during his convalescence. Five days before he was released from hospital, I gave birth to Laura. We spent a year living together, during which time we took care of his home and I prepared his meals. It was a very stressful time.

Eileen, a 35 year old business analyst and mother of two, experienced a similar intergenerational tug of war while caring for an aging family member:

Several years ago, when I was pregnant with my twins, I took care of my mom's aunt, who was in her nineties and determined to live alone. She required home care, but it was only available to her 12 hours per day. Invariably, she would require more help when the health care aide wasn't there, and I was constantly woken by the phone and then had to make the 30 minute drive to her house at all hours of the night. It got worse when the babies were born because my husband went to school at night and I would have to take the little ones with me if she fell — which happened a lot. I ended up having to put her in a nursing home, which, to this day, I still feel horrible about.

Heather, a 31 year old information broker and mother of one, continues to find herself scrambling to meet the needs of all the family members who currently depend on her:

My mom is 69 and my in-laws are 79 and 82 so I do have quite a bit of responsibility for all of their care. My mother-in-law is currently in the hospital and my sister-in-law and I are doing all her personal care twice a day because of the shortages in nursing staff. My mom is alone and doesn't drive so I take her on errands and such. It is like juggling three families at the same time. There are times I wish we lived further away. I hope I don't sound mean, but it's very, very hard to do it all.

Be Prepared

If you haven't had to deal with any elder care responsibilities yet, consider yourself lucky. Health care analysts estimate that the majority of us will be required to care for aging relatives at some point during our adult lives. While it's impossible to avoid the problem altogether — family members do age and require extra care — there are some steps you can take to prevent elder care from becoming a major problem for your family.

> ## "WORTH QUOTING"
>
> "When the time comes, I am prepared to play a part in it all. I've seen in my parents' generation that resentment flourishes when the child on home turf carries the load. That isn't fair."
>
> • Jane, 38, architect and mother of two

Plan ahead

Don't wait until you're in the midst of a crisis before you consider the possibility that one or both of your parents could become seriously incapacitated. Long before the first serious medical problem rears its ugly head, you should take the time to sit down and talk with your parents about important medical, legal and financial issues that relate to their care. These issues are difficult to talk about, but it's important to get them out in the open: if you don't plan ahead, you could find yourself racing to court in the midst of a crisis in an effort to gain power of attorney over a parent who is too ill to make his or her own decisions.

Explore your options

Encourage your parents to consider various housing options while they're still in good health. If they find residential care facilities that they like, they may wish to put their names on the waiting lists for these places, even if they don't currently have any need for such accommodations. If their names come up and they still don't have any need for residential care, they can always ask to have their name bumped further down the waiting list.

> ## "WORTH QUOTING"
>
> "I found that it worked best if I went to see him (her father) the same day each week. Then he knew when to expect me and I knew to keep my calendar clear on Wednesdays and to book any of his appointments on Wednesday."
>
> • Doreen, 43, writer

Sanity Savers

If your parents require help with light housework or grocery shopping, hire a college student to help them for a couple of hours each week. You'll be amazed how much saner you feel knowing that there's someone else to help share the load.

Put a support network in place

Start making contact with people who will be in a position to help you and your parents if they suddenly require care. Establish contact with your parents' family doctor and keep the lines of communication open. If your parents' health situations change, the doctor may help you to determine what type of care is needed and where you can find it. Find out what types of community resources are available to your parents. The local information bureau and/or the local senior citizens centre should be able to tell you how to get in touch with organizations offering meals-on-wheels or home-care services.

Do your homework

Find out what elder care services, if any, your employer offers. Do you have access to an elder care referral service? Does your employer subsidize the costs of adult day care services? The human resources department and/or the administrator of your company health plan should be able to provide you with information on the services available to you.

Etc.

Here's a tax deduction you'll want to know about if you're responsible for caring for an aging parent. If an elderly relative on a low income lives with you because of a mental or physical health problem, you may be able to deduct some or all of your housing costs from your income tax. Call your local Revenue Canada office for details or visit the Revenue Canada web site at *http://www.rc.gc.ca.*

Don't overdo it

Don't agree to take on more elder care responsibilities than you can reasonably handle out of a feeling of duty to your parents. "The I-must-do-it-all syndrome is the easiest trap to fall into and the hardest one to climb out of," writes journalist Virginia Morris in a recent article in *Ladies Home Journal*. "Don't let yourself get sucked up in the emotional eddy of feeling resentful about having to do so much, guilty that you aren't doing more and even guiltier for feeling resentful. Scrambling to do more that you can handle will jeopardize your health, your marriage, your friendships, your career — even your sanity."

Don't shoulder the burden on your own

If you happen to be the closest living relative to your parents, you could find yourself stuck with the lion's share of the care giving responsibilities unless you speak up and ask for help. While the sister who lives 500 miles away can't fly in daily to help your aging mother wash her hair, she can fly into town as often as her schedule permits and give you a badly-needed break. She can also follow up with your parents' doctors and take care of other tasks that can easily be handled by phone. She can also play an active role in helping you to make important decisions about your parents' care.

Understand you will sometimes have to make tough choices

Respect your parents' feelings and wishes as much as possible, but don't feel racked with guilt if you have to occasionally make decisions that they don't agree with — like putting their house on the market and moving them into a long-term care facility. You'll feel better about these decisions, by the way, if they are made in consultation with other family members.

Join a caregiver's support group

It's highly therapeutic to be able to express your feelings to a group of people who understand exactly what you're going through. Call your local senior citizens centre, health unit or the geriatric ward of your local hospital to find out if there's such a support group running in your community.

Don't beat yourself up for not feeling like Florence Nightingale

Accept the fact that you're going to experience a variety of emotions: guilt, helplessness, anxiety, resentment and even anger. The rate of burnout and depression amongst caregivers is extremely high, so you've got to make a point of taking care of your own emotional health.

"WORTH QUOTING"

"A mother dressing a daughter will feel a sense of pride, especially as the daughter begins to do things. A daughter dressing a mother will still see that woman as her mother, and maybe feel sorrow that she has to help her."

• elder care expert Tim Braubaker, quoted in *Minneapolis Star Tribune*

Look for the silver lining
Seniors don't just take: they also do a lot of giving. Consider what the Vanier Institute of the Family had to say about seniors in *From The Kitchen Table to the Boardroom Table*: "A recent study on Aging and Independence, conducted by Statistics Canada, revealed that 67 percent of Canada's older seniors (aged 75 and over) receive help regularly on such things as housework and cooking, home maintenance and personal care. But then, too, 59 percent of older seniors give help regularly in these areas, and in other areas such as child care, shopping and transportation. Very often, this help is received from, and given to, family — spouses, sons, daughters, grandchildren and other relatives."

Getting the Support You Need at Work

Elder care isn't just a family issue; it's also a workplace issue. Employers who choose to ignore the problem do so at their own peril because the workplace fall-out can be considerable. Consider the facts for yourself:

➢ A study conducted by the Conference Board of Canada revealed that many caregivers experience a variety of serious work-related problems.

➢ A study conducted by the Canadian Aging Research Network (CARNET) revealed that individuals who have elder care responsibilities experience more stress, less job satisfaction, more problems balancing work and family pressures and a higher rate of absenteeism than co-workers who don't have these types of responsibilities.

➢ According to an article in the *Canadian HR Reporter*, employees with elder care responsibilities miss 4.2 days of work per year to attend to the needs of aging relatives.

➢ A recent study by the National Alliance of Caregiving in the US revealed that 10 percent of employees with elder care responsibilities are absent for at least six days per year. What's more, many caregivers are forced to head home early or come in late, switch to part-time or less demanding work, or leave the workforce altogether.

➤ Another study — this one by the Families and Work Institute in New York — revealed that 39 percent of workers with elder care responsibilities reported being distracted at work, 25 percent had changed jobs because of the responsibilities, 22 percent had considered quitting their jobs and 14 percent had dropped out of the workforce entirely.

According to the Conference Board, potential employee problems related to elder care responsibilities include the following:

➤ rearrangement of work schedules

➤ absenteeism

➤ tardiness

➤ stress, depression and sleep disorders

➤ turning down promotions or relocations

➤ excessive phone calls

➤ unavailable for overtime work or job-related travel

➤ requests for reduced hours

➤ higher staff turnover

➤ health problems

➤ decreased quality and/or quantity of work

➤ increased work accidents

➤ increased incidence of time off work without pay

➤ inability to accept extra projects or responsibilities

Make sure that studies citing the workplace ramifications of elder care responsibilities catch your employer's eye as you make

> ## "WORTH QUOTING"
>
> "Partial absenteeism — late arrivals, long lunch breaks, early departures — takes its toll ... but not nearly as much as the workday interruptions faced by caregivers who talk on the phone with loved ones and service providers. This situation can arise even with employees who don't physically care for parents or whose parents live elsewhere. Estimated at one hour per week per caregiver, this factor is the biggest drain of all on employee productivity, amounting to over half of the estimated cost ..."
>
> • Tibbett L. Speer, in a recent article in *American Demographics*

your best case for flextime, tele-work, or family-friendly work policies (see Chapter 4).

It Takes an Entire Village ...

The problems posed by the need to care for aging relatives are so complex and so far-reaching that changes are needed to our very social fabric. At least that's the word from the Conference Board of Canada. In their recent report on the elder care issue, they suggested that family-friendly leave legislation should be implemented which would allow workers leaves of absence for many different reasons, including elder care responsibilities. The Board felt that pension policies should be revised to ensure that workers who leave their jobs in order to care for aging relatives are not penalized in terms of pension credits. Tax deductions and/or family allowance payments should be made to those providing care to elderly relatives. And finally the Board recommended that the elderly should be guaranteed some base standard of care as part of the national health insurance program.

The Conference Board maintained that employers should help employees by agreeing to pick up the tab for some of the costs associated with elder care (subsidizing the costs of travelling to see an elderly relative and/or paying for the costs of dependant care) and/or by establishing onsite or near-site elder care centres or intergenerational centres (centres where both elder care and child care services are offered). Note: while such bells and whistles are likely to be beyond the financial means of small employers, some might choose to participate in elder care consortiums — groups of employers who band together to set up elder care facilities.

Finally the Board recommended that employers should provide information to employees that would help them to make informed choices about elder care-related issues and make counselling and personal support services available to them as well. Employers should also offer flexible work arrangements as much as possible and ensure that existing work/family policies meet the needs of employees with elder care responsibilities.

You can download a copy of this report entitled "Eldercare and the Workplace" from the Conference Board of Canada web site *http://www2.conferenceboard.ca/pubs/htm.* or order a copy by calling (613) 526-3280.

Clearly, dealing compassionately and effectively with the eldest members of your extended family requires both hard work and patience. Support services vary considerably from province to province, so do your homework carefully (start with the resources in Appendix A and B). And, if you still have energy, the next chapter addresses the topic of your significant other — keeping some sanity in the modern marriage!

FACTS & FIGURES

Aging relatives aren't the only family members who may requires special care. According to Statistics Canada, 6.5 percent of disabled adults live with their parents.

Chapter 9

For Better and For Worse: Inside the Modern Marriage

You've been looking forward to date night all week. You leave work at 5:00 pm on the button, pick up a sinfully expensive take-out dinner at the gourmet pasta shop around the corner from work, and make a quick pit stop at the local video store to rent a copy of that new romantic comedy that all the women at work have been raving about. You arrive home, set the table, light the candles, pour the wine, and sit back and wait for that special guy in your life to arrive home from work.

You're enjoying your second glass of wine when the phone rings. He's just come out of a meeting at work and he's got some paperwork to finish up before he can call it a night. His boss has invited him out for a drink and he really can't say no — not after landing that big promotion.

You put the pasta dinner in the fridge and make yourself some scrambled eggs and toast. Then, you put on the video and flop out on the couch. By the time he walks through the door at 11:30 pm, you're sound asleep. So much for date night ...

It's a scene that gets played out over and over again in bedrooms across the country. One partner's unavailable, the other one's hurt. Sometimes the victim is played by the leading lady; other times it's the leading man. In this particular game of bedroom politics, nobody wins.

While no marriage is perfect, couples in dual income families face particular challenges that can lead to conflict and even divorce. At the heart of the problem is the time crunch that leaves couples with little time or energy for one another.

Consider the facts for yourself:

➤ According to Dr. Peter Hanson, author of the bestselling book *The Joy of Stress*, working couples face a "time famine" that can put their relationships in jeopardy. Hanson recently told *Maclean's* magazine that working couples spend an average of 12 minutes per day in private conversation with one another. Is it any wonder that so many relationships are in trouble?

➤ A recent study by Catalyst, a New York consulting firm, revealed that 56 percent of working couples cite a lack of time as the biggest challenge that they face in their relationships with their partners.

➤ A similar study by the New York-based Families and Work Institute confirmed that the time crunch is the biggest problem facing today's working couples.

In the first part of this chapter, we're going to be talking about how this time crunch is playing out in the bedrooms of the nation: how couples feel about their relationships with one another, how the lack of time together is impacting on intimacy and what couples can do to stay connected despite their crazy schedules.

Time Out!

When couples break up in the movies, there's invariably another man or another woman to blame. An affair is an amazing plot device — something that gives the characters a reason to scream and yell and even boil one another's pets. (I've never quite forgotten that particular scene from *Fatal Attraction*. Have you?)

In real life, the events that lead to marriage breakdowns aren't usually this dramatic. People simply wake up one day and realize that they no longer care much about the person who's sitting across the breakfast table. According to University of Washington psychology professor John Gottman, who was interviewed in a recent article in *Woman's Day*, only 20 percent of divorces are caused by an affair: "Most marriages die with a whimper, as people gradually turn away from one another."

Because working couples face so many other demands on their time — particularly if they have young children as well as full-time jobs — it's easy for them to neglect to set aside time to spend as a couple. "Many couples find their biggest challenge is simply finding time together," wrote journalist Jill Smolowe in a recent article in *Time*. "Work hours conflict; travel demands interfere. Even relatively compatible schedules do not guarantee couples a daily hour of uninterrupted time together."

Judith S. Wallerstein and Sandra Blakeslee, authors of *The Good Marriage: How and Why Love Lasts*, agree that a couple's relationship can suffer because of work-related pressures: "Just as work intrudes on the family, it also penetrates the relationship between husband and wife," the authors write. "They postpone intimacy, sex, just being together, and having fun. Obviously, time together is an important measure of a marriage: 'quality time' does not work any better for a couple than it does for children."

The experts aren't the only ones talking about this issue, of course. It's a hot topic of conversation around the water cooler. Consider what these working women* had to say about their relationships with their partners:

> *I work two jobs and he works one and goes to school. Throw in kids, housework and laundry and it isn't difficult to see why we hardly spend any time together. It's taking a toll on our marriage. We seem to have grown apart to a degree.*

> The logistics of getting together, just the two of us, are overwhelming enough that we tend not to do it. It's more of a momentum problem. It just seems like

---

* In order to protect the privacy of the survey respondents, names have not been included in this chapter.

too much effort to have a real date. Besides, by the time we think of doing it, it's already too late at night.

There is so little time left at the end of the day and week for just us that our leisure time is in danger of being spent doing individual things that we enjoy independently: sewing, playing hockey, or running.

We're always racing around trying to get caught up, which never happens. We do tons of things with the kids and at home, but we need to get out together more.

I feel that with each child, my husband and I have less and less time and energy left for one another. We love our children and we love raising them together, but sometimes I wonder if things will ever be the way they were before we had children. Sometimes days can go by without us spending any significant time or communicating in any real way together. I just hope our relationship is strong enough to ride out this time in our lives.

"Worth Quoting"

"It's very easy to become absorbed in work if your relationship is having difficulties. This can torpedo a relationship. If your partner would rather be working than spending time with you, or vice versa, that's a sure sign that there are major troubles in the relationship. Sometimes 'work' is used as an excuse to avoid other problems and the cycle becomes entrenched. Although 'overtime' situations will arise from time to time, it is important to break this cycle as well."

• A recently separated
mother of three

The Stranger in Your Bed

You worked all day, came home and made dinner, cleaned up the kitchen, bathed your kids, read them bedtime stories, folded three baskets of laundry, paid some bills and spent some time talking with your mother on the phone. Now that you're ready to head to bed the last thing on your mind is sex. What you want is sleep, glorious sleep.

Forget all those comparisons between sex and chocolate. For most working women, the real contest is between sex and sleep. The man who can tempt you to keep your eyes open a half-hour longer has to be a modern-day Casanova indeed. Consider what he's up against as he whispers sweet nothings in your ears:

> *There's not much time for romance with 17 month old twins! By the time they are in bed and the house is back in order, I'm ready to go to bed to read and fall asleep.*

> Lately, I have had to work extra hours due to deadlines at work, so I have been working after the baby goes to bed at night. This leaves little quality time for my partner. Let's call it birth control.

> *My romantic life is pretty non-existent right now. If you're talking about sex — well we manage a quickie once a week or so. But romance? I don't even remember what that is.*

Women aren't the only ones to feel the sexual fallout from exhaustion, of course. It can often be a problem for both partners. "The kids need the attention, work needs attention, other duties need attention, but they all drain our energy," admits one working mother. "By the time we get everyone off to bed, neither of us feels like doing much except zoning out."

According to Dr. Michael A. Perelman, a clinical psychologist and co-director of the Human Sexuality Program at New York Hospital in Manhattan, fatigue is probably the number one cause of sex-related problems — especially for men. "Many men erroneously presume that they should be able to function regardless of how they are feeling," he recently told *Prevention* magazine. "Nothing could be further from the truth for most men older than 30. Fatigue can push a man over the edge of his ability."

Chronic work-related stress can also put out the fires of passion. When the body is under stress, it produces fewer sex hormones. That can lead to a lack of desire in both sexes, impotence in men, and the inability to achieve an orgasm in women.

Conflicts are most likely to arise if one partner is experiencing a marked decline in interest but the other is just as keen as ever — a phenomenon the psychologists like to call "desire discrepancy."

FACTS & FIGURES

More than 40 percent of women and 30 percent of men regularly have no interest in sex, can't have an orgasm, or suffer from some other type of sexual dysfunction, according to a recent study published in the *Journal of the American Medical Association*.

(Don't know what I'm talking about? Think of that classic scene in *Annie Hall* when Annie and Alvy each complain to their psychiatrist about how often they have sex. "We have it constantly. I'd say three times a week," says Annie. "We have it hardly ever," says Alvy. "Maybe three times a week.")

You can find yourselves caught in a particularly nasty Catch 22 if you and your partner get out of the habit of having sex. You're not having sex, so your sexual desire drops; and because your sexual desire drops, you don't bother having sex. If you find yourself dealing with this all-too-common situation, your best bet is to start having sex again, even if you don't feel particularly inspired at first. "You have to take action and behave in sensual ways," psychotherapist Melody Lowman told a reporter from *Newsday*. "The feelings will follow."

Lana Holstein, M.D., offered similar advice in a recent article in *Prevention* magazine. She suggested that couples treat sex like exercise until their libidos have a chance to reset: "Like exercise, you don't necessarily want to do it when you put on your sneakers and start out. But you know you should. You know that, by the end, you'll feel better. So you have to be willing to start a sexual connection from zero, or even minus one on the scale of desire. Once you have made love, you are usually glad you did — just like exercise."

Some couples choose to accept the fact that their sex life is going to be less active at certain chaotic periods in their lives and look for other ways to stay connected:

> *I think we have come to terms with the fact that, for the moment, romance is on hold. We have been together for a very long time — since we were 16 — so we get some consolation from the fact that romance has to be put on the back burner for a while, but that we can go back to it when conditions are more favourable!*

Romance has taken on a new meaning for us. It used to be a "romantic" night if we went out for dinner and walked home under the stars — all the more traditional things you think about. Now, we have to find quick little intimacies — a love note propped up on a counter top, a quick bear-hug, a voicemail message.

We find romance where we can and in little tiny blocks: a note in the lunch-bag, a flower from the grocery store, a special breakfast, a walk in the moonlight (with our toddler in tow!), or a call in the middle of the day just to say, "I love you."

Here are some other tips on staying connected with your partner when your wacky schedules are threatening to tear you apart.

Communicate

Find out what's bothering your partner and let him know what's eating you. "Talk it out. Fight it out if you have to, but get those feelings out in the open so that you can discuss them," says one working woman. "Communication is the key to staying together — mostly keeping up with what each of you is doing at home and at work," insists another. "We find that we're more likely to get angry with one another if we haven't been communicating effectively." ("The toilet's still making that noise. Why didn't you fix it?" says she. "I can't get the part I need. Didn't you know that?" says he.)

Invest in your relationship with one another

While you might be tempted to divide your energies between work and your children, it's important to take care of your relationship with your partner, too. "My biggest problem was feeling guilty about spending time alone with my husband," says one working mother. "I work full-time and felt that I should spend all the time I possibly could with my son. After all, I was leaving him all week. How dare I want to 'get away' from him during part of the weekend, too." She and her

> ## "Worth Quoting"
>
> "Sex is not just sex. It's a major glue that keeps two people together."
> — Bernie Zilbergeld, Ph.D., sex therapist, quoted in a recent article in *Prevention* magazine.

partner started setting aside time to go out alone, and that's made a tremendous difference in their relationship. "I still feel guilty sometimes, but I can say that we have a stronger marriage and a better family life due to our times spent together."

Find ways to make your partner feel special

"I used to watch my husband play softball when we were dating," says one working mother. "I never missed a game. For a while, my attendance was really sporadic and that was really upsetting him. Now that I know how important it is to him that I be there, I've made it my goal to try to attend his games on a regular basis."

Spend time together on a regular basis

"We have lunch together three times a week, although this usually turns into a business meeting," says one working woman who runs a business with her partner. "We try to go out once a month without the kids and do something fun, even if it's just taking a trip to the movie theatre or having dinner out with friends. We also take one weekend each January to flee the kids and the business and vow not to talk about either for three whole days. (This is very difficult!)"

Don't let your To Do List take over your life

"Put less emphasis on fighting dust bunnies and more on trying to enjoy the time you do spend with one another," suggests one working mother.

Look for stress-free ways to squeeze in a date

"When we don't have the time or the money to go out on an official date, we have one at home," explains one working mother. "We feed the kids, put on a video for them and cook something fancy for just the two of us. We then break open a bottle of wine, put the kids to bed and watch a video together."

Find creative ways to enjoy having fun together regularly

"We like to do simple things like getting a bottle of wine and the new issue of *Cosmopolitan* and giving one another the quizzes!" says one woman.

Be zany together

"Be irresponsible occasionally," suggests one working mother. "Fling your deadlines to the wind and find a pile of leaves to jump in while the kids are in school."

Plan a great escape

"About two years ago, my husband and I were slowly growing apart and I decided a trip to Nantucket was what would help us," says one working mother. "I booked the room, got the baby-sitter, packed the car, and off we went. It was the best thing we did that year. We had only each other to worry about, we walked around the island, rediscovered each other in the bedroom and just enjoyed our time."

Look at the big picture

"Remember that your partner is going to be around for a lot longer than your children will — that this person is a lifelong friend and that even though there isn't much time left for one another when you have young children, you need to work at keeping the relationship strong."

Invest in yourself

"Do things together, but don't forget to take a few minutes for yourself every once in a while," advises one working woman. "It's easier to connect with your partner when you're connected with yourself!" Don't allow your own needs to get overlooked, adds another working woman: "There has to be some individual time too in order to recharge the batteries. Otherwise, there is no energy to put into romance. I think the one thing becoming a mother did was deprive me of the time I need for solitude. Sometimes I just want to go lock myself in the bathroom and soak — alone! — in the tub. If I can get sufficient 'me time,' I am more available to my husband when we can sneak some time in."

Career Tug-of-War

It isn't easy being part of a dual-income couple. What should be a partnership sometimes turns into an out-and-out tug-of-war: "Today's typical marriage is a dual-career affair. That means two sets of job demands,

"Worth Quoting"

"A few weeks ago, I called a sitter on a Tuesday and booked her for that Saturday night. I told my husband that the planning was up to him. We went out for an early dinner in a very hip part of town and then walked around and window shopped for a few hours afterward. It was so much fun! It reminded us of what a good time we can have together and why we married one another in the first place."

- A mother of three

two pay cheques, two egos — and a multitude of competing demands on both spouses' time, attention, and energy," wrote journalist Jill Smolowe in an article in *Time* magazine.

What Smolowe and others are just starting to talk about is the career tug-of-war — a problem that is taking its toll on more marriages than most of us would care to admit.

My, Dear, You're Looking a Little Green

Your boss just announced that you're getting a promotion that's accompanied by a $10,000 jump in pay. Part of you is jumping with joy; the other part of you is wondering how your partner will feel about relinquishing his status as primary breadwinner now that you're bringing home more bacon than he is.

While many men pretend not to be bothered by the fact that they are being out-earned by their wives (something that's now happening in approximately 20 percent of marriages), they aren't being completely honest with themselves or their partners, writes Smolowe in *Time* magazine. "They discuss their wives' higher earnings with phrases like 'I say more power to her,' and 'I don't feel threatened by it.' Inevitably, such statements are followed by the words, 'I have a strong ego,' a defensive refrain that seems to betray a discomfort not yet resolved." Some of these men then go on to sabotage their spouse's success, either by refusing to do his share of housework or by having an affair.

Sometimes it's the women themselves who feel uncomfortable with their career success, notes marriage therapist Cloe Madanes, who was quoted in a recent article in *Psychology Today* magazine: "While a successful male is lauded for his achievements, the successful woman fears losing the love of her spouse, of her children, and of her parents if she appears too financially strong. Heaven forbid she earn more than her husband."

> ## "WORTH QUOTING"
>
> "We are struggling to be a couple again. It seems like we are just going through the motions of day-to-day life and not really considering our relationship."
>
> • A working woman

Have Spouse, Will Travel

In 1990, in 94 percent of job transfers that involved couples, the woman was the so-called "trailing spouse" — the one who agreed to leave her job and relocate to another city for the sake of her partner's career. Today, the situation has reversed itself, according to US outplacement firm Challenger, Gray and Christmas: more men than women are being asked to pack up house and follow their spouse to a new location.

While most men are prepared to give at least lip service to the idea of being supportive of their wives' careers, the true test comes when they're given an opportunity to walk the walk. It's one thing, after all, to say that both partners' careers are equally important; it's quite another to pack up your bags so that your partner can accept an out-of-town promotion.

Men are right to be afraid of what being the "trailing spouse" may mean to their lives. Men who do decide to play the role of the trailing spouse can find themselves having an even tougher go of the transition than women in the same situation. Consider what Smolowe had to say about this issue in her article in *Time* magazine:

> Feelings of resentment, helplessness and dependency that have long plagued displaced working women promise to be harsher for men. While potential employers rarely find it odd that a wife has given up a job to trail her husband, they often question the dedication of a candidate who puts his wife's career first. Friends betray their prejudices and heighten anxieties with questions like, "But what are you going to do?" Moreover, some men are ill prepared to take a back seat role.

As you can see, there are no easy solutions to the challenges of being part of a dual income family. That's why it's so important to find the time you both need to recharge your batteries on a regular basis. One of the best ways to do that is by spending time with close friends — the subject of our next chapter.

Facts & Figures

Talk about getting that long distance feeling. A recent survey of 189 companies conducted by Windham International, a New York relocation consulting firm, revealed that 13 percent of executives who are relocated are not accompanied by their spouses — up from seven percent just two years earlier.

Chapter 10

Making Room for Family, Friends and Community

It's hard enough to find time to spend with the people who live under the same roof as you. It's even more of a challenge to find room in your schedule for everyone else who is lined up for a slice of your time: other family members, friends and members of the community.

In this chapter, we're going to talk about ways of coping with these conflicting demands on your time: how to stay connected with far-flung relatives and friends and how you can find ways to give something back to your community without hitting the overload button.

The Theory of Relativity

You run into one another at weddings and funerals. You may even manage to exchange cards over the holiday season, too. But beyond that, how much time do you get to spend with members of your family? Not a lot, according to the latest statistics:

➤ Forty percent of Canadians live more than 100 kilometres away from their mothers and 49 percent live more than 100 kilometres away from their fathers — something that can limit the amount of time they spend together, according to the Vanier Institute of the Family. "As the distance (between parents and children) increases to between 100 and 200 kilometres, the frequency of monthly visits begins to decline. Visiting less than once a month becomes more common. When the distance between children and parents increases to over 1000 kilometres, it becomes quite common for children not to visit with their parents at all" (*Source: Profiling Canada's Families*).

➤ One-fifth of grandchildren never visit their grandparents and over one-quarter never phone or write.

As depressing as those statistics may be, it's not all doom-and-gloom on the family front, however. Over one-third of siblings who live apart visit with one another at least once a week. What's more, an even larger proportion write or phone one another weekly.

If you hold down a full-time job during the day and have child care and household responsibilities to attend to in the evening, it's easy to let weeks — even months — go by without making contact with your relatives.

Here are some quick tips on ways to stay connected.

Find ways to eliminate some of the hassle of using snail mail

If you want to get into the habit of writing a letter a month to your grandmother, sit down at the beginning of the year and address and stamp a dozen envelopes. You'll be more likely to sit down and write the letter if the envelope is ready to go. Don't underestimate how much your letters may mean to an older person, by the way. Anne, a thirty-three year old executive secretary and mother of one, was glad she had made the effort to write to one of her husband's aunts when she discovered that the elderly woman had kept every one of her notes.

Encourage your kids to get in on the act

Children love to send and receive letters. With a little encouragement from you, they will become prolific correspondents. If they're having trouble coming up with ideas, encourage them to ask older family members to pass along stories about their growing up years — a subject that never fails to enthral members of all generations.

If you are too busy to write a letter by hand, zap off an e-mail instead

Better yet, send off a whole batch of e-mails to your various online relatives. You can either do a group e-mail — in which case everyone gets the same message from you — or you can customize each message for each recipient, but "recycle" the same core paragraphs again and again by cutting and pasting them into subsequent e-mails. Don't forget to attach copies of the latest baby pictures. After all, isn't that why your parents decided to spring for their e-mail account in the first place? And don't let the fact that you may not have Internet access at home stop you from using the easiest and cheapest communications means ever. Set up a free e-mail account through one of the many companies offering this service while you are taking advantage of free Internet access at your local library, school or community centre.

Get a lively dialogue going by setting up a family mailing list!

Go to Onelist.com (*http://www.onelist.com*) and follow the simple instructions to set up your free mailing list. I've set up a number of different mailing lists this way — including one for my entire extended family and one for my sisters only.

Start a family newsletter

Rather than saddling one family member with the job of editing each issue, rotate the job from family member to family member.

Try to find fun alternatives to sending holiday greeting cards

For example, have a family recipe swap instead. Send a copy of your favourite holiday recipe to everyone on your card list and encourage them to send you a copy of their favourite recipe instead of a card. In the end, you'll have the makings for a terrific family cookbook rather than a pile of greeting cards that are destined for the recycling bin.

Get in the habit of getting together

Start a tradition whereby you come from the four corners of the earth to congregate in Prince Edward Island during the first week in August — or some such thing! If you can't afford to do it annually, at least try to do it every five to 10 years — perhaps to mark a special family milestone like someone's seventy-fifth birthday or fiftieth wedding anniversary.

Girlfriend Power

You just got passed over for a major promotion at work. Your kids are giving you grief. And your husband has stopped doing his share of the housework. Who are you going to call? One of your girlfriends.

The bonds between women are powerful indeed. In fact, as anyone who has been through a major life crisis can tell you, it's your girlfriends who keep you sane. The busier and crazier your life gets, the more you need your friends.

"My friends are important to me because they are another sounding board or shoulder," explains Stephanie, a 25 year old administrative assistant and mother of one. "My husband is a great friend and listener, but sometimes you just need a girlfriend."

"I love my husband and my children, and I literally thank God every day for them," says Marilyn, a 43 year old technical writer and mother of three. "But I also thank God for my friends, who listen to me gripe, or buy me just the right Christmas gift, or take the baby for two hours while I go to the dentist/hair stylist/for an interview/on a date with my husband, or suggest lunch or a shopping trip at just the right time."

The challenge, of course, is to find time for one another when you're both leading insanely busy lives.

Here are a few tips for including your girlfriends in your busy life:

Meet at the gym.

You've got to exercise anyway. (Or at least you should be!) Why not turn your exercise routine into an opportunity to socialize with a friend?

Do lunch

If your evenings are tied up with household chores and your weekends are packed with kid-related activities, why not try to meet a group of friends for lunch instead? "I try to meet my friends for lunch during the work week. Since I am going to lunch anyway, this doesn't take away time from my work or family," says Marie, a 41 year old software engineer and mother of two.

Talk on the phone while you're doing something else

"Get a cordless phone so you can chat while you're washing dishes, folding laundry or sitting in the yard watching the kids," suggests Gayle, a 28 year old graphic designer and mother of one.

Put technology to work for you

"I have a very close relationship with four friends I went to elementary school with," says Jennie, a 30 year old web site producer and mother of one. "They live all across the country. We e-mail as a group usually a couple of times a week and have a reunion once a year in a fun place."

Make a date

Don't keep uttering vague promises about how you'll have to get together "soon." Find an excuse to get together in person this month. "It helps to have a goal to build a day out around, like a craft show, lunch or shopping," says Gayle. If you and your friends are a literary bunch, you might consider starting your own book club. (Hey, if Oprah can do it, why not you?)

Seize the moment

Realize that a 30 second phone call is better than no call at all. Don't wait until you have an hour-long block of time to chat on the phone with your friends. You could be retired by the time that happens. Instead, pick up the phone and gamble that you'll be able to spit out a sentence or two before someone walks by and interrupts you. "My best friend has young kids like I do, so we both understand if we suddenly have to hang up because one of our kids has had a diaper explosion or is hanging from the ceiling fan!" explains Cindy, a 34 year old planner and mother of two.

Let her know that you miss her
If your life is totally insane right now and you can't find enough hours in the day to spend with your friend, be sure to let her know how much you miss her. Send her a card, dash off a two-line e-mail, send her flowers or leave her a cheery message on her voice mail at work. While these gestures are no substitute for a heart-to-heart talk that lasts until the wee hours of the morning, they'll help to keep your friendship strong until you can wrestle your To Do List back under control again.

Projects and Causes

We're a nation of volunteers, according to the folks at Statistics Canada. In 1997, 7.5 million of us donated 1.1 billion hours of our time to various projects and causes. Thirty-three percent of women and 29 percent of men were active volunteers that year and donated, on average, 149 hours of their time over the year.

Volunteer work can be very rewarding — if you can fit it into your schedule. Not everyone can.

"I would love to be doing some volunteer work, but at this point, I just don't see how I could fit it in and do a good job," admits Kirste, a 33 year old assistant investment advisor and mother of two. "I've decided that my charitable work will have to take the form of donations right now. I guess it's a bit of a cop-out, but something has to give."

"When I was young, I was always volunteering for something," adds Marie, a 41 year old software engineer and mother of two. "I had lots of time and little money. Now it's the other way around. That means that for 'good

> ### "WORTH QUOTING"
>
> "Time with friends allows you to be yourself — not someone's employee, someone's mommy, someone's maid, or someone's daughter: just yourself!"
>
> • Suzanne, 29, attorney and mother of one

causes,' I tend to send money."

"I don't volunteer," admits Heather, a 30 year old portfolio manager and mother of three. "I feel guilty about that. It seems very selfish to be so involved in your own life that you don't take time to enrich the lives of others. My career is very demanding and I want to spend time with my young son and my husband whenever I can."

Heather is wise to be cautious — and to admit to herself and others that this isn't the right time in her life to be taking on volunteer work. Some women, like Victoria, a 41 year old community college instructor and mother of three, find it much harder to say no:

> In truth, I do too much volunteer work. I do small things for the church. I make meals for new moms in my mothers' club. I chair a committee for the PTA. I am president of my baby-sitting co-op. I am organizing the holiday gift collection for my daughter's child care program. And I am making fundraising calls for my college's 20 year reunion. I would guess I spend 10 to 20 hours a week — probably more right now — on volunteer work.

Here are some tips on making volunteer work a rewarding part of your life rather than just one more item on your To Do List.

Don't over commit yourself to volunteer work
Decide how many commitments you can reasonably juggle at any one time and stick to it. "I volunteer at my kids' school. I join one big committee and then do little single-day projects throughout the year," says Judy, a 44 year old sales representative and mother of two. "I volunteer about once a month with a group of friends from church," adds Stephanie, a 25 year old administrative assistant and mother of one. "I would like to do more, but I have found that this is enough for now."

Only volunteer for causes you believe in
You don't have time to support every cause, so make sure that the ones you give your time to are the ones that are most important to you. If you lost a family member to heart disease, you may be willing to brave those cold February winds to go canvassing for

the Heart and Stroke Foundation because it's important to you to support that particular cause.

Only take on tasks that you will enjoy
If you find it a struggle to balance your own cheque book, don't let anyone talk you into doing the books for the local minor hockey association. Similarly, if you can't stand cooking, don't offer to whip up batch after batch of Nanaimo bars for the fundraiser at your church.

Look for projects lasting a limited period of time rather than ongoing ones
"In general, any volunteering I do is on special projects with a beginning, middle, and an end — not ongoing projects that take up a definite amount of time each week," says Marie, a 41 year old software engineer and mother of two. "The only volunteer work I do now is the occasional one-time stint for my older daughter's school," adds Marilyn, a 43 year old technical writer and mother of three. "I'll sign up to bake for one of the parties — or to be a 'field trip mom' or edit the school newsletter once." By picking projects with a definite end in sight, you have more control over what you do, so that when other aspects of your life need attention you'll be better able to handle it.

Volunteer on your own terms, not theirs
"I will volunteer for the school as long as it doesn't require my presence at a certain time and place," explains Phyllis, a 37 year old information consultant and mother of two. "For example, I have sewn library book bags for the older kids. I had a deadline to finish them, but I didn't have to attend a meeting or commit specific times to the activity."

Just say no
You're not doing anyone a favour if you agree to take on more than you can reasonably handle. "I'd love to do more, but I'd be too stressed out," admits Marilyn. "I refuse a lot of requests — people think that because I work at home, I must have lots of free time — but it's always hard to do. Still, I've gotten better at saying no with each child!"

While it can be challenging to set aside time for volunteer work, friends, or family, it's definitely worth the effort. If you get in the habit of reaching out to one special person in your life each day — by phone, letter or e-mail — you'll find yourself feeling a lot more connected with those around you.

In the next chapter, we'll be talking about another time-consumer, albeit one not nearly as enjoyable as keeping in touch with friends and family — housework!

Chapter 11

The Martha Stewart Syndrome: Who Says it's a Good Thing?

Imagine how different our lives would be if the predictions of the science fiction writers of the 1950s and 1960s had come true. When they gazed into their crystal balls and contemplated life in the new millennium, they predicted that housework would be a thing of the past — that we'd all have access to high-tech robots that would cook, clean and attend to our every whim. A half-century later, we're still waiting for that robot-in-shining armour to appear on the horizon, broom and dustpan in hand.

Here's the latest dirt on women and housework:

➤ Canadian women spend two-and-a-half times as much time on household tasks as Canadian men. According to the most recent figures from Statistics Canada, women spend 139 minutes per day on housework while men spend just 54 minutes. Figure 11.1 shows exactly how much less time the average man spends on household tasks — something that should give your hubby some food-for-thought next time the topic comes up!

➤ A 1992 study of dual-career families in both the US and Sweden revealed that men overestimate the amount of work they do around the house and that middle-class men are no more likely to do housework than their blue collar counterparts.

FACTS & FIGURES

Here's something to chew on the next time you're cooking dinner for your family. The replacement cost of household work in 1986 was nearly $200 billion — nearly 40 percent of Canada's gross domestic product.

• Source: Vanier Institute of the Family

Figure 11.1: **Battle of the Sexes: The Average Time Spent on Housework by Women and Men (minutes per day)**

Activity	Women	Men
Cooking/Washing Up	70	22
House Cleaning and Laundry	65	13
Maintenance and Repair	4	19
Total	139 minutes	54 minutes

Source: Statistics Canada General Survey, 1992

➤ The average American working woman spends 25 hours per week on housework — significantly less than the 38 hours per week put in by her non-employed counterparts, according to *Good Housekeeping* magazine.

Labour-saving devices like microwaves and dishwashers haven't been the ticket to freedom that they first promised to be. According to John P. Robinson and Melissa Milkie, who recently wrote an article on the subject for *American Demographics*, women who own these devices spend almost as much time on housework as those who don't: "The average woman aged 18 to 50 spends 57 minutes a day cooking. The difference between those with microwaves and those without is less than 10 minutes ... Women with automatic dishwashers spend a minuscule minute less than those without them cleaning up meals." That's not just bad news for appliance manufacturers, of course. It's also dreadful news for women! Despite the introduction of a fleet of small and large appliances to the home, we've actually managed to create more work for ourselves, not less. "Anecdotal evidence suggests that we have more dishes and clothes than we used to, and we probably wash them more often," write Robinson and Milkie in *American Demographics*.

Obviously, the topic of this chapter is housework — one of the greatest sources of frustration for most working women. We're going to start out by looking at Martha Stewart Syndrome — that strange affliction that has overworked working women tuning into a television show or reading decorating magazines that seem to bear only a passing resemblance to reality. Then we're going to focus on some practical strategies for taking some of the stress out of housework: lowering your expectations, conquering clutter, creating a housework schedule, finding ways to reduce the amount of cleaning you have to do, taming the laundry monster, looking for shopping shortcuts and saving time in the kitchen. We'll wrap up the chapter by talking about my favourite sanity saver of all: getting other people to do the work!

The New Domesticity: Why You Can't Stencil Your Way to Happiness

Are you a Dr. Jekyll and Ms. Hyde when it comes to housework: someone who rushes around the house doing just enough cleaning to keep the health department happy — and then flopping out on the couch to watch an episode of *Martha Stewart Living?*

Apparently, a lot of us working women are leading this strange double life: slamming Martha in front of our co-workers, but then sneaking home a copy of her latest book or magazine in a brown paper bag. There's no denying it. According to the folks at Martha Stewart Omnimedia, 75 percent of the domestic diva's fans are working women. I, for one, consider this to be one of the greatest mysteries of our generation: how is it that huge numbers of perennially exhausted working women are choosing to spend what little leisure time they have watching a woman who can devote an entire half-hour television segment to the art of making a bed? Do we not feel bad enough about our less-than-pristine houses without tuning into a woman who preaches a new standard of perfectionism that no average working woman can attain?

Consider what writer Margaret Talbot had to say about Martha Stewart in a recent article in the *New Republic*:

> To spend any length of time in Marthaland is to realize that it is not enough to serve your guests homemade pumpkin soup as a

> ### "WORTH QUOTING"
>
> "I started a needlework sampler when I was about five months pregnant with my son. He is 14 months old and it is still unfinished. I may have to change the date from his date of birth to the date of his high school graduation!"
> • Suzanne, 29, attorney

first course. You must present it in hollowed-out, hand-gilded pumpkins as well. It will not do to serve an Easter ham unless you have baked it in a roasting pan lined with, of all things, "tender, young, organically-grown grass that has not yet been cut."

Some women feel that Martha Stewart's appeal has something to do with our desire for order. Consider what Marilyn, a 31 year old writer, has to say:

I think Martha Stewart appeals to the orderly side of us that never gets satisfied. She is what we might have seen our mothers as being when we were very young. She creates an atmosphere of "home" when all we feel is "house." The fact is, a houseful of squalling babies and little girls with their hair flying as they throw Happy Meal toys at each other across the table make a home richer than all the perfectly painted walls and matching china settings.

Karen, a 34 year old technical writer, believes that Martha Stewart's appeal is linked to our quest for perfection.

I think we've become largely a generation of women who are all trying too hard to do it all and do it "right." Both moms who work outside the home and moms who stay at home seem obsessed with trying to be perfect — everything from raising the perfect children to having the perfect house to parenting perfectly according to whatever the latest textbook theory is. Martha Stewart fits right in with that quest for "perfection."

Amber, a 33 year old public health nurse, thinks that we're captivated by Martha's ability to put herself first:

I think the appeal of Martha Stewart is the fact that she leads an idealistic, organized life with apparently few or any other demands for her time. She can make herself and her projects her priority while the rest of us have our children, work, cleaning and cooking as our priorities. I think that while we busy women would never give up our lives, we use her to fantasize about what it would be like to be able to do what we want, when we want, without feeling guilty about wasting time.

Some women feel that Martha Stewart isn't a particularly good role model for women, despite her proven track record as a businesswoman. "She creates unrealistic expectations for today's woman and makes us nostalgic for the fifties — the so-called good-old-days when women didn't have the equal opportunities at work that they are beginning to have today," says Donna, a 48 year old acupuncturist.

Other women — particularly working women with young children — refuse to take her seriously: "Martha Stewart's approach is so far removed from the daily grind that I just laugh when I read the magazine my mother passes along," says Andrea, a 38 year old teacher and writer. "Actually, I think she appeals more to women with no kids or grown-up kids than she does to those of us in the trenches."

Perhaps that's why I find it so hard to understand the whole Martha Stewart phenomenon. With four kids and a full-time job, I'm definitely in the trenches.

"Worth Quoting"

While Martha certainly raised the bar when it comes to housekeeping standards, she wasn't the first person to use TV to show North American women what they should aspire to achieving on the home front. In her book *Where The Girls Are: Growing Up Female With The Mass Media*, Susan J. Douglas talks about the unreasonably high housekeeping standards modelled by two of the most popular 1950s TV shows: "To even approach the level of material comforts that *Leave It to Beaver* and *Father Knows Best* suggested everyone had, millions of families needed Mom in the workforce. And to have their houses approach the standards of tidiness and cleanliness also set by these shows, Mom had to come home from work and mop till she dropped."

Learning to Love the Dust Bunnies

While the best way to reduce housework-related stress is to abandon all hope of following in Martha Stewart's footsteps, there are some other things you can do to bring your stress level back down to earth. Here are a few tips on keeping your sanity in the face of the dust.

Lower your expectations

It's pretty tough to keep your house in showroom condition when you work outside the home. After all, you've got plenty of other demands on your time more important than dusting and chasing a vacuum cleaner around the room. That's why one of the first steps to reducing the amount of stress you feel is to give yourself permission to cut corners on the housework front. Rather than focusing on having an immaculate home, focus on having a home that is clean enough to keep the health unit off your back, suggests Gayle, a 27 year old graphic designer. "Nobody cares if your house is dusty as long as it's sanitary. They won't care that the living room is a mess as long as your bathroom is clean."

Keep the big picture in mind

Sometimes it helps to remind yourself that you have more important things to attend to than dusting knick-knacks or fluffing throw cushions. That's a lesson that Marilyn, a 43 year old technical writer, learned after she became a mother:

> Soon after my first child was born, I was complaining to an older friend that my house was always a mess. It really bothered me that I was suddenly living in visible chaos. My friend said something like, "You have the rest of your life to clean your house," and she was right. I try to remember that whenever the mess and the craziness are getting to me. I can now read bedtime stories to my children while surrounded by sippy cups with last night's water in them and an overflowing laundry basket.

Don't bite off more than you can chew

Rather than promising yourself that you'll keep the house spotless seven days a week, commit to something a little more realistic. Otherwise, you'll just be setting yourself up for disappointment. "I have a contract with myself that I must do one hour of house "stuff" each day: cleaning, paying the bills, laundry and so on," says Rose, a 23 year old teacher. "It's amazing what I get done in an hour. If I don't get everything finished, it waits until the next day."

Be selective

Spend your cleaning time attending to the spots in your home that get the most use: the kitchen counters, the front foyer and the bathrooms. Who cares if there's a quarter inch of dust on the dining room table? You can wipe it off the next time you plan to entertain.

> ## "Worth Quoting"
>
> "Accept less than perfection. There is no way you can be a perfect mother, perfect housekeeper, perfect cook, perfect wife, perfect employee, and so on. Good enough is fine in most cases."
>
> • Heather, 39, customer service representative

Conquering Clutter

Feel like you're constantly surrounded by a sea of clutter? You're probably not far from wrong! According to Pam Young, author of *Get Your Act Together*, the average person manages to accumulate approximately one grocery bag's worth of clutter each week — a mind-boggling 52 bags of clutter per person per year!

You don't have to be a rocket scientist to figure out that clutter is enemy number one when you're trying to make some serious inroads with the housework. After all, you're not going to be able to do much with that vacuum cleaner if you can't even find the floor!

Rather than chasing piles of clutter around the house while you're trying to vacuum or dust, get rid of the stuff you don't need once and for all. You won't just save yourself time each time to go to clean your house: you'll also feel a whole lot better for it! Consider what Don Aslett, author of *Is There Life After Housework?* has to say about the benefits of clutter-busting: "Everything stashed away or hidden — discreetly or indiscreetly — is also stashed in your mind and is subconsciously draining your mental energy. Once discarded, it's discarded from your mind, and you're free from keeping mental tabs on it."

Getting rid of clutter is the easy part, of course. Getting it to stay away for good is the more formidable challenge. If you're serious about wanting to live in a clutter-free environment, you'll need to get rid of clutter on a regular basis. Mary, a 36 year old research biologist, has found ways to make clutter-busting a part of her weekly routine:

> I have a cardboard box that I use to collect clutter around the house. Once every week on a Saturday, I walk around the house and pick up everything on the dining table, kitchen counter, and end tables and put it in the box. When I have time, I go through the box and toss stuff we don't need or want, put toys away, file stuff that needs to be filed, and put catalogues or magazines away or in the recycling bin. This has made a world of difference in clutter control for me.

You'll also need to learn how to be as ruthless as possible when deciding what to keep and what to throw away. Marcia, a 34 year old psychologist and mother of four, is a firm believer in getting rid of as much stuff as possible. "Toss, toss, toss," she advises. "When games are missing some of their pieces, throw them out. After you read a magazine, throw it out. Yeah, you might someday want to remember Heloise's Hint number 345, but it's not worth having your July 1975 *Good Housekeeping* magazine sitting around your house for 20 years!"

Convinced of the merits of reducing clutter, but don't know how to get started? Here are some practical tips on conquering the clutter at your house.

The Front Hall

Hang a row of hooks across the back of your closet so that your toddler or preschooler can start hanging up her own coat. (If you don't teach your child to master this skill by age five, your front hall will look like a war zone for the next 10 years.) Make sure that there's a convenient place for your children to store their mittens and hats. Otherwise, they'll simply end up in the middle of the floor. Something as simple as a laundry basket tucked inside the front hall closet is all that's needed to eliminate this perennial source of clutter.

SANITY SAVERS

"I never leave a room without carrying something out that belongs elsewhere. And I'm trying to teach the children the same thing."

• Marilyn, 43, technical writer

Provide a convenient spot for your school-aged children to deposit backpacks and other paraphernalia. "Buy Rubbermaid storage bins with tops — one for each child," suggests Lisa, a thirty-five year old fitness consultant. "Put each child's name on the top of his or her bin using permanent marker and keep them near the back door. That way, when your children come home from school, they can store all of their school stuff in their bin."

Store out-of-season coats and jackets in another part of the house. The average front hall closet is too small to tackle four seasons worth of garments. The same goes for shoes and boots: you don't need your summer sandals and your winter boots cluttering up the closet at the same time!

The Kitchen

Organize your cupboards by theme: baking supplies should be clustered together, as should cookbooks, pots and pans, dinner plates and so on. Once you've come up with your cupboard organizing system, make sure that each member of the family understands what goes where. Otherwise, you're likely to find the breakfast cereal mixed in with the cleaning supplies. For the small fiddly stuff like spice jars, try separating them into two or three shelves, grouped by letter. That way, you'll only have to go through A to I, J to R, or S to Z, rather than all those little bottles.

If your child enjoys doing art projects at the kitchen table, use a fishing tackle box to store all her art-related bits and pieces. The top tray is ideal for crayons, pencils, markers, scissors and rulers; while the storage area underneath is great for holding foam pieces, pom-poms, fabric scraps and other bits and pieces.

Get in the habit of cleaning out the refrigerator each time you bring in a new load of groceries. If you don't, you'll end up with a smorgasbord of prehistoric leftovers that aren't fit for man or beast.

Don't allow family members to leave school papers, newspapers, unpaid bills and other bits of paper on the kitchen counter. Not only does it look awful to have that much paper laying around, you'll risk throwing out your credit card statement along with last week's newspapers.

Set up a mini-office in one of your kitchen cupboards. "A friend of mine just passed on a great tip," says Lisa. "She suggested that I buy file folders in different colours for different areas of my life — green for financial information, red for unpaid bills, orange for household information, yellow for medical information, blue for the kids' stuff — and that I install a plastic file holder on the inside of one of my kitchen cabinets. Now, each night I sort through all the day's mail and school work and file each piece in the appropriate folder. Then, on the weekend, I take the folders up to my home office and file the papers in the big filing cabinet."

The Family Room

Provide adequate storage space for all the entertainment-related clutter. If you and your children are movie buffs, you'll need a bookcase or storage chest to hold all of your videos. If you're music lovers, you'll need a place to store all your CDs. Find creative ways to handle the piles of magazines and newspapers. "One idea I got from my Mom was to put current catalogues and magazines in one of those fancy wicker or twig baskets and toss the old catalogue or magazine out when a new one arrives," says Mary, a 36 year old research biologist. "The baskets don't look as messy as a pile does."

Come up with creative spots to store your child's toys. A toy box isn't a good idea for toys that have dozens of pieces as they will simply get mixed in with other toys. A better idea is to provide your child with a series of see-through containers with snap-on lids so that he or she can store all the pieces together.

Set some house rules about eating and drinking in the family room. A lot of family room clutter consists of dirty dishes, half-eaten bowls of popcorn that inevitably get spilled and other food-and-beverage-related messes.

Sanity Savers

"Make a list of jobs that take ten minutes or less to do. Have each family member tackle at least one of the jobs on the list every day."
- Cindy, 26, marketing assistant and mother of one

The Bedrooms

Don't keep a lot of unnecessary clutter in the bedroom. After all, this is supposed to be your sanctuary at the end of a long day. Rather than keeping piles of books and magazines on your night table, just keep the novel or magazine that you happen to be reading at the time. Store the rest of these reading materials on a bookshelf elsewhere in the house where they can be retrieved easily when you need them.

Help your children to keep clutter under control in their own rooms by providing them with plenty of storage space. A bookcase can be used to store books, trophies and large toys; a desk with drawers can be used to store writing supplies and school papers; and a well-designed closet organizer can take care of a lot of the other kid-related clutter. Run a thin strip of cork board around the perimeter of your child's bedroom at a height of about three feet off the ground. Your child can then use push-pins to display his or her most recent works of art on this mile-long bulletin board.

If one of your children has a stuffed animal collection that is taking over her room, you might suggest that many of these animals find a new home in a hammock suspended from the ceiling. (Just make sure your child realizes that the hammock is for the animals' use only, not for that of a budding trapeze artist.) Encourage your children to sort through their toys regularly so they can get rid of the ones that they no longer use or that are missing important pieces. If your children can't bear to part with the toys right away, suggest that you put them in a box in the basement for now. If they haven't asked to play with anything in the box six months from now, it's probably safe to donate it to a local women's shelter or toss it in the trash.

Clean out each family member's bedroom closet before the start of a new season. That way, you'll have a

> ## SANITY SAVERS
>
> "I have two large bulletin boards in our family room. The boys put what they consider to be their best works of art on the bulletin board. The rest goes into a box under each of their beds. Periodically, we go through the box and decide what goes into a scrapbook and what gets thrown away. (I used to save absolutely every paper they even scribbled on, but there's just too much now.) Also, the box is great to have when an aunt or family friend sends a gift to one of the boys and they want to send some of their artwork in their thank-you note."
>
> • Karen, 34, technical writer-editor and mother of two

good idea of what each person needs to complete his or her summer or winter wardrobe before you hit the clothing stores. Store out-of-season clothing in sealed plastic containers or empty suitcases and then stash everything under the bed. The clothing is still within reach if you have an unseasonably warm or cold day, but it's not taking up valuable closet real estate the rest of the time.

The Bathroom

Rather than having three brands of shampoo on the go all at once, see if you can find one brand of shampoo that is right for each member of the family. Unless your tub is clean and clutter-free enough to make Martha Stewart proud, pass on the see-through shower curtain and the plain-glass shower doors.

Store your children's bath toys in a mesh laundry bag, and then hang the bag from the taps or the spout. Stash as much clutter as possible in the medicine chest and in the cupboard under the sink. Just one quick word of caution: be sure to store all of the hazardous materials in your bathroom safely out of your child's reach.

Remember that clutter-busting is an ongoing task. The secret to taming the clutter monster is to eliminate clutter on a daily or weekly basis. So pop on everyone's favourite CD and set the timer for 15 minutes after dinner each evening. You'll be amazed how much clutter you'll be able to eliminate if the whole family tackles the task at once.

"WORTH QUOTING"

"June Cleaver made having a spotless house look so effortless. ... I resolved early on to become a slob when I grew up, since housework seemed to produce nothing but misery. (I succeeded spectacularly, by the way.)"

•Susan J. Douglas, *Where The Girls Are: Growing Up Female With The Mass Media*

Cleaning 101

Once you've managed to conquer the piles of clutter in your life, your next step should be to come up with a game plan for keeping your house clean and clutter-free. That means looking for ways to minimize the amount of time you have to spend cleaning and scheduling clean-ups on a regular basis.

Looking for some quick-and-painless ways to stay on top of the housework during the week? Here are a few ideas:

➤ Keep a set of cleaning supplies under each sink. That way, the cleaners, sponges and paper towels will be readily available for quick clean-ups as the need arises.

➤ Tidy up the bathroom counter while you're blow-drying your hair or while your child is playing in the bathtub.

➤ Use the squeegee on the shower walls as soon as you're finished your shower. This will help to minimize the amount of soap scum build-up you have to deal with the next time you clean the bathroom. (Hint: you can reduce the amount of elbow grease required to keep those shower walls sparkling if you seal them with car wax the next time they're clean.)

➤ Use comforters rather than blankets on the beds in your house. It's a lot easier to pull up a comforter than to fuss with a blanket, and your house looks 110 percent cleaner if the beds are made. Comforters with removable, washable covers are faster than separate blankets and sheets.

➤ Instead of leaving all of the household tasks until the weekend, tackle a couple of small jobs each day. Come up with a weekly agenda that works for you: e.g. bills get paid on Sunday nights, the microwave gets wiped down on Monday nights and so on.

➤ Stuck with a particularly boring job? Do more than one thing at once. Never dry your dishes, for example — let them air-dry as you spend that time sweeping the kitchen floor, putting away laundry or doing some other mundane task.

See Figure 11.2 for a checklist to help organize the cleaning chores.

Figure 11.2

A Date with Dirt

The checklist below should help you to identify the types of jobs that you should plan to do daily, weekly, and annually.

Daily:
- ☐ Make your bed.
- ☐ Pick up any items that happen to be lying around and put them back where they belong.
- ☐ Do the dishes after every meal and wipe the counters and stove.
- ☐ Clean up spots and spills.
- ☐ Take out the garbage.
- ☐ Hang up clean clothes and put dirty clothes in the clothes hamper.
- ☐ Get rid of old newspapers, junk mail and other paper-related clutter.
- ☐ Do laundry (if necessary).

Weekly:
- ☐ Vacuum carpets and door mats.
- ☐ Mop floors.
- ☐ Dust.
- ☐ Change the sheets on the beds.
- ☐ Clean all bathroom and kitchen surfaces.
- ☐ Clean the toilets.
- ☐ Wipe down the inside and outside surfaces of your microwave.

Monthly:
- ☐ Dust the woodwork.
- ☐ Vacuum the upholstery.
- ☐ Clean out the refrigerator.
- ☐ Wash and disinfect trash containers and the fronts of your appliances and kitchen cupboards.

Annually:
- ☐ Clean your oven.
- ☐ Degrease your stove hood and exhaust fan.
- ☐ Turn your mattress over.

Obviously, there's no one-size-fits-all cleaning checklist. You'll have to customize the list a little to make it fit with your lifestyle. If you have long-haired pets, you may want to vacuum more frequently. Similarly, if you have a newborn baby who spits up on a dozen outfits per day, you'll want to keep "laundry" in the daily category!

An Ounce of Prevention

Your mother was right: an ounce of prevention is worth a pound of cure. Rather than spending hours trying to get rid of dirt, why not prevent it from becoming a problem in the first place? Here are few tips that may help you to cut down on the amount of time you spend cleaning.

Stop dirt in its tracks

Place floor mats on the inside and outside of each exterior door and encourage family members to wipe their feet on them before they enter the house. This will dramatically reduce the amount of dirt that gets tracked into your house.

Give soap problems the slip

Put liquid soap dispensers rather than bar soap beside each sink. You'll eliminate the need to spend hours scraping soap sludge off the soap dish, sink and counter.

Start your own fan club

Open the window or turn on the bathroom fan while you are having a shower. This will help to slow the growth of mildew in your bathroom.

Wipe your problems down the drain

Get into the habit of rinsing and wiping down the shower walls after you're finished showering. This can help to reduce the build-up of soap scum and mineral deposits.

You can reduce the amount of time you spend cleaning your house if you decorate with the right types of materials. Here are a few dirt-defying decorating tips from interior designer and mother of one, Cathy Fountain:

➤ Go with mat or stain finishes rather than glossy finishes on walls, countertops and floors. High gloss finishes serve to emphasize spills and scratches.

ETC.

Eight men praised for their housekeeping finesse recently battled it out in a contest sponsored by Proctor and Gamble, makers of Mr. Clean. The contestants got the chance to strut their stuff in a specially designed cleaning obstacle course designed to showcase their talents in folding laundry, mopping floors, changing diapers and more. Now there's a group of men who won't have any trouble getting dates!

> When you're choosing paint colours, go for mid-tone rather than dark or light colours. Middle-range colours tend to do a better job of hiding dirt.

> If you really want to hide the fingerprints and the ketchup splatters, sponge paint your walls or use other faux finishing techniques to create patterns within the paint.

> If you decide to use wallpaper in the kitchen or bathroom, look for high-quality washable middle-range colours in vinyl.

> Use egg shell finishes in all areas of your house except for the kitchen and bathroom, where you should opt for a more washable pearl finish.

> Paint any exposed woodwork with semi-gloss paint that can be wiped down easily.

> When you're shopping for carpets, look for Berber carpets that are full of texture. The texture will help to disguise dirt and you won't have the ugly vacuum lines that you get on plush carpets.

SANITY SAVERS

Don't want to become a slave to housework? Here are some features you'll want to avoid the next time you renovate or move, as they tend to collect dirt and/or require more elbow grease to maintain:

> indented or embossed tile or floor coverings
> indoor-outdoor carpet
> highly textured walls and ceilings
> unfinished wood
> extremely high ceilings
> carpet in the kitchen or bathroom
> windows that are difficult to reach.

Taming the Laundry Monster

There is no middle ground when it comes to doing laundry. You either love it or hate it! Some women make it part of their daily routines. Others avoid it until everyone's down to their last pair of underwear!

"I do laundry almost every night," says Karen, a 34 year old technical writer-editor. "I would never have time to do it on the weekends if I let it pile up. It's easy to throw a load in before dinner, take a minute to throw it in the dryer after dinner, and then fold it while I'm watching TV after the kids are in bed. Putting it away is the hardest part. Sometimes it sits folded in the laundry room all week and we just keep pulling from the pile each morning when we're looking for clean clothes. It often makes me wonder why we have dressers!"

"Laundry works best for me if I get one load done during the week and leave the rest for the weekend," says Irene, a 41 year old regulatory affairs officer. "I've taken to getting most of it washed on Friday nights so that it's not hanging over me all weekend."

"Laundry happens when it happens," confesses Jane, a 37 year old architect. "Usually it has to yell at us before it gets any attention. I try to leave that particular chore until the weekend because it is just one more thing to juggle during the week. Who wants to leave forgotten wet clothes in the washing machine for three days! Ironing, of course, is another story: it never happens!"

While there aren't many of us who actually look forward to doing laundry, there's a lot you can do to tame the laundry monster. Here are a few tips:

➤ Teach family members to sort their laundry as they take it off. You can help them to do this by placing three different laundry hampers in your bathroom: one for darks, one for lights and one for colours.

➤ If you find that you're having to do laundry every couple of days, you might want to expand your wardrobes a little. "I bought my husband and my daughter lots of socks and underwear. That way, if I run behind on the laundry, they don't run out," says Debbie, a 39 year old sales development manager.

➤ Don't buy clothes that need ironing and you'll save yourself a lot of time and headache!

➤ Don't go on a search and rescue mission trying to find your daughter's favourite jeans. If she can't be bothered to get her clothes into the laundry hamper, she is clearly willing to live without them.

➤ Hate matching socks? Assign each member of the family a particular sock colour and buy him or her a dozen identical pairs. Then, instead of spending hours trying to find the mates for the various socks, you'll just need to sort the socks by colour and bundle them into pairs. If two family members are both vying for black, for example, assign one solids and the other patterns or stripes.

➤ Give other members of the family a chance to pitch in. At the very least, let them assume responsibility for putting away their own clothes. "My husband and I often fold laundry together in the evening," says Vicki, a 41 year old community college instructor.

➤ When taking clean clothes out of the dryer or off the line, automatically put it into individual baskets for each person. That way, everyone gets to put away their own laundry — even small children can manage this.

➤ Don't think you have a hope of ever catching up on laundry again? Toss everything into laundry baskets and head for the nearest laundromat. Pop in a dozen loads at once and you should have your laundry all caught up within a couple of hours. What's more, you can use the time you spend at the laundromat doing something that's good for you — like gabbing on the payphone with a girlfriend or flipping through the pages of *People* magazine.

Looking for ways to cut back on the amount of time you spend in the laundry room? Here are a few more tips.

"Worth Quoting"

"Laundry is a sore subject in my house. I do it all — from finding the dirty clothes to washing, folding, ironing — yuck! No matter how much I cajole, bribe, or yell, the clothes never fully get into the hamper, and in my travels I will find dirty socks under the bed, underwear within the bed folds and my husband's laundry mixed in with clean laundry in a basket I have yet to put away! It drives me nuts!"

• Eileen, 35, business analyst and mother of two

Sort your laundry into piles in the laundry room

Tackle the loads in priority order. If you're running out of bras, get them in the washer before you tackle that mountain of sheets and towels.

Toss a load of laundry in the machine each night before you go to bed

In the morning, move the wet clothes into the dryer and toss another load into the washing machine. Before you head out the door to go to work, take ten minutes to fold the clothes as they come out of the dryer. Then, when you arrive home from work, toss the next load of wet clothes in the dryer. After dinner, take ten minutes to fold the second load of laundry. Follow these steps each day and you'll never have to waste an entire Saturday catching up in the laundry again.

Take the baskets of clean laundry into the family room
Fold everything while you watch TV or visit with family members. Clothes that need to be hung up should go on hangers right away. There's no point folding a shirt and then unfolding it to put it on a hanger when you take it upstairs! Routine mending can be done in the same manner and you won't miss a thing!

Don't bother trying to match up socks when you're folding laundry
Just toss all the socks into an empty laundry basket and tackle them when you're on the phone or watching TV. (Hint: if you've got teenagers who like to live on the phone, let them know that they're welcome to stay on the phone as long as they'd like as long as they do light housework while they're talking: matching up socks, picking up clutter, dusting and more.)

Dine and Dash: Eating on the Run

There's no denying it: unless you're a natural-born Julia Child, cooking can be a major headache. Just think about the number of steps that are involved in making a simple dinner. You have to decide what to make, taking into account your family member's various dietary needs and preferences. You have to check to make sure you have all the necessary ingredients and make a trip to the grocery store to pick up anything you're missing. You have to do all the necessary preparation: peeling potatoes, slicing carrots and so on. Then you have to do the actual cooking — the easiest step in the whole process, in my humble opinion. Then, after your family gulps down the product of all your hard work in 20 minutes or less, making snide remarks about your cooking, you find yourself stuck with a sink full of pots and pans to wash. Is it any wonder that so many of us are ready to hang up our aprons for good?

While there's no way to eliminate all the work from meal preparation, you can make it less of a nightmare for yourself if you approach it in a semi-methodical fashion. That means setting aside time to plan, taking advantage of grocery shopping short-cuts, and making the most of the time you spend in the kitchen.

Is There Life After Frozen Dinners?

It's easy to get hooked on frozen dinners. You simply walk in the door from work, throw a plastic tray in the oven, and presto! — ten minutes later you've got something to eat. While these products can be a godsend on occasion, most of us don't like to use them on a daily basis: they're pricey, they often contain too much salt and fat and, despite advertising claims to the contrary, they tend to be a little bland.

What many of us have forgotten is that there are many tasty and nutritious dinners that can whipped up in roughly the same amount of time that it takes to cook a frozen dinner in the microwave: things like vegetable omelettes, vegetable stir fries, spaghetti, fajitas and more. (See Appendix B for some web site references which will help you out in a bind.)

The secret, of course, is to have the ingredients on hand when you need them. (After all, it's hard to do a vegetable stir fry when the only thing vegetable-like substance you can find in your refrigerator is a bag of bean sprouts that's long since turned into compost!) That means planning your meals in advance and making a grocery list based on the week's menus.

"But I'm too busy to do that," you protest. You're absolutely right. But you're also too busy to run to the grocery store three times each week in order to pick up frozen fish sticks and chicken nuggets. You're going to have to spend some time on meal planning regardless. The question is would you rather do it in advance and enjoy meals that are actually worth eating, or would you prefer to have to figure out what you're going to have for dinner

Etc.

Looking for some recipes that you'll actually enjoy making? Pick up a copy of Janet and Greta Podleski's wacky yet wonderful low fat cookbook, *Looneyspoons*. It's available in most bookstores or at your local library, but you can also order a copy from Granet Publishing Inc., 99 Northfield Drive East #206, Waterloo, Ontario N2K 3P9 1-800-470-0738. You can find out more about the book at *http://www.looneyspoons.com*

each night as you're driving home in the car and then settle for whatever meal you can throw together in a hurry? (See Figure 11.3 for a checklist of kitchen staples.)

Home Economics Revisited

Need some more reasons to take the time to plan your meals properly? Consider the health benefits as well. According to a 1996 study published in the *International Journal of Obesity*, women who plan their meals and shop accordingly are far more likely to keep nutritious food in their homes.

LeeAnne, a 28 year old newspaper publisher, feels that her family eats better and the stress of making meals is significantly reduced when she takes the time to plan ahead. She explains:

> I think one of the most efficient things I've done is to sit down and make a weekly menu list. I miss some weeks but I try to sit down each week and plan each night's dinner. I make a grocery list to go along with it, so I know what ingredients I have to pick up. Then, each night, I don't have to think about what we're having: I simply need to throw the ingredients together and I know that they are all in the fridge because I've already done the shopping from my list. I plan simple menus for busy work nights (sometimes just grilled cheese sandwiches and cut up veggies will suffice) and more complex meals for quieter days such as weekends and so on. This has greatly reduced our supper-time stress.

Here are some additional tips on planning your weekly menus and hitting the grocery store.

Keep a list of your all-time favourite recipes
It'll save you a lot of time when you sit down to plan the next week's menus.

Plan at least one week's worth of menus at a time —
even longer, if you can manage it.
One woman I know made a list of her family's 35 favourite meals and fit them into a five week schedule.

Checklist of Kitchen Shortcuts

You'll never run out of dinner ideas if you keep your kitchen well-stocked. Here are some staples that every busy cook should have on hand:

Packaged and Bulk Goods:
- ❏ pasta
- ❏ canned soups (especially cream of mushroom, cream of celery and chicken broth)
- ❏ canned beans (kidney beans, black beans, chick peas)
- ❏ canned tomatoes
- ❏ canned refried beans
- ❏ mild green chillies
- ❏ roasted red peppers
- ❏ rice
- ❏ salsa
- ❏ taco shells
- ❏ frozen burritos
- ❏ fajita shells
- ❏ tomato sauce
- ❏ tomato paste
- ❏ spaghetti sauce
- ❏ salad dressing
- ❏ red wine vinegar
- ❏ vegetable dip
- ❏ non-fat bean dip
- ❏ dried fruit
- ❏ rice cakes
- ❏ canned tuna
- ❏ canned salmon
- ❏ couscous
- ❏ olive oil
- ❏ textured vegetable protein (TUP)
- ❏ instant noodles (use miso instead of the salty soup mix)

Checklist of Kitchen Shortcuts, *cont.*

Fruit and Vegetables:
- ❏ fresh vegetables ("salad in a bag," broccoli coleslaw, baby carrots, potatoes, onions, mushrooms, green peppers, tomatoes)
- ❏ frozen vegetables
- ❏ fresh fruit
- ❏ frozen berries
- ❏ canned fruit
- ❏ canned or frozen fruit juices.

Meat and Alternatives:
- ❏ smoked, pre-cooked ham
- ❏ smoked, pre-cooked chicken
- ❏ frozen fish fillets
- ❏ ground beef
- ❏ individually frozen chicken breasts, steaks, hamburger patties, pork chops
- ❏ tofu (firm for stir frying; soft for sauces and desserts)
- ❏ peanut butter
- ❏ frozen pre-packaged veggie burgers and hot dogs
- ❏ tahini
- ❏ tempeh

Milk and Alternatives:
- ❏ dairy products
- ❏ evaporated milk
- ❏ cheese (block or shredded)
- ❏ sour cream
- ❏ eggs
- ❏ calcium-enriched soy milk

Bread
- ❏ tortilla shells
- ❏ pitas
- ❏ bagels
- ❏ prebaked pizza shells
- ❏ whole wheat buns

FACTS & FIGURES

According to a recent article in *Better Homes and Gardens* magazine, 23 percent of consumers now consider the ideal recipe to be one that contains no more than three ingredients while 58 percent want recipes with eight ingredients or less.

Assign meals to each family member when you plan

Food tastes better when someone else cooks and assigning dinners ahead of time allows people to plan. In addition, you are apt to get less complaining if your kids learn how much preparation time goes into a meal.

Cut out quick, easy, healthy recipes when you see them

Tape them where you'll easily see them (the fridge, the inside of the cupboard). Then you'll have a bank of new ideas to try when your culinary creativity is running on empty.

Keep a running grocery list in your kitchen

"In our house, we have a white board hanging in the eating area of the kitchen," says Danielle, a 34 year old software developer. "We use it to keep a running grocery list. That way, whoever is going to the store knows exactly what we need."

Time your grocery trip so that you hit off-peak hours

The last thing you want to be doing is wasting your valuable leisure time standing in line at the checkout. "I love to go grocery shopping at midnight," admits Beth, a 32 year old speech-language pathologist. "I'm alone. There are hardly any people in the store. I can take the time to comparison shop and use coupons. What's more, it's quiet and peaceful and an escape after the clamour of getting the kids to bed."

Don't avoid the frozen foods aisle entirely.

It's a good idea to keep a few convenience foods on hand. "I keep frozen fish sticks and frozen french fries on hand for a quick dinner on days when I forget to take the meat out of the freezer," says Heather, a 39 year old telephone company employee.

Look for healthy convenience foods like salads in a bag or peeled baby carrots

You pay a slight premium for these products, but they guarantee that you'll be getting the nutrients you need, no matter how crazy your week ends up being.

*Take advantage of grocery stores
that deliver*

Some stores even allow you to phone
or fax in your grocery order or order
online. "I don't have the time or
patience to go to the grocery store, so
I do my grocery shopping online about
once a week," says Marilyn, a 43 year
old technical writer. "It only takes
about 20 minutes. It's really convenient, and even with the delivery
charge — 10 percent of the order — I
still save money because I tend not to
do any impulse buying."

Etc.

Doing your grocery shopping on the
Internet may sound like a load of science fiction mumble jumble, but it's
actually already an option for many
Canadians. The Peach Tree
http://www.thepeachtree.net, for
example, offers online grocery shopping services to people living in
Vancouver, Vancouver Island, Edmonton, Winnipeg, rural Manitoba,
Toronto, North Bay and St. John's.

Look for Shortcuts in the Kitchen

Now that you've got a fridge full of gro-
ceries, it's time to do something with them! Here are some tips on
making the most efficient use of the time you spend in the
kitchen.

*Do as much food prep as you can on your
non-working days*

Chop onions and green peppers, brown hamburger, hard-boil
some eggs, create a veggie tray and slice a brick of cheese and
wrap it into lunch-sized portion sizes. These simple tasks will
save you a lot of time and effort on the days when you have to go
to work.

Try some batch cooking

"I cook several meals at once on the weekend," says Angela, a 27
year old promotions and advertising manager. "The meals get
frozen and then heated up during the week. It saves us a lot of
stress in deciding what's for dinner and who's responsible for
making it. I don't mind cooking for three or four hours on the
weekend because my husband's responsible for caring for the
children while I cook."

Keep track of the meals you have on hand

"We try to 'cook ahead' on the weekends so we have food ready to go in the freezer," says Tricia, a 33 year old software designer and graduate student. "We'll buy a big package of chicken breasts on sale, grill them all at once and freeze the leftovers. I keep track of these 'ready to serve' meals on a list on the fridge door. I simply cross each item off the list as it is eaten."

Use your crockpot

This amazing kitchen appliance allows you to toss in some raw ingredients in the morning and come home at the end of the day to a delicious, slow-cooked meal. It's the closest thing to magic I've ever seen!

Keep it simple

"Since we both work full-time, making elaborate dinners is not part of our daily routine," says Mary, a 35 year old research biologist. "There are a lot of healthy, easy-to-prepare foods that we take advantage of — pasta, pasta products and frozen meats. We don't always stick with traditional meals like meat, potatoes and vegetables. We'll make a meal out of a big salad with veggies and bread; chili; cheese, sausage and crackers; or nachos."

Running into a rut when it comes to making meals? The following recipes can be prepared in next to no time at all and they require very few ingredients. What's more, they can all be made with healthy, low-fat ingredients.

➢ vegetable stir fry (with or without chicken, beef, or pork)

➢ omelettes

➢ fajitas

➢ burritos

➢ tacos

➢ shepherd's pie

➢ pasta with vegetables

➢ chicken cacciatore (just use commercial spaghetti sauce for the sauce!)

➢ soup and salad

➢ soup and sandwich

➢ stuffed pitas (vegetarian or with meat)

➤ pizza

➤ barbecued anything (chicken, steak, hamburgers, veggieburgers, sausages)

➤ whole wheat crackers topped with salmon or tuna

➤ chili

➤ meatballs

➤ skillet supper (vegetables, pasta, ground beef, tomatoes, and whatever else you have on hand)

➤ smoked pre-cooked ham or chicken

➤ fish with lemon

➤ grilled cheese sandwiches and veggies and dip

➤ macaroni and cheese

➤ tofu cutlets

➤ hummous, pita and vegetables

➤ spaghetti

➤ scrambled eggs

➤ frozen perogies.

Learn the Art of Delegating

Now we come to the very best housework strategy of all: convincing other people to share the load! Unless you enjoy being a live-in maid, you owe it to yourself to introduce the other members of your house to the toilet brush and the vacuum cleaner.

His and Hers Chore Lists

The battle of the sexes has largely been resolved in the bedroom and the boardroom, but it's still being fought out in the bathroom and the kitchen. Studies have shown that housework is right up there with sex and money when couples are asked to name the issues about which they fight the most. Despite the fact that couples today think they're buying into an equal partnership, women continue to assume responsibility for the majority of the responsibilities at home. "Couples are always shocked to find themselves warring over housework," noted marriage therapist Evelyn Moschetta in a recent article in *Ladies' Home Journal*.

Here are some tips on preventing battles over housework from coming between the two of you.

Don't be afraid to ask for help

Your partner might not be a selfish jerk — just an unthinking jerk! "I find that if I tell my husband specifically what needs to be done and what time frame he has to do it in, he will help around the house," says Eileen, a 35 year old business analyst. "He just doesn't see dirt like I do!"

Draw up a job list together and then carve out your turf

Try as much as possible to ensure that neither partner gets saddled with jobs that he or she especially hates doing. If you both hate the same jobs, then either alternate weeks of tackling the most hated tasks or hire someone else to come in and do them for you — a solution we'll be returning to in a minute. Marie, a 41 year old software engineer, decided to take responsibility for major household tasks and to leave the real nitty-gritty stuff to her partner. She explains:

> I am more of a "big project" person while my husband is more of a maintainer. He really gets pleasure from puttering around fixing things and making things right. I just love to sink my teeth into a big project that requires research and planning. So, he pays the bills, does the cooking, and does a lot of the recurring chores. Then, I do all the one-ofs such as deciding if we need more or less life insurance, buying our houses, getting ready for the arrival of our children, deciding how to invest our money, planning vacations and so on.

Hang up the job list in a spot where you both can see it
That way, you won't feel obligated to remind him that he has to do the bathrooms this weekend, and he won't feel the need to hint about how nice it would be to have a home cooked meal for a change!

Be flexible
Don't be afraid to do one of his jobs if he's putting in a lot of overtime or to let him do one of yours if you're dealing with a major crisis at work. The job list isn't a legal document, for Pete's sake! It's simply a game plan for getting things done. On the other hand, you won't want to let him off the hook entirely. No matter how crazy his schedule may be, if he wants to reap the financial rewards of being part of a dual-income household, he can darned well remember to pick up his own socks!

Live and let live
You like to fold the towels and stack them neatly. Your husband prefers to roll them up like pint-sized sleeping bags. Who cares how the damned things are folded so long as they all fit in the linen closet! Is it worth having a major meltdown over such a non-issue?

Getting Your Kids in on the Act
Your partner isn't the only person who should be on your housekeeping hit list, of course. If you have children, it's important to get them involved, too — not just because it helps to reduce your burden (although that sounds like a pretty good reason to me!), but also because you'll be giving them the opportunity to pick up some valuable life skills. (What college-aged male is going to have trouble getting a date once word gets out that he's a gourmet chef and his bathroom is always immaculate?) You can get an idea of what jobs are suitable for children of various ages by checking out the list in Figure 11.4. Keep in mind that the earlier you encourage your children to help out, the faster they'll master the skills, within reason. The important thing is to get them into the habit, even if it's something as simple as peeling garlic or putting away cutlery for a pre-schooler.

Figure 11.4

The Age-Appropriate Job Jar

Use the following suggestions as a guideline for determining what your children of various ages can realistically accomplish around the house.

Three and four year olds:

❏ picking up toys and putting them away (sorting is a little harder!)

❏ matching clean socks

❏ making their bed

❏ putting their clothes in their drawers

Four and five year olds:

❏ sweeping the floor

❏ helping with meal preparation

❏ dusting the furniture

❏ setting the table

❏ taking out the compost

Six and seven year olds:

❏ taking out the garbage and the recycling

❏ cleaning out the car

❏ making a simple meal (cereal or a sandwich)

❏ vacuuming their rooms

❏ sorting and straightening out toys

❏ emptying the dishwasher or the dish rack

❏ sorting laundry

❏ setting and clearing the table

Eight and nine year olds:

❏ cleaning bathroom mirrors

❏ cleaning toilets, countertops and sinks

❏ folding laundry and putting it away

❏ weeding the garden

❏ putting away groceries

❏ raking leaves

Ten to 12 year olds:

❏ washing windows

❏ mending clothes

❏ changing the sheets

❏ doing their own laundry

❏ cleaning the bathtub or shower stall

❏ mowing the lawn

❏ washing the car

❏ shovelling snow

Teenagers:

❏ cleaning out the refrigerator

❏ defrosting the freezer

❏ organizing the basement or the garage

❏ cleaning light fixtures

❏ making dinner

Here are some tips on getting your children involved in helping with household tasks:

➤ Assign each child a couple of chores that are age appropriate. Use Figure 11.4 and your own good sense as a guideline. (Obviously, you don't want to let your three year old handle toxic chemicals!)

➤ Don't load on too many jobs at one time. Keep in mind how overwhelmed you feel when you've got a mile-long To Do List. Your kids will end up feeling the same way.

➤ Teach your kids the basics and then let them try to figure things out on their own. You'll frustrate them to no end if you follow them around the house, burdening them with unwanted advice.

➤ Rather than insisting that your house be immaculate, settle for good enough. Your kids will thank you for it!

To properly prepare your children for adulthood, ensure that they learn to cook as well as the basics in nutrition — they likely won't pick it up elsewhere. Here are some tips on getting them started in the kitchen.

Make sure that you have a kid-friendly work area
If the counter is too high for them to work at comfortably, consider having them work at the kitchen table instead.

Plan to be on hand to supervise and to lend a hand when needed
Cooking is a skill that requires time to master. Besides, the kitchen is one of the most dangerous spots in the house, so you don't want to leave the budding chefs in your family on their own while they're cooking up a storm.

Give your kids a crash course in nutrition
Don't assume that your kids automatically understand that meals need to include foods from a variety of food groups. Pull out a copy of Canada's Food Guide and show them what types of foods belong in each food group, and have them make a list of their favourite types of food. This information will prove useful as they go about planning family menus. While you're at it, go over the basics of food handling and food safety as well. Explain about the need to keep hot foods hot, and cold foods cold, as well as details they may not have thought about, like how long to store leftovers before discarding them. Food poisoning is surprisingly common — protect your kids!

Set your kids loose on your cookbook collection
Encourage them to pick out some new recipes to try. Then, have them check to see which ingredients you already have on hand and which ones need to be added to your grocery list. (Note: don't be surprised if the recipes they want to try aren't quite what you would pick out yourself. Half of the fun of cooking, after all, is trying something fun or unusual.)

Teach your kids the fundamentals of cooking
Include information such as how to measure ingredients, how to mix wet and dry ingredients and so on. By showing them the basics, you will increase their chances of producing meals that they can be proud to take to the dinner table.

Put some fun into the menu by planning themed meals
Decorate your table and choose some music that fits the cuisine you're sampling, or try something totally wacky like adding food colouring to the mashed potatoes on "green food" night.

SANITY SAVERS

"Do not turn on the TV, except for special occasions. It's amazing how much more gets done without the TV on. My daughter gets her homework done, my baby gets lots of attention, and my husband cleans the kitchen after I make dinner."

• Silke, 34, civil engineer and mother of two

Encourage your kids to write down all those recipes your family is test-driving
You might even want to encourage them to create their own family cookbook — a great gift idea for friends and relatives.

Pitch in when it comes time to clean up
Most kids find it overwhelming to be faced with a sink full of dishes after spending an hour making a meal. They're more likely to volunteer for cooking patrol again if you offer to help clean up the mess.

Call in the Pros

If your partner keeps forgetting to clean the bathrooms and your children are nowhere to be found when it's time to mop the floor, perhaps it's time for you to wave the proverbial white flag and call in the pros.

"We hired someone to come in and clean our house every two weeks," says Susan, a 34 year old librarian. "It was less expensive than I expected and it has saved not only my sanity, but our marriage."

Marie, a 41 year old software engineer, was initially reluctant to pay other people to do jobs that she could do herself, but she's since had a change of heart:

> It took me a long time, but I finally learned that there are just some chores that I am not willing to do. Before that, if I knew I was capable of doing something, I thought I "should" do it. Finally, I realized that living my life by a list of "shoulds" was only making me crazy. Now, someone comes every other week to tend to our lawn and garden and someone else comes every week to clean our house. I pay someone to change my oil and wash my car — both of which I'm capable of doing myself — and if something breaks, I either pay someone to fix it or throw it out and get a new one.

> ## SANITY SAVERS
>
> "Get a long cord on your kitchen phone. I do the dishes, sweep the floor, and clean the table while I'm talking on the phone to my friends."
>
> • Heather, 39, customer service representative

Yes, it costs more money to live this way, but part of the advantage of having two incomes in our family is that we have more money. In return, almost all of my spare time is spent doing family things or personal things — not doing mindless chores that only have to be done over again later anyway! Family and my hobbies are what is important to me: not being able to say "Look how this floor sparkles. I did it myself!"

Anne, a 33 year old executive secretary, notes that there are some fringe benefits to signing on with a cleaning service:

Absolutely the smartest thing I have done to get organized is to hire a cleaning service to come every other week. Not only do they tackle the big jobs but, almost more importantly, knowing that they are coming forces me to declutter the house every other week. The day before they come, we have a "No Clutter Day" which means everything must find a home or get thrown out. It's an external deadline that forces me to deal with our "stuff" before the clutter gets out of hand.

Debra, a 44 year old music production co-ordinator, is also a firm believer in hiring other people to help with household tasks:

I hire anyone I can: a housekeeper, a college girl to run errands and drive, a neighbourhood kid to walk the dog. If there's an able body looking for work, I try to find something for them to do to relieve myself of the chores. This year, I hired a young college couple to address my Christmas cards and to wrap the gifts. It gave me the freedom and time to bake cookies and do holiday projects with my daughters.

Don't forget that you always have the option of bartering your skills. If you enjoy gardening but consider your sewing machine to be the enemy, offer to weed a friend's garden if she'll hem your son's jeans.

How to Hire a Cleaning Service

You've decided to take the plunge and hire someone to clean your house. You flip open the Yellow Pages and find yourself staring at a page of ads. So how do you go about finding the cleaning service that's just right for you?

Ask friends and family members if they can recommend a good cleaning service in your area. You increase your chances of being satisfied with the cleaner you choose by relying on word of mouth. Then do some preliminary screening by phone. Find out how long the company has been in business and then call the Better Business Bureau to find out if there are any complaints registered against the company.

Arrange for someone from the cleaning service you're considering to come to your home and provide you with a written estimate. Make sure that the estimate clearly indicates which jobs are — and are not — included in the price. That way, if you're getting an estimate from a second company, you'll be able to compare apples to apples. Ask the cleaning service representative to supply a list of references. Then, pick up the phone and call each person on the list. Don't just accept the cleaning service representative's claim that the company is bonded and insured. Ask for proof.

Don't feel guilty about having someone else do your cleaning. Just keep reminding yourself that it's one of the few things in your life that you can actually download to someone else. Instead of beating yourself up because you can't manage to find personal fulfilment while scrubbing a toilet, focus on finding fun ways to spend your newfound free time.

While housework is never going to be your favourite pastime, as you can see, there's plenty you can do to reduce the amount of time you spend cleaning house. That's great news for any working woman!

Conclusion

Thirty Steps to a Saner You

It's midnight. Over the past 18 hours, you've managed to get two children dressed, drive them to day care, put in eight hours at work, pick up your children from day care, make dinner, wash the dishes, do three loads of laundry, balance the cheque book, and bake a batch of muffins for the charity fundraiser at work. By all accounts, it's been a fabulously productive day. So why aren't you jumping for joy?

For one thing, you're too exhausted! For another, you're feeling slightly bummed. One more day has whizzed by and you still haven't had a chance to read the novel you got for your birthday, take that hour-long bubble bath you've been craving, or show your face at the gym. Once again, you managed to tackle all of the items on your To Do List, but you didn't manage to do a single thing to take care of your own needs.

Running on Empty

You don't have to be an auto mechanic to know that you risk doing serious damage to your car engine if you run out of oil — that you could, in fact, burn it out entirely. What you might not realize is that the same thing can happen to women who refuse to heed the internal "warning light" that tells them that they're running on empty. They risk burning themselves out.

"Worth Quoting"

"What I need more than anything is a little time to myself. I really treasure the hour or so at night when the children are finally asleep and my husband is unwinding in the living room. I get into bed and watch the soap opera I recorded that day, or read, or thumb through some catalogues. I also keep a diary each day, so I write in that before I go to sleep."

• Marilyn, 43, technical writer and mother of three

205

Don't know what I'm talking about? Let me explain. Each time you deprive yourself of sleep, cut out your workout because you're too tired to make it to the gym, skip a meal because you're too busy to cook, or pass up the opportunity to enjoy a fun night out with friends because you've got to head back into the office, you're failing to do the preventive maintenance that your body and soul require.

Wanted: One Fairy Godmother

What every working woman needs, of course, is a fairy god-mother: someone who will show up and wave her magic wand whenever you need a helping hand.

Tempted to skip lunch to finish work on that report? Presto! The report is finished and there's a gourmet meal sitting on your desk.

Spending your weekend doing housework? Presto! The work is done and you have time to read that murder mystery that's been gathering dust on your night table for the past six months.

The baby starts fussing in the middle of the night? Presto! Your partner hops out of bed and quiets the baby before you even wake up. (Now you can see why they call it a magic wand!)

I hate to be the bearer of bad news but there's a distinct shortage of fairy godmothers these days. That means that you're going to have to learn how to take care of your own needs, like it or not. In the remaining pages of this book, I'm going to give you a crash course in being your own fairy god-mother. There's just one catch: there's no magic wand.

Thirty Steps to a Saner You

While I can't give you a magic wand that will make all your problems go away, what I can offer you are 30 strategies for staying sane.

"Worth Quoting"

"Remember snow days? As a child, when it snowed, I would get up in the morning and immediately turn on the radio to see if school was going to be closed — and how I rejoiced when it was! A free day, completely unplanned, in which I could do anything I wanted ... As adults, we need to create our own snow days, or at least snow time — a time for unplanned, unexpected events."

• Stephan Rechtschaffen,
Timeshifting

Here goes:

1. **Find a job you love and a boss you like.** If you work full-time, you put in approximately 2,000 hours at work each year. Do you want to spend that much of your life doing something you hate for someone you can't stand?

2. **Don't worship work.** As much as you may enjoy your job, it can't give you a hug when you're having a bad day and it won't visit you when you're old and grey. No matter how successful you are and how much your career means to you, you need to find ways to have a balanced life.

3. **Don't let your job make you sick.** No pay cheque is more valuable than good health. If you're suffering from headaches and other stress-induced ailments, it's time to make some changes to your working situation or to switch jobs entirely.

4. **Create a cushion for yourself.** Block off more time for each appointment or task than they should reasonably require. That way, you should always be ahead of schedule rather than scrambling to keep up.

5. **Learn which deadlines matter and which ones don't.** If you're too busy to meet every deadline on your To Do List, find out which ones are important and then give yourself permission to let the rest go.

6. **Know when it's best to play by the rules and when you can cut yourself a bit of slack.** Tap into the office grapevine and find out which company policies are seldom complied with — and which ones are carved in stone.

7. **Don't be afraid to ask for what you want.** Don't wait for your boss to read your mind and recommend you for a promotion; schedule a meeting so that you can present her with a list of ten compelling reasons why she should do just that.

8. **Be your own publicist.** You have to be prepared to blow your own horn if you want to do well at work. It's not enough to do a bang-up job. You have to make a point of letting others know about your achievements.

9. **Invest in your career.** Sign up for workshops and regularly read up on new developments in your field. The more marketable you are, the more control you are able to exercise over your career and your life.

10. **Leave work at work.** Unless they're paying you the big bucks to be on call 24 hours a day, don't waste your personal time sweating about problems you're facing at work. Instead, use that time to work on your relationships with the people you care about.

11. **Figure out if you'd be better off — or worse off — working for yourself.** If you're sick of working nine-to-five for a boss who won't cut you any slack when it comes to family issues, then you might want to consider parachuting out of your current situation. If, on the other hand, you've got workaholic tendencies, perhaps being your own boss isn't the best bet after all. (There's no one to tell you it's time to go home!)

12. **Declutter your life.** Get rid of as much clutter as possible. You won't just reduce the amount of work you need to do to keep your home or office in order, you'll also eliminate the stress that comes from having too much stuff around you.

13. **Don't let other people waste your time.** Watch the way you use your time just as carefully as you watch the way you spend your money.

14. **Learn to distinguish between emergencies and situations that are merely masquerading as emergencies.** Otherwise, you'll be in panic mode 90 percent of the time — and for no good reason. (Hint: there's no such thing as emergency housecleaning!)

15. **Don't play Martha unless you want to.** If you have the time or inclination to follow in Martha Stewart's footsteps, then go for it. If you don't, don't sweat it. Remember, she who has the fewest handmade centrepieces doesn't necessarily finish last.

16. **Master the art of cutting corners.** Who says you have to dust every room in your house at least once a week? If certain rooms don't get used very often, let the dust build up until

you're actually going to use them. There's enough to be done around the house without creating make work projects for yourself.

17. **Find ways to take the drudgery out of tasks that you hate.** Listen to music while you pick up around the house. Do your taxes while you watch an episode of *Frasier*. Talk on the phone with a friend while you scrub the pots and pans.

18. **Say "no" as often as you can.** Rather than saying "yes" each time someone asks you do something, say "no" first. If you think about it and decide that you really would like to be involved after all, you can always call the person back and volunteer your services on your own terms.

19. **Don't waste time volunteering for projects you don't care about.** Only agree to support causes that you truly believe in. Otherwise, you'll resent others for being a drain on your time.

20. **Downsize your To Do List.** Don't commit to doing more than what you know you can reasonably accomplish. Otherwise, you're simply setting yourself up for failure.

21. **Don't allow your kids to pack their schedules with every extra-curricular activity going.** They might have the stamina for it, but you won't.

22. **Double up as much as possible.** Make two batches of spaghetti sauce at the same time — and fold a load of laundry while you're waiting for the noodles to cook. Don't take this to extremes, however: multitasking during a romantic moment won't score you any points with your partner.

23. **Give yourself permission to drop some balls.** Pick up the ones that matter. Leave the rest on the floor.

24. **Take care of yourself.** Eat properly, exercise regularly, get the sleep you need and find healthy ways to cope with stress. Don't sacrifice your health for the sake of your job or your family. (Remember, martyrs don't have the greatest long-term survival stats.)

25. **Take time to dream.** It's easy to get caught up in the details of everyday living. Every once in a while, take yourself out to lunch or dinner and spend the entire meal thinking about what you want out of life and how close you are to getting it. If you're still miles away from achieving your goals, perhaps it's time to map out a new path.

26. **Do something crazy at least once a month — once a week if you can manage it.** Leave a goofy phone message in your best friend's voice mail. Chase your two year old around the house. Play frisbee with your partner.

27. **Take mini-vacations.** Take a day off work every now and again to do something you wouldn't normally have time to do — like visiting an art gallery, taking in a concert or having lunch with an equally busy friend. Or stay home alone and spend the entire day lying on the couch reading.

28. **Spend as much time as possible with the people you love.** Pare down your commitments so that you have time for what matters most in your life.

29. **Define success on your own terms.** When it comes to personal and professional satisfaction, there's no such thing as one-size-fits-all.

30. **Above all, keep your sense of humour.** It's the ultimate weapon in your battle against the insanity around you!

Appendix A

Directory of Organizations

Organizations for Women in Business

Canadian Association of Women Executives and Entrepreneurs
2175 Sheppard Avenue East, Suite 310
North York, Ontario
M2J 1W8
Tel: 416-756-0000
Fax: 416-491-1670
Web site: *www.cawee.net*
E-mail: *cawee@taylorenterprises.com*

Canadian Federation of Business and Professional Women's Clubs
56 Sparks Street, Suite 308
Ottawa, Ontario
K1P 5A9
Tel: 613-234-7619
Web site: *www.bpwcanada.com*
E-mail: *bpwcanada@ibm.net*

Canadian Women's Foundation
133 Richmond Street West, Suite 504
Toronto, Ontario
M5H 2L3
Tel: 416-365-1444
Fax: 416-365-1745
E-mail: *info@cdnwomen.org*

Centre for Women in Business
Mount Saint Vincent University
Halifax, Nova Scotia
B3M 2J6
Tel: 902-457-6449
Web site: *www.msvu.ca/cwb*
E-mail: *cwb@msvu.ca*

National Action Committee on the Status of Women
234 Eglinton Avenue West, Suite 203
Toronto, Ontario
M4P 1K5
Tel: 416-932-1718
Fax: 416-932-0646
E-mail: *nac@web.net*

Status of Women Canada
350 Albert Street, 5th Floor
Ottawa, Ontario
K1A 1C3
Tel: 613-995-7835
Fax: 613-957-3359
Web site: *http://www.swc-cfc.gc.ca*

Women Business Owners of Canada Inc.
1243 Islington Avenue,
Suite 911
Toronto, Ontario
M8X 1Y9
Toll Free: 1-888-822-WBOC (9262)
Tel: 416-236-2000
Fax: 416-236-1099
Web site: *www.wboc.ca*

Women Entrepreneurs of Canada
3 Church Street, Suite 604,
Toronto, Ontario
M5E lM2
Tel: 416-361-7036
Web site: *www.wec.ca*
E-mail: *wec@wec.ca*

Women-Focused Entrepreneurial Training
Federal Business Development Bank
BDC Building
5 Place Ville Marie, Suite 12525
Montreal, Quebec
H3B 2G2
Tel: 514-283-5904
Web site: *www.bdc.ca*

Women and Rural Economic Development
379 Huron Street
Stratford, Ontario
N5A 5T6
Toll Free: 1-800-790-9949 (within Ont.)
Tel: 519-273-5017
Fax: 519-273-4826
Web site: *www.wred.org*
E-mail: *wred@sentex.net*

Women's World Finance/Atlantic Canada
Canadian Affiliate of Women's World Banking
P.O. Box 1142
58 Dorchester Street
Sydney, Nova Scotia
B1P 5Z1
Tel: 902-562-8845
E-mail: *wwfcba@yahoo.ca*

General Business Organizations

Alliance of Manufacturers and Exporters Canada
1 Nicholas Street, Suite 1500
Ottawa, Ontario
K1N 7B7
Tel: 613-238-8888

Business Development Bank of Canada
150 King Street, Suite 100
P.O. Box 23
Toronto, Ontario
M5H 1J9
Tel: 416-973-0341
Web site: *www.bdc.ca*

Canadian Association for Home-Based Business
1200 East Prince of Wales Drive,
Ottawa, Ontario
K2C 1M9
Tel: 613-724-7964
Fax: 613-232-4559

Canadian Association of Family Enterprise
1163 Sylvestor Street
P.O. Box 136
Lefroy, Ontario
L0L 1W0
Tel: 705-456-4900

The Canadian Chamber of Commerce
BCE Place
181 Bay Street
P.O. Box 818
Toronto, Ontario
M5J 2T3
Tel: 416-868-6415

Canadian Council of Better Business Bureaus
7330 Fisher Street South-East,
Suite 368
Calgary, Alberta
T2H 2H8
Tel: 403-531-8686
Fax: 403-531-8697

Canadian Direct Marketing Association
1 Concord Gate, Suite 607
Don Mills, Ontario
M3C 3N6
Tel: 416-391-2362
Web site: *www.cdma.org*

Canadian Federation of Independent Business
4141 Yonge Street, Suite 401
Willowdale, Ontario
M2P 2A6
Tel: 416-222-8022
Web site: *www.cfib.ca*
E-mail: *cfib@cfib.ca*

Canadian Franchise Association
5045 Orbitor Drive
Building 12, Suite 201
Mississauga, Ontario
L4W 4Y4
Toll Free: 1-800-665-4232
Tel: 905-625-2896
Fax: 905-625-9076
Web site: *http://www.cfa.ca/*

Canadian Importers Association
210 Dundas Street West, Suite 700
Toronto, Ontario
M5G 2E8
Tel: 416-595-5333

Canadian Organization of Small Business
10010-107A Avenue, Suite 102
Edmonton, Alberta
T5H 4H8
Tel. 403-423-2672

Canadian Professional Sales Association
145 Wellington West, Suite 610
Toronto, Ontario
M5J 1H8
Tel: 416-408-2685
Web site: *http://www.cpsa.com*

Canadian Standards Association
178 Rexdale Blvd.
Rexdale, Ontario
M9W 1R3
Tel: 416-747-4000

Retail Council of Canada
121 Bloor Street East
Suite 1210
Toronto, Ontario
M4W 3M5
Tel: 416-922-6678

Provincial Women's Directorates

British Columbia Ministry of
Women's Equality
P.O. Box 9899
Stn. Prov. Govt.
Victoria, British Columbia
V8W 9T9
Tel: 250-387-1223
Web site: *www.weq.gov.bc.ca*
E-mail: *minister@weq.gov.bc.ca*

Human Rights and Citizenship
Branch
Alberta Community Development
Standard Life Centre, Room 800
10405 Jasper Avenue
Edmonton, Alberta
T5J 4R7
Tel: 403-427-3116
Fax: 403-422-3563
Web site:
www.gov.ab.ca/~mcd/mcd.htm

Manitoba Women's Advisory
Council
107-175 Carlton Street
Winnipeg, Manitoba
R3C 3H9
Tel: 204-945-5969

Manitoba Women's Directorate
100-175 Carlton Street
Winnipeg, Manitoba
R3C 3H9
Tel: 204-945-3476
Web site: *http://www.gov.mb.ca/wd/*
E-mail: *RMitchell@chc.gov.mb.ca*

New Brunswick Women's
Directorate
Centennial Building
Room 413, King Street
Fredericton, New Brunswick
E3B 5H1
Tel: 506-453-2143

Newfoundland Women's Policy
Office
Executive Council
4th Floor, Confederation Building
West Block
St. John's, Newfoundland
A1B 4J6
Tel: 709-729-5098
Web site:
www.gov.nf.ca/exec/wpo/wpo.htm
E-mail: *dmeade@nwp.nf.ca*

Nova Scotia Department of
Human Resources
Women's Directorate
P.O. Box 943
Halifax, Nova Scotia
B3J 2V9
Tel: 902-424-5820

Ontario Women's Directorate
900 Bay Street, 6th Floor
Mowat Block
Toronto, Ontario
M7A 1L2
Tel: 416-314-0300
Web site: *http://www.gov.on.ca/owd*

Prince Edward Island Women's Secretariat
P.O. Box 2000
Charlottetown, Prince Edward Island
C1A 7N8
Tel: 902-368-5570

Saskatchewan Women's Secretariat
7th Floor
1855 Victoria Avenue
Regina, Saskatchewan
S4P 3V5
Tel: 306-787-1548
Web site: *www.womensec.gov.sk.ca*

Secretariat à la Condition Feminine
1050 des Parlementaires
3rd Floor
Quebec City, Quebec
G1R 5Y9
Tel: 418-643-9052
E-mail: *cond.fem@mes.gov.qc.ca*

Women's Advisory
Department of the Executive
Government of Northwest Territories
P.O. Box 1320
Yellowknife, Northwest Territories
X1A 2L9
Tel: 867-920-3106

Yukon Women's Directorate
P.O. Box 2703
Whitehorse, Yukon
Y1A 2C6
Tel: 867-667-3030
Web site: *www.yukonweb.com/government/womensdir/*
E-mail: *elda.ward@gov.yk.ca*

Work and Family

Conference Board of Canada
255 Smyth Road
Ottawa, Ontario
K1H 8M7
Tel: 613-526-3280
Fax: 613-526-4857

Work/Family Solutions
P.O. Box 93091, Brampton S.P.O.,
499 Main Street South
Brampton, Ontario
L6Y 4V8
Toll Free: 1-800-284-5742
Tel: 905-454-8504
Fax: 905-454-8582
E-mail: *work.familysolutions@sympatico.ca*

Work, Family and Life Consulting Services
122-20820-87th Avenue
Langley, British Columbia
V1M 3W5
Tel: 604-882-2555
Web site: *http://wso.net/wfl/*
E-mail: *wfl_con@compuserve.com*

Work-Life Harmony Enterprises
207 Shaughnessy Blvd., Suite 601
North York, Ontario
M2J 1J9
Tel: 416-497-8942
Fax: 416-492-8799
E-mail: *nspinks@netcom.ca*

Child Care

The Canadian Child Day Care Federation
Suite 401-120 Holland Avenue
Ottawa, Ontario
K1Y 0X6
Tel: 613-729-5289

Canadian Council of Social Development (CCSD)
441 MacLaren
4th Floor
Ottawa, Ontario
K2P 2H3
Tel: 613-236-8977

The Canadian Day Care Advocacy Association
323 Chapel Street,
Ottawa, Ontario
K1N 7Z2
Tel: 613-594-3196

Child Care Advocacy Association of Canada
323 Chapel Street
Ottawa, Ontario
K1N 7Z2
Tel: 613-594-3196
Fax: 613-594-9375

Child Care Resource and Research Unit (CRRU)
Center for Urban and Community Studies
University of Toronto
455 Spadina Avenue
Suite 305
Toronto, Ontario
M5S 2G8
Tel: 416-978-6895

Family Service Canada
220 Laurier Avenue West
Suite 600
Ottawa, Ontario
K1P 5Z9
Tel: 613-722-8610

Unit for Child Care Research
School of Child and Youth Care
University of Victoria
Victoria, British Columbia
V8W 2Y2
Tel: 250-721-7979

Vanier Institute of the Family
94 Centrepointe Drive
Nepean, Ontario
K2G 6B1
Tel: 613-228-8500

World Organization for Early Childhood Education — Canada (OMEP)
Faculty of Education
Laval University
Quebec City, Quebec
G1K 7P4
Tel: 418-656-7891

Surfing with a Briefcase: The Best Web Sites for Working Women

Eager to tap into all the terrific resources that are available online, but don't have hours to spend surfing? Here's the answer to your cyber-prayers: a directory of the very best web sites for working women. These sites are packed with information and resources on the following topics: career; elder care; health; housework, laundry and more; work/family programs; and working moms.

Career Web Sites	
Career City *www.careercity.com*	The site features articles on issues of interest to working women: what it's like to be part of a dual-income couple, the truth about the glass ceiling and more.
***Chatelaine's* Ask an Expert — Job Expert** *www.chatelaine.com/experts/job*	An archive of past and current columns from *Chatelaine's* career expert Karen Wright. There are articles on job sharing, coping with a difficult boss, changing careers and many other work-related topics.
Electra *http://www.electra.com/*	The site features articles on career, health and relationships. The career area contains some good material on avoiding work-at-home scams, deciding whether you've got the personality to work from home and more.

iVillage *www.ivillage.com/career/*	One of the best online resources for working women, this site features advice from many well-known career experts, message boards, a chat area and tons of helpful articles. There's also a Work From Home area on the site.
Sanity Savers *www.sanitysavers.com*	As the name implies, this is the official web site for this book! You'll find an archive of articles on the joys and challenges of being a working woman, links to other great web sites and a whole lot more.
WomenConnect.com *www.womenconnect.com*	This site contains articles from *Working Woman* and *Working Mother* magazines, chat areas, message boards and more.
Women's Wire Work Channel *www.womenswire.com/work/*	The site is packed with useful information on virtually every aspect of being a working woman. You'll find a job interview tool kit, message boards, a chat area and articles galore.

Elder Care Web Site

Caregiver Network Inc. *www.caregiver.on.ca*	This web site is packed with useful information on virtually every aspect of elder care imaginable. There's a detailed resource guide, leads on products and services of interest to caregivers and much more.
The Caregiver's Handbook *http://www.acsu.buffalo.edu/~drstall/hndbk0.html*	An online guide to caring for an aging relative. While some of the content will only be of interest to Americans, much of it is applicable to Canadians as well.

Health	
Better Health *www.betterhealth.com*	Part of the ivillage community of web sites, Better Health offers messages boards, chat areas, articles on a variety of health-related topics and a whole lot more. My favourite feature of the site is the Digital Conscience tool which allows you to sign up for weekly e-mails motivating you to reach your health-related goals.
Healthy Way™ *www.sympatico.ca/healthyway/*	You'll find information on job stress, nutrition, exercise, children's health, aging and much more at this Canadian web site. There's an excellent article called "Trusting Health Information Online" that should be required reading for every surfer! The LifeView® Health Risk Assessment is also definitely worth a look: I was surprised to see what good news I got, given my insane lifestyle!
Women.com Health and Fitness *http://women.com/index/health.html*	A useful site that's packed with information on a variety of issues related to women's health. Take the Stress Quiz and find out how well you're really coping.

Housework, Laundry and More	
Betty Crocker *www.bettycrocker.com/onhand/frame-bot.html*	Fridge looking pretty bare? No time to grocery shop? Don't panic. You can use this handy little tool to figure out what you can make with the stuff you do have around the house.
Canadian Living's Food and Nutrition archive *www.canadianliving.com/features/fnarchives.htm*	Need some quick and easy meal ideas? You'll find plenty of inspiration here.

Mr Clean — Professional Cleaning Tips *www.mrclean.com/hints/tips.html*	Timesaving cleaning tips from Don Aslett, author of *Is There Life After Housework?*
Speed Cleaning Rules *www.thecleanteam.com/Rules.html*	Practical tips from the book *Speed Cleaning* that will cut down on the amount of time you spend cleaning your house.
The Tide Clothesline® Tips & Time Savers *www.tide.com/tipsTimeSavers/*	The site is packed with useful tips on winning the laundry war. There's even laundry trivia to amuse yourself with as you're folding all those loads of clean clothes.

Working Moms

Baby Centre *www.babycenter.com*	Bulletin boards, online chats and extremely detailed information on a variety of pregnancy and parenting-related topics for parents with children age three and under. Packed with useful information on working during pregnancy, choosing child care, the joys and challenges of being a working mother and more.
Beatrice's Web Guide — "Chats for Moms" *www.bguide.com/webguide/parenting/plus/d0505Chat.html*	Links to some of the best places to connect with other moms online.
Canadian Parents Online *www.canadianparents.com*	A popular web site for Canadian families. Packed with articles, links, resources, bulletin boards and more.
Crayola Family Play *www.familyplay.com*	Need an activity to keep your kids entertained while you're making dinner? You'll find a smorgasbord of quick and easy activities for children ages three to 12 as well as articles on a variety of different parenting-related topics.

Parenting Q & A *www.parenting-qa.com*	Contains information on a variety of parenting-related topics. The section on work/family is particularly good.
ParentSoup *www.parentsoup.com*	Bulletin boards, online chats, parenting articles, an impressive roster of big name experts and more.
ParentsPlace *www.parentsplace.com*	Bulletin boards, online chats, parenting articles and more. Contains a detailed child care area which, while aimed at American parents, will also be useful to Canadian parents.
Stork Site *www.storksite.com*	One of the original pregnancy-related web sites, Stork Site is one of the best places online to find answers to your pregnancy-related questions and/or chat with other pregnant moms.
The Unofficial Guide to Childcare *www.childcare-guide.com*	The web site for my book *The Unofficial Guide to Childcare*. Contains book excerpts, parenting articles, tips sheets and more.
The Unofficial Guide to Having a Baby *www.having-a-baby.com*	The web site for my book *The Unofficial Guide to Having A Baby*. Contains book excerpts, parenting articles, tip sheets and more.
Working Moms Refuge *www.moms-refuge.com*	Contains articles about the joys and challenges of being a working mother. Also home to the famous "Whack Martha" game!

Appendix C

Bibliography

Books

Alexander, Roy. *Commonsense Time Management.* New York: Amacom, 1992.

Alvi, Shahid. *Eldercare And The Workplace.* Ottawa: The Conference Board of Canada, 1995.

Aslett, Don. *Is There Life After Housework?* Cincinnati: Writer's Digest Books, 1985.

Bravo, Ellen. *The Job/Family Challenge.* New York: John Wiley and Sons, Inc. 1995.

Bredin, Alice. *The Home Office Solution.* New York: John Wiley and Sons, Inc., 1998.

Brook, Paula. *Work Less Live More.* Toronto: Doubleday Canada Limited, 1997.

Canadian Women Entrepreneurs In Growth Sectors: A Survey. Montreal: Business Development Bank Of Canada, 1997.

Caring Canadians, Involved Canadians: Highlights From The 1997 National Survey Of Giving, Volunteering and Participating. Ottawa: Statistics Canada, 1998.

Culp, Stephanie. *You Can Find More Time For Yourself Every Day.* Cincinnati: Betterway Books, 1994.

Davidson, Jeff. *The Complete Idiot's Guide To Managing Your Time.* New York: Alpha Books, 1995.

Davidson, Jeff. *The Complete Idiot's Guide To Reaching Your Goals.* New York: Alpha Books, 1998.

Dlugozima, Hope. *Six Months Off.* New York: Henry Holt and Co., 1996.

Douglas, Susan. *Where the Girls Are: Growing Up Female with the Mass Media.* New York: Times Books, 1994.

Easto, Larry. *How To Succeed In Your Home Business.* Willowdale: Home Business Press, 1993.

Financing a Small Business: A Guide For Women Entrepreneurs. Montreal: Business Development Bank of Canada, 1995.

Gilberd, Pamela. *The Eleven Commandments Of Wildly Successful Women.* New York: Macmillan Spectrum, 1996.

Ginsberg, Laurence and Bruce McDougall. *The Complete Idiot's Guide To Being An Entrepreneur in Canada.* Scarborough: Prentice Hall Canada Inc., 1996.

Goldman, Katherine Wyse. *Working Mothers 101.* New York: Harper Collins, 1998.

Lague, Louise. *The Working Mom's Book Of Hints, Tips, and Everyday Wisdom.* Princeton: Peterson's, 1995.

Lichtenberg, Ronna. *Work Would Be Great If It Weren't For The People: Ronna And Her Evil Twin's Guide To Making Office Politics Work For You.* New York: Hyperion, 1998.

Lockwood, Georgene. *The Complete Idiot's Guide To Organizing Your Life.* New York: Alpha Books, 1998.

McKenna, Elizabeth Perle. *When Work Doesn't Work Anymore.* New York: Dell Publishing, 1997.

Myths & Realities — The Economic Power Of Women-Led Firms In Canada. Scarborough: Bank of Montreal's Institute For Small Business, 1995.

Omichinski, Linda. *You Count, Calories Don't.* Winnipeg: Hugs International, 1999. Order by calling 1-800-565-4847.

Omichinski, Linda and Heather Wiebe Hildebrand. *Tailoring Your Tastes.* Winnipeg: Tamos Books, 1995. Order by calling 1-800-565-4847.

O'Shea-Roche, Annette, and Sieglinde Malmberg. *Partners At Home And At Work.* North Vancouver: Self-Counsel Press, 1994.

Parlapiano, Ellen H. and Patricia Cobe. *Mompreneurs A Mother's Practical Step-by Step Guide to Work-at-Home Success.* New York: The Berkley Publishing Group, 1996.

Passoff, Michelle. *Lighten Up! Free Yourself From Clutter.* New York: Harper Collins, 1998.

Peel, Kathy. *The Family Manager's Guide For Working Moms.* New York: Ballantine Books, 1997.

Podleski, Janet and Greta. *Looneyspoons: Low-Fat Food Made Fun!* Ottawa: Granet Publishing Inc., 1996.

Pollar, Odette. *365 Ways To Simplify Your Work Life.* Dearborn Financial Publishing, Inc., 1996.

Price, Susan Crites and Tom Price. *The Working Parents Help Book.* Princeton: Peterson's Career Focus Books, 1996.

Priesnitz, Wendy. *Bringing It Home. A Home Business Start-Up Guide For You And Your Family.* St. George: The Alternate Press, 1995.

Rechtschaffen, Stephan M.D. *Timeshifting — Creating More Time To Enjoy Your Life.* New York: Doubleday, 1996.

Robinson, Bryan Ph.D. *Overdoing It How To Slow Down And Take Care Of Yourself.* Deerfield Beach: Health Communications, Inc., 1992.

Roblin, Lynn R.D. and Bev Callaghan RD. *Suppertime Survival.* Toronto: Macmillan Canada: 1996.

Sachs, Judith. *Break The Stress Cycle! 10 Steps To Reducing Stress For Women.* Holbrook: Adams Media Corporation, 1998.

Sisson, Brenda and Heather McDowall Black. *Choosing with Care.* Toronto: Addison-Wesley, 1992.

Sprinkle, Patricia H. *Women Who Do Too Much.* New York: Harper Paperbacks, 1996.

Thomas Yaccato, Joanne. *Balancing Act: A Canadian Woman's Financial Success Guide.* Scarborough: Prentice Hall Canada Inc., 1996.

Wallerstein, Judith S. and Sandra Blakeslee. *The Good Marriage: How and Why Love Lasts.* New York: Houghton Mifflin Company, 1995.

Wilen, Joan and Lydia Wilen. *Shoes In The Freezer, Beer In The Flower Bed.* New York: Fireside, 1997.

Winston, Stephanie. *Stephanie Winston's Best Organizing Tips.* New York: Fireside, 1995.

Magazine, Newspaper and Online Articles and Reports

"Adding Balance To Work And Family Life Is Only A Phone Call Away." *Business Wire* 16 September 1997.

Alston, Alyce C. "Office Hours: In Praise Of Office Gossip." *Fortune* 19 August 1985: 253.

Ander, Roseanna. "Ensuring Parents Can Care For Their Sick Children." Harvard Center For Children's Health *<http://www.hsph.harvard.edu/children/newsltr/96_97/win97_3.htm>*

Armour, Stephanie. "Elder Care Challenges Employers—Special Concerns Need Addressing." *USA Today,* 19 August 1998: 06B.

"As More Women Relocate, HR Helps Husbands." *HR Wire* <*http://www.HRWire.com*>

Bagnall, Janet. "Sisterly Solidarity Falls Apart At Work, Poll Suggests." *The Toronto Star* 16 September 1996: E1.

Barham, Lisa J., Benjamin H. Gottlieb, E. Kevin Kelloway. "Variables Affecting Managers' Willingness To Grant Alternative Work Arrangements." *The Journal of Social Pyschology* 138 June 1, 1998: 291(12).

Berry, Judy O. and Julie Meyer Rao. "Balancing Employment and Fatherhood." *Journal of Family Issues* 18.4 July 1997: 386-402.

Billings, Laura. "7 Work Problems — Solved." *Redbook* 1 March 1998: 53(2).

Boase, Sharon. "Shouldering Shift Work." *Hamilton Spectator* 29 September 1998.

Bourette, Susan. "Women Gain Most of Canada's New Jobs." *The Globe and Mail* 9 January 1999: A1 & A2.

Brethour, Patrick. "Absenteeism Gender Gap Widens; Family Demands Hit Women Harder." *The Globe and Mail* 4 September 1996: B5.

Bruzzese, Anita. "Mentoring Helpful For Personal, Professional Growth." Gannett News Service, 12 March 1998.

"Can I Talk To You About A Raise?" womenCONNECT.com 1 February 1999 <*http://www.womenconnect.com*>

"Can This Marriage Be Saved? He's Jealous Of My Success." *Newsday* 19 December 1995: B19.

"Careers: The Maternal Wall A New Study Shows That Even The Most Elite Working Moms Face Discrimination." <*http://www.elibrary.com/get doc.cgi*>

Casamassima, Christy. "Battle Of The Bucks." *Psychology Today* 28 13 March 1995: 42(6).

"Catalyst Study Finds Dual-Career Couples Want Freedom And Control." *Catalyst* <*http://www.catalystwomen.org*>

Chisholm, Patricia and Sharon Doyle Driedger. "Coping With Stress." *Maclean's* 109 8 January 1996: 32(5).

Connor, Lee A. Lusardi. "Can You Afford To Stop Working?" *Redbook* 1 November 1996: 50(3).

Couch, Mark P. "Work-Family Issue Changing From Child Care To Elder Care." Gannett News Service 13 March 1996.

Coutu, Diane. "The Wages of Stress." *Harvard Business Review* 76. 6 (1998): 21+.

Cummins, H.J. "Looking After Mom And Dad." *Minneapolis Star Tribune* 15 June 1998: 01E.

Cummins, H.J. "Proposals Aim To Boost Family Time For Workers — Clinton Plans Rival GOP's." *Star Tribune* 25 June 1996: 01A.

Cummins, H.J. "The Middle Ages — For Millions Of Americans Caring For Elderly Parents, It's A Period Of Added Responsibility And Emotional Stress." *Newsday* 15 August 1998: B01.

Curley, Suzanne. "Rush ... Work ... Worry ... Hurry ... It's No Wonder That Millions of Us Are Sleepless in America." *Newsday* 1 July, 1995: B01.

Curtius, Mary. "Careers/Playing Politics; New Alliances; Finding the Right Mentors — Inside And Outside Your Workplace — Can Be A Key To Success." Home Edition, *Los Angeles Times* 10 August 1998: D2-8

Davenport, Thomas H. and Keri Pearlson. "Two Cheers For The Virtual Office." *Sloan Management Review* 39 22 June 1998: 51(15).

De Tureen, Veronique. "The Family Dinner/Mealtime Nourishes With More Than Its Plateful Of Food. When Served With Conversation And Camaraderie, It Feeds The Soul And Develops The Character Of Those Around The Table." *Star Tribune* 24 January 1996: 01T.

"Depression Prevails Among Caregivers." *HR Wire* 6 April 1998 *<http://www.HRWire.com>*

Deutschman, Alan and Mark D. Fefer. "Managing/Cover Stories: Pioneers Of The New Balance. More Managers Are Striking Deals For Flexible Work Schedules. They Have More Time For Their Kids and — Surprise — Their Careers Are Prospering." *Fortune* 20 May 1991: 60.

Doherty, Gillian, Martha Friendly and Mab Oloman. "Women's Support, Women's Work: Child Care In An Era Of Deficit Reduction, Devolution Downsizing and Deregulation." Status of Women Canada March, 1998. *<http://www.swc-cfc.gc.ca/publish/research/ccare-e.html>*

Dominitz, Nathan. "Making Flextime Work For You And Your Boss." Gannett News Service 28 July 1995.

"Don't Short-Circuit Your Own Career." Contemporary Women's Issues Database. 21 July 1995.

Dorr, Dave. "It's Time For Happy People To Come Out Of The Closet." *St. Louis Post-Dispatch* 12 January 1999: D1.

Drago, Robert. "Share The Load At Home, Dad — Reduce Job Hours." *Wisconsin State Journal* 21 June 1998: 2B.

Dranov, Paula. "Keep Your Job — Even If Nobody Else Does." *Cosmopolitan* 221 1 October 1996: 214(4).

Dunnett, Paul. "Boost Benefits Value To Lure Top Talent." *The Globe and Mail* 27 January 1999: B10.

Eberlein, Tamara. "Get The Best Maternity Leave For You (And Your Baby)." *Redbook* 190 1 December 1997: 108(7).

Eichler, M. "Marriage and Divorce." *The 1998 Canadian Encyclopedia.* Toronto: McClelland and Stewart, 1998.

"Elder Care Is A Looming Reality For Boomer Women." Contemporary Women's Issues Database 10 1 November 1997: 1+.

"Eldercare Looms Large." Contemporary Women's Issues Database 11 1 November 1998: 10.

Erdich, Louise. "A Woman's Work: Too Many Demands, And Not Enough Selves." *Harper's* 286 May 1993: 35+.

"Failure To Communicate Costs Seven Weeks A Year." *HR Wire* *<http://www.HRWire.com>*

Falter-Baras, Suzanne. "Balancing Agendas — Work, Family And The Law." Contemporary Women's Issues Database 1 June 1997.

"Family Ties Big Reason Employees Reject Transfer." *HR Wire* *<http://www.HRWire.com>*

Fast, Janet and Moreno Da Pont. "Changes In Women's Work Continuity." *Canadian Social Trends* Autumn 1997: 2-7.

Fisher, Anne B. "Work: Welcome To The Age Of Overwork." *Fortune* 30 November 1992: 64.

Fisher, Paul. "Connected: The Great Kitchen Con: Trick Cooking Gadget For This, Gizmos For That But Have Labour-Saving Devices Actually Made Life Easier? Paul Fisher Thinks Not." *The Daily Telegraph* 26 March 1998.

Friedman, Stewart D., Perry Christensen and Jessica DeGroot. "Work and Life: The End Of The Zero-Sum Game." *Harvard Business Review* 76.6 (1998): 119-129.

Gadd, Jane. "Who's Got The Jobs From Hell? Statscan Reveals All." *The Globe and Mail* 13 January, 1999: A1 & A7.

Gale, Elaine. "Time To Read: 'We Hoot And We Holler'" *Minneapolis Star Tribune* 24 July 1995: 01E.

"Gen-X Women What Challenges, Advancement, Hard Work." *HR Wire* <*http://www.HRWire.com*>

Gibb-Clark, Margot. "A Model For Maintaining The Work-Life Balance." *The Globe and Mail* 5 January 1999: B6.

Gibb-Clark, Margot. "A Strategy That Puts The Stress On Stress." *The Globe and Mail* 26 October 1998: B15.

Gibb-Clark, Margot. "Corporate Concierges Deliver." *The Globe and Mail* 25 September 1998: B23.

Gibb-Clark, Margot. "Female Civil Servants Seen Facing Hurdle." *The Globe and Mail* 25 January, 1999: B15.

Gibb-Clark, Margot. "Fewer People Work 'Normal' Week." *The Globe and Mail* 19 September, 1996: B11.

Gibb-Clark, Margot. "The Male Way Still Rules On Corporate Boards." *The Globe and Mail* 28 January, 1999: B11.

Gibb-Clark, Margot. "The 'Wallace Factor' Seen To Be Swaying The Courts." *The Globe and Mail* 4 February 1999: B10.

Gibb-Clark, Margot. "Worker Morale Higher in Canada Than US: Survey." *The Globe and Mail* 10 February 1999: B11.

Gibson, Valerie. "I'm Blaming It On Martha Stewart." *The Toronto Sun* 3 December 1998 <*http://www.canoe.ca/CNEWSLifeColumns*>

Goodman, Ellen. "Demands of Home,Work Create a New 'Time Bind'." *Star Tribune* 9 June 1997: 11A.

Goodman, Ellen. "Women Still Looking For The Payoff." *Rocky Mountain News* 14 September 1997: 4B.

Graves, Ginny. "The 9 Habits Of Highly Successful Sleepers." *Good Housekeeping* 226 1 March 1998: 82(3).

Green, Sarah Jean. "Work? Aye, There's The Rub." *The Toronto Star* 10 January 1999: E1.

Griffin, Margot. "Caring For Your Parents." *The Toronto Star* 3 May 1998: E8.

Groves, Martha. "Careers/Playing Politics; The Rumor Mill; Gossip Can Be A Useful Thing. But If It Gets Out Of Hand, Watch Out!" Home Edition, *Los Angeles Times* 10 August 1998: D2-4.

Habib, Marlene. "Women Jeopardizing Their Health, Study Says." *The Globe and Mail* 9 February 1999: A2.

Hales, Dianne. "How To Keep The Fires Burning — Little Things You Can Do Every Day To Keep Your Relationship Strong And Passionate." *Newsday* 21 November 1995: B17.

Hammonds, Keith H. "Balancing Work And Family."
http://businessweek.com/1996/38/b34931.htm>

Hark, Lisa. "A Grocery List And Meal Plan Helps With Weight Loss." Heart
Information Network *<http://www.heartinfo.com>*

Harris, Lynn and Lois Joy Johnson. "Sleep: How Much Is Enough...And
Other Secrets Of A Good Night's Rest." *Ladies Home Journal* 114 1
June 1997: 88(4).

Hickey, Mary C. "The Exhausted Woman." *Ladies Home Journal* 111 1
March 1994: 86(4).

Holcomb, Betty. "Beat The Clock-Watchers." *womenCONNECT.com* 19
January 1999.

"Holiday Stresses Getting To You?" Working Moms' Internet Refuge
<http://www.momsrefuge.com/games/index.html>

Hollander, Sarah. "Closeup Women's Work Is A Work Of Art." *Newsday* 31
March 1993: 29.

"How Kids Feel About Working Moms." *Working Mother* September 1998: 20.

"Ideal Recipe: Three Ingredients At Most." *The Examiner* 23 September 1998: 1B.

"Important Studies In The Field." Work & Family Connection
<http://www.workfamily.com/studies.htm>

"Industry Canada: National Survey Of Giving, Volunteering and
Participating — 1997." M2 *PressWIRE* 24 August 1998.

Irvine, Martha. "Companies Offering Perks to Workers."
womenCONNECT.com 29 September 1998
<http://www.womenconnect.com>

Irvine, Martha. "Many Americans Just Aren't In The Mood, US Sex Survey
Finds." *The Globe and Mail* 10 February 1999: A2.

"Is Exercise Resistance Affecting Your Health?" *Health News,* University of
Toronto Faculty of Medicine 16.4 (1998) 1-3.

"Is The Mrs. A Tad Stressed? It's Likely Your Fault." *National Post* 2
December 1998.

Jackson, Maggie. "Businesswomen Finding Their Stride Successful
Examples Refusing to Act Like Men To Move Upward." *Rocky
Mountain News* 12 October 1997: 12G.

Jackson, Maggie. "Is Your Company Your Hometown." women
CONNECT.com 2 October 1998 *<http://www.womenconnect.com>*

Johnson, Tracy. "Quit Watching" *Report on Business Magazine* 15.8 (1999):
58-62.

Kesterton, Michael. "Thought Du Jour" *The Globe and Mail* 14 January 1999: A22.

Kidd Stewart, Janet. "Couples Find Costs, Benefits To Commuter Marriages." *The Dallas Morning News* 3 March 1998: 5C.

Knowlton, Leslie. "Burnout. Job Stress Seems To Be Growing — Especially For Mental Health Workers." *Newsday* 9 September 1995: B01.

Lawlor, Julia. "Coping With Elder Care-Issue Edging Out Day Care At Companies." *USA Today,* 19 July, 1994: 01.

Lawlor, Julia. "The Dropout Blues Some Who Leave Work Force To Stay At Home Meet New Risks, Emotional Struggles." *Rocky Mountain News* 26 October 1997: 2G.

Lee, Catherine M. and Linda Duxbury. "Employed Parents' Support From Partners, Employers, And Friends ..." *The Journal Of Social Psychology* 138 1 June 1998: 303(20).

Lee Svitak, Dean. "A Meal To Share." *Star Tribune* 5 June 1996: 01T.

Leive, Cynthia. "The Overtime Escape From Overload." *Newsday* 18 May, 1997: G12.

Leo, John. "Sexes: Why Men Don't Do Chores Ralph and Wanda Tidy Up The Crisis In Housework." *Time* 30 June 1986: 90.

Lewis, Diane E. "Study Of Female Executives Finds Alliances Do More Than Networks." *Star Tribune* 10 November 1997: 03D.

Lewis, Robert. "The Spirit Of The Volunteers." *Maclean's* 21 December 1998: 04.

Litchfield, Jane. "Husband, Meet Housework." *Chatelaine* 71 1 May 1998: 80(4).

MacDonald, Sue. "How To Reduce Stress." Gannett News Service 7 November, 1995.

Mackay, Harvey. "Hate Your Job? Try Finding Something About It You Like." *Minneapolis Star Tribune* 25 January 1996: 02D.

Mattox, William R. Jr. "Families On The Go Can Still Share Dinnertime." *St. Louis Post-Dispatch* 18 April 1997: 07B.

Matus, Jordan. "This Way Up. (How To Move Up The Corporate Ladder) *Men's Health* 13 01 November 1998: 114(2).

McGlone, Peggy. "Moms At Work: Finding A Balance." *The Star Ledger* 21 January 1998.

"Memo To TV Moms: Get Real!" *Working Mother* March 1998: 16.

"Men More Likely To Lie On Résumés, Study Says." *The Examiner* 7 December 1998: A7.

"Mentors Help Crack The Glass Ceiling." *HR Wire*
<http://www.HRWire.com>

Mitchell, Alanna. "Family-Friendly Job Plans Doing More For Men: Study."
The Globe and Mail 8 January 1997: A1 and A6.

"More Working Together Stats" Blue Point Books
<http://www.west.net/~bpbooks/qwsidx.html>

Morris, Virginia. "The Parent Trap: 5 Mistakes Not To Make In Caring For
Your Aging Parents." *Ladies Home Journal* 114 1 March 1997: 108(4).

Muoio, Anna. "How To Make Your Career Move." *Fast Company* 1 October
1997: 93.

Nachman, Barbara. "Are You Eating Or Exercising While Reading This?
Welcome To Multi-Tasking." Gannett News Service 29 September 1998:
ARC.

"NC State Sociologist: Give Dad His Due And Duties." North Carolina State
University News Service <http://www.ncsu.edu/news>

Nemeth, Mary. "Sandwich Generation — Middle Aged People Caring For
Both Children And Elderly Parents." *Maclean's* 107 10 January 1994:
34(2).

"Networks Empower Women, Yield Bottom-Line Results." *HR Wire*
<http://www/HRWire.com>

Neuborne, Ellen. "Debate Rages On Swapping Overtime For Comp Time."
USA Today 19 March 1997: 04B.

Olson, A. Andrew. "Long-term Networking: A Strategy For Career Success."
Management Review 83 1 April 1994: 33(3).

Pearce, Michael R. "From Carts To Clicks." *Ivey Business Quarterly* 63.1
Autumn 1998: 69-71.

"Personal File. Can This Marriage Be Saved? He Refuses To Help With The
Housework." *Newsday* 14 April 1998: B12.

Peterson, Karen. "In An Unsteady World, Girlfriends Endure." *USA Today* 5
December 1995.

Peterson, Karen S. "Some Sandwiched Between Generations." *USA Today* 17
July 1995.

Picard, André. "Health Care's Next Frontier." *The Globe and Mail.* 22 March
1999: A8-A9.

Rhodes, Ann. "How To Help Aging Parents." *Chatelaine* 67 1 September
1994: 105(4).

Robinson, John P., Melissa Milkie and Kevin Heubusch. "Dances With Dust Bunnies: Housecleaning In America." *American Demographics* 19 1 January 1997: 36(6).

Rogoznica, June. "Thirty Ways to Get More Time This Minute." womenCONNECT.com 31 August, 1998
< *http://www.womenconnect.com*>

Rosner, Bob. "Working Wounded — On The Road Again." womenCONNECT.com 6 January 1999
<*http://www.womenconnect.com*>

Saltzman, Amy. "Companies In A Family Way." *US News & World Report* 122 12 May 1997: 64.

Schellenberg, Grant. "The Changing Nature Of Part-Time Work." The Canadian Council on Social Development
<*http://www.ccsd.ca/xs_pt.htm*>

Schellhardt, Timothy D. "Tech Temps On Top." *The Globe and Mail* 14 January 1999: C7.

Schieszer, John. "When Job Stress Makes You Sick." *St. Louis Post-Dispatch* 23 April 1995: 21.

Scoffield, Heather. "Nortel Leaves Employees At Home." *The Globe and Mail* 27 May l998: B27.

Scott, Katherine and Clarence Lockhead. "Are Women Catching Up In The Earnings Race?" The Canadian Council on Social Development
<*http://www.ccsd.ca/gen_bg.htm*>

"Secretary Of State Fry Says 1996 Census Confirms Women's Hidden Contribution To The Economy." Status of Women Canada 17 March 1998 <*http://www.swc-cfc.gc.ca*>

Segell, Michael. "The Secrets Of Sleep." *Esquire* 122 1 October 1994: 123(7).

Sharp, David. "So Many Lists, So Little Time." *USA Weekend* 17 March 1996: 004.

"Shirking Office Parties Can Endanger Career, Says Office Etiquette Expert." *The Examiner* 6 February 1999: B7.

Silverstein, Stuart. "Work & Careers; What Those Long Work Hours May Mean About Your Home Life." Home Edition, *Los Angeles Times* 25 May 1997: D5.

"Slow Gains For Today's Working Women: New Report Finds While There." *Sacramento Observer* 22 January 1997: PG.

"Small Businesses Offer Home/Life Balance." *HR Wire*
<*http://www.HRWire.com*>

Smith, Marguerite T. "Work And Family: Fighting To Have It All — The Question Of The '90s: How Can You Have A Rewarding Career While Raising A Family?" *Money* 1 January 1990: 130.

Smolowe, Jill. "Living: When Jobs Clash With Two Salaries And Two Egos, Family Life Gets Harder All The Time." *Time* 3 September 1990: 82.

"Social Class Irrelevant To Men And Housework." Contemporary Women's Issues Database 1 1 July 1992: 9.

"Social Trends — Elder Care" *Canada and the World* Backgrounder 1 May, 1998.

Speer, Tibbett L. "The Unseen Costs Of Eldercare: Employers Can Help Employees Help Their Aging Parents, And Save Money In The Process." *American Demographics* 18 1 June 1996: 20(3).

Spillman, Susan. "What Women Can Learn From Men At Work." *Cosmopolitan* 221 01 October, 1996: 124(2).

Stains, Laurence Roy. "Can Your Sex Life Be Saved?" *Prevention* 50 1 February 1998: 92(8).

Stevens, Liz. "It's Difficult To Even Meet." Gannett News Service 24 July 1995.

Stoffman, Judy. "Alzheimer's Explosion Predicted." *The Toronto Star* 24 January 1999.

"Survey: Women Work, Take Care Of Families — And Like It — Study Challenges Idea Women Must Choose." *Star Tribune* 11 May 1995: 01D.

Tahmincioglu, Eve. "Job Cuts, Bigger Workload Is Stressing People Out." Gannett News Service 24 April 1995.

"Taking Care Of Yourself First." *HR Wire* <http://www.HRWire.com>

Talbot, Margaret. "Le Très Riches Heures de Martha Stewart: Money Time, And The Surrender Of American Taste." *The New Republic* 214 13 May 1996: 30(6).

Tergesen, Anne. "Personal Business: Telecommuting: Making Stay At Homes Feel Welcome." *Business Week* 3599 12 October 1998: 155.

"The Re-Division of Labor: How Working Parents Can Share Family Responsibilities." Work & Family <http://www.parenting-qa.com>

"Time Out To Survive." *The Globe and Mail* 27 July 1998: B11.

Tonnessen, Dianna. "Stress — 18 Ways To Tame Tension." *Newsday* 23 October 1995: B13.

"Two Careers, One Marriage: Making It Work In The Workplace." Catalyst <http://www.catalystwomen.org>

"US Couples Differ In View Of 'Fair' Share Of Household Jobs." North Caroline State University News Service <http://www.ncsu.edu/news>

Walkom, Thomas. "Hard Labour Of Love." *The Toronto Star* 31 October 1998: B1 & B4.

Walter, Kate. "Elder Care Obligations Challenge The Next Generation." *HR Magazine* 41 1 July 1996: 98(5).

Wartik, Nancy. "Sex Underdrive." *Harper's Bazaar* 1 October 1997: 134(2).

Weeks, Jerome. "Cleaning Up Housework Myths: Our Perception Of 'Clean' May Need Some Polishing." *The Dallas Morning News* 3 September 1998: 1C.

Wells, Jennifer. "Stuck On The Ladder." *Maclean's* 20 October 1997: 60.

Welsh, John. "Working Couples No Slouches When Satisfying Sex At Stake." *Wisconsin State Journal* 10 September 1998: 1A.

Wheeler, Carla. "Impressing The Boss: It Takes A Little Work." Gannett News Service 28 April, 1997.

"When Did Being Happy Become Politically Incorrect?" Secret Society of Happy People <http://www.sohp.com/home/index.htm>

"When Women Employees Tend To Move On." *HR Wire* <http://www.HRWire.com>

Whitman, David. "The Myth of AWOL Parents." *US News & World Report* 1 July 1996: 54.

Wigmore, Dorothy. "Are You Stressed Out On The Job?" *Contemporary Women's Issues Database* 6 1 September 1992: 32.

Wild, Russell. "Handle Stress Before It Hurts Your Health." *The Dallas Morning News* 19 May 1997: 3C.

Wilkinson, Julia. "Welcome Back: Returning To Work After Maternity Leave." womenCONNECT.com 8 February 1999 <http://www.women connect.com>

Williams, Steve and Steve Schwade. "No More Sleepless Nights: News You Can Use To Help You Snooze." *Prevention* 46 1 May 1994: 72(11).

Wolfe, Warren. "Workplace — The Hidden Cost Of Alzheimer's" *Minneapolis Star Tribune* 10 September 1998: 01D.

"Women Assume Added Role As Eldercare Providers." Contemporary Women's Issues Database 1 February 1996: 8.

"Women Get Low Marks In Heart-Disease Prevention." *The Examiner* 9 February, 1999: A3.

"Women Making It To The Top." CatalystWomen.org *<http://www.catalyst women.org/press/infobriefl.html>*

"Work and Elder Care — Facts For Caregivers And Their Employers." Facts on Working Women *<http://www.dol.gov/dol/wb/public/wb_pubs/elderc.htm>*

"Working Moms At Risk For Cardiovascular Disease." *HR Wire* *<http://www.HRWire.com>*

"Working Moms: Facing Friendly Fire." *HR Wire* *<http://www.HRWire.com>*

"Working Mothers See Gains In U.S. Companies." *The Toronto Star* 22 September 1996: F4.

"Working Parents." *The Globe and Mail* 25 January 1999: B15.

"Working Women Give High Heels The Boot." *HR Wire* *<http://www.HRWire.com>*

Yaccato, Joanne Thomas. "Here's Looking At You, Kid. (Costs Of Being A New Mother) *Chatelaine* 69 1 June 1996: 38(1).

Recommended Readings

Culp, Stephanie. *611 Ways To Do More In A Day*. Cincinnati: Betterway Books, 1998.

Douglas, Ann. *Family Finance 101*. Scarborough: Prentice Hall Canada, 1999.

Douglas, Ann. *The Unofficial Guide to Childcare*. New York: Macmillan, 1998.

Douglas, Ann, and John R. Sussman. *The Unofficial Guide to Having A Baby*. New York: Macmillan, 1999.

Fortang, Laura Berman. *Take Yourself To The Top*. New York: Warner Books, Inc., 1998.

Podleski, Janet and Greta. *Looneyspoons: Low-Fat Food Made Fun!* Ottawa: Granet Publishing Inc., 1996.

Vanier Institute of the Family. *From the Kitchen to the Boardroom Table*. Ottawa: Vanier Institute of the Family, 1998.

Vanier Institute of the Family. *Profiling Canada's Families*. Ottawa: The Vanier Institute Of The Family, 1994.

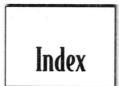

Index

Academy of Management Executive, The
(Aspelin), 40
After-hours schmoozing, 41, 42
After-school child care programs, 132, 133
Aging relatives. *See* Elder care
Akyeampong, Ernest, 53
Alcohol, 17, 22
Aslett, Don, 175
Aspelin, David J., 40

Babbar, Sunil, 40
Batch cooking, 193
Bathroom, 180
Bedrooms, 178-180
Bennion, Daniele, 70
Bibliography, 223-236
Billings, Laura, 102
Black, Heather McDowall, 107
Blakeslee, Sandra, 149
Braubaker, Tim, 141
Breast-feeding, 119-122
Breast pads, 121
Breast pumps, 120, 121
Business Development Bank of Canada, 82

Caffeine, 17, 22
Caggiano, Christopher, 78
Canada Life Assurance Company, 70
Canada's Food Guide to Healthy Eating, 16
Career advancement opportunities, 31
Career web sites, 217, 218
Caregiver's support group, 141
Carlson, Richard, 25
Chatman, Jennifer, 48
Chickenpox, 130
Child care, 123-134
    after-school program, 132, 133
    backup plan, 129, 132
    employer responsibilities, 125
    finding, 123-125
    latchkey kids, 133, 134
    new child care arrangements, 126-128
    organizations/agencies, 216
    sick child, 128-131
Child care referral services, 68

Child care-related benefits, 64-68
Child care subsidy programs, 67, 68
Children's illnesses, 130, 131
Choosing With Care (Sisson/Black), 107
Cigna Corporation, 71
Cleaning, 180-184
Cleaning checklist, 182
Clemmer, Jim, 81
Clutter
    desktop, 33, 34
    e-mail, 34, 35
    household, 175-180
Coffee, 17, 22
Collard, Betsy, 50
College students, 119, 140
Common cold, 130
*Complete Idiot's Guide to Managing Your
    Time* (Davidson), 33
Compressed work week, 60, 61
Conference Board of Canada, 144, 145
Conjunctivitis (pink eye), 130
Cooking, 187-195
Cooney, Teresa M., 136
Coyle, Karen, 49
Crockpot, 194

Davidson, Jeff, 33
Desire discrepancy, 151
Desktop Surveillance program, 12
Diet, 15-17
Directory of organizations, 211-216
Dirt prevention, 183, 184
Dlugozima, Hope, 70
Douglas, Susan J., 108, 173, 180
Dual-career families, 99, 100, 148, 155-157.
    See also Marriage
Duxbury, Linda, 96

E-mail
    clutter, 34, 35
    employer surveillance, 49, 50
    staying in touch, 161
    waste of time, as, 32
Ear infection, 130
Eating habits, 15-17

Elder care, 135-145
  Conference Board of Canada recommen-
    dation, 144, 145
  preparedness, 139-142
  web sites, 218
  workplace support, 142-144
"Eldercare and the Workplace", 144
*Eleven Commandments of Wildly Successful
  Women, The* (Boucher), 50
*Embattled Paradise: The American Family in
  an Age of Uncertainty* (Skolnick), 100
Emergency child care services, 66, 67
Employee benefits, 69-71
Exercise, 17-20
External support team, 47

Face time, 40-42
Fairy godmother, 206
Family, 159-162. *See also* Marriage
Family newsletter, 161
Family room, 178
Fisher, Anne B., 10
Flextime, 58-60
Flight cancellation, 37
Fountain, Cathy, 183
Franchises, 85
Friends, 162-164
*From the Kitchen Table to the Boardroom
  Table*, 142
Front hall, 176, 177
Frozen dinners, 188
Fuchs, Victor, 110

Gastroenteritis, 130
Gee, E. M., 136
Gender gap. *See also* Women
  absenteeism, 55
  lying on résumés, 44
  personality conflicts at work, 40
  symptoms of stress, 11
Gender politics, 43-45
General business organizations, 212-214
General Social Survey on Time Use, 2
Get Your Act Together (Young), 175
Girlfriends, 162-164
*Good Marriage: How and Why Love Lasts,
  The* (Wallerstein/Blakeslee), 149
Gossip, 42, 43
Gottman, John, 149
Greenblat, Donald W., 23
Grocery shopping, 193

Groves, Martha, 42

Haas, Robert, 72
Hanson, Peter, 148
Head lice, 131
Health-related websites, 219
Heart disease, 14
Henderson, Karen, 135
Hesoid, 42
Holstein, Lana, 152
Home, working from, 61-64
Home and Garden channel, 3
Home-based business. *See* Self-employment
Horowitz, Sara, 62
Housework, 169-204
  bartering, 203
  bathroom, 180
  bedrooms, 178-180
  children's tasks, 197-202
  cleaning, 180-184
  clutter, 175-180
  cooking, 187-195
  delegating, 195-202
  dirt prevention, 183, 184
  family room, 178
  front hall, 176, 177
  husband's tasks, 195-197
  kitchen, 177, 178
  laundry, 184-187
  Martha Stewart syndrome, 171-173
  meal preparation, 187-195
  outside cleaning service, 202-204
  tips, 174, 175
  websites, 219, 220
Human Resources Development Canada, 125
Husband-wife relations. *See* Marriage

Impetigo, 130
Insomnia, 21-24
Internet websites, 217-221
Is There Life After Housework (Aslett), 175

Job sharing, 56-58
John Nuveen and Company, 71

Karoshi, 11
Kiechel, Walter III, 42
Kitchen, 177, 178

Latchkey kid, 133, 134
Late-night snacks, 23

Laundry, 184-187
Lichtenberg, Ronna, 41, 43
Lifestyle changes, 14-24
Lighten Up! Free Yourself From Clutter (Passoff), 33
Looneyspoons (Podleski), 188
Loveira, Susan, 49
Lowman, Melody, 152

Madanes, Cloe, 156
Male/female differences. *See* Gender gap
Marriage, 147-157
    career tug-of-war, 155, 156
    job transfers (following your spouse), 156, 157
    sex life, 150-153
    staying connected with your partner, 153, 155
Martha Stewart syndrome, 171-173
Maternity leave, 114, 116, 117
Maternity wardrobe, 116
McKenna, Elizabeth Perle, 1
Meal preparation, 187-195
Meetings, 35, 36
Milkie, Melissa, 170
Morris, Betsy, 104
Morris, Virginia, 140
Mothers. *See* Working mothers

Nannies. *See* Child care
Netscape Communication Corp., 70
Networking, 46
New Four Food Groups, 16
Nielsen, Dorise, 45
No, saying, 166
Nutrition, 15-17

Office politics, 39-51
Online grocery shopping, 193
Onsite day care services, 65, 66
Organizations, directory of, 211-216
Osborn, Susan, 42
Outside cleaning service, 202-204

Passoff, Michelle, 33
Peach Tree, The, 193
Pediculosis (head lice), 131
Perelman, Michael A., 151
Pertussis (whooping cough), 131
Physical fitness, 17-20
Picard, André, 136

Pink eye (conjunctivitis), 130
Pregnancy. *See* Working mothers
Prioritize, 28, 30
Provincial women's directorates, 214, 215

Rechtschaffen, Stephan, 206
Recommendations/tips, 206-210
Red measles, 130, 131
Relatives, 159-162
Relaxation, 24
Robinson, John P., 170
Rubella, 131
Runner's high, 17

Sabbaticals, 69-71
Scarlet fever, 131
Scharlach, Andrew, 135
Schor, Juliet, 10
Secret Society of Happy People, 51
Self-employment, 75-93
    common mistakes, 87-90
    motivation zappers, 90-92
    myths, 83-87
    questions to ask, 76-82
    time management, 92, 93
Sexual dysfunction, 152
Shea, Kathleen V., 25
Sick child, 128-131
Sisson, Brenda, 107
Six Months Off (Dlugozima), 70
Skolnick, Arlene, 100
Sleep, 20-24
Smokers, 22
Smolowe, Jill, 156, 157
Speer, Tibbett L., 143
Spinks, Nora, 6, 58
Stanek, John, 51
Step In, 82
Step Up, 82
Stewart, Martha, 171-173
Strategies for staying sane, 206-210
Strep throat, 131
Stress
    lifestyle changes, 14-24
    symptoms, 13
    workplace, 25, 26
Sugar highs, 16
Swiss, Deborah, 96

Talbot, Margaret, 171
Tax deduction, 140

Tele-working, 61-64
Time cushion, 32
Time management
    meetings, 35, 36
    self-employment, 92, 93
    work, 36, 37
Tips/recommendations, 206-210
To Do Lists, 29-32
Trailing spouse, 157

Unofficial Guide to Child Care, The
    (Douglas), 124

Voice messages, 37
Volunteer work, 164-166

Walker, Judith, 96
Wallerstein, Judith S., 149
Websites, 217-221
*Where The Girls Are: Growing Up Female
    With The Mass Media* (Douglas), 173
Whooping cough, 131
Wilkins, Kathryn, 27
Women. *See also* Gender gap
    bank overtime, 59
    glass ceiling, 44
    shoes, 47
Women and the Work/Family Dilemma
    (Swiss/Walker), 96
Work environment
    alternative work options. *See* Work-life
        programs
    clutter, 33-35
    e-mail. *See* E-mail
    elder care, 142-144
    employee benefits, 69-71
    face time, 40-42
    gender politics, 43-45
    gossip, 42, 43
    meetings, 35, 36
    mothers. *See* Working mothers
    office politics, 39-51
    self-employment. *See* Self-employment
    stress reduction, 25, 26
    time management, 36, 37
    to do lists, 29-32
Work-family crunch, 54, 55
Work-life programs, 55-74
    approaching your employer, 72-74
    benefits to employer, 71, 72
    child care-related benefits, 64-68

compressed work week, 60, 61
flextime, 58-60
job sharing, 56-58
other employee benefits, 69-71
sabbaticals, 69-71
tele-working, 61-64
*Work Would Be Great If It Weren't For The
    People* (Lichtenberg), 43
Working mothers, 95-122
    anger, 108
    announcing pregnancy at work, 112-114
    breast-feeding, 119-122
    children, effect on career, 96-99
    dual-career families, 99, 100
    emotions, 106-110
    full time vs. part time, 100, 101
    guilt, 106
    help at home, 119
    jealousy, 108
    maternity leave, 114, 116, 117
    pregnancy discrimination, 114, 115
    research studies, 110, 111
    resistance from co-workers, 103-105
    returning to work after pregnancy, 118,
        119
    sadness, 107, 108
    satisfaction, 108, 109
    sick child, 128-131
    staying connected to children, 111, 112
    websites, 220, 221
    working during pregnancy, 115, 116
    worry, 107

Young, Pam, 175

Zilbergeld, Bernie, 153

About the Author

If anyone knows what it's like to have too many balls in the air, it's Ann Douglas! A busy mother of four and a prolific writer, Ann is constantly scrambling to balance the needs of her family with the demands of her writing career. Ann is the author of seven books for adults and two books for children, one of which was recently chosen as a Book of the Month Club selection. She is also the child care expert for Parent Soup, a major online service for parents; a columnist for Canadian Parents Online, Canada's most respected parenting web site; and a regular contributor to two of the leading US web sites for families: Crayola Family Play and Stork Site. Ann's work has appeared in some of North America's most respected magazines and newspapers, including *Chatelaine*, *Homemaker's*, *Canadian Living*, *Cottage Life*, *The Globe and Mail*, and the *Chicago Tribune*. Ann and her husband Neil live in Peterborough, Ontario, with their four children (ages two through 11). She can be reached via e-mail at pageone@kawartha.com.

Other Books by Ann Douglas

For Adults

Family Finance 101: What Every Parent Needs to Know About Financial Planning. Scarborough: Prentice Hall Canada Inc., 1999.

The Unofficial Guide to Having A Baby. New York: Macmillan Publishing USA, 1999. (With John R. Sussman, M.D.)

The Unofficial Guide to Childcare. New York: Macmillan Publishing USA, 1998.

The Complete Idiot's Guide to Curling. Scarborough: Prentice Hall Canada Inc., 1998. (With Rod Bolton.)

The Complete Idiot's Guide to Canadian History. Scarborough: Prentice Hall Canada Inc., 1997.

The Complete Idiot's Guide to Canada in the '60s, '70s, and '80s. Scarborough: Prentice Hall Canada, 1999.

For Children

The Family Tree Detective: Cracking the Case of Your Family's Story. Toronto: Greey de Pencier, 1999.

Baby Science: How Babies Really Work. Toronto: Greey de Pencier, 1998.